Be prepared...
To learn...
To succeed...

Get **REA**dy. It all starts here. REA's preparation for the NJ ASK is **fully aligned** with the Core Curriculum Content Standards adopted by the New Jersey Department of Education.

Visit us online at
www.rea.com

READY, SET, GO!®

NJ ASK

Mathematics
Grade 4

Staff of Research & Education Association
Piscataway, New Jersey

Research & Education Association
Visit our website at
www.rea.com

The Performance Standards in this book were created and implemented by the New Jersey State Department of Education. For further information, visit the Department of Education website at *www.state.nj.us/njded/cccs.*

Research & Education Association
61 Ethel Road West
Piscataway, New Jersey 08854
E-mail: info@rea.com

Ready, Set, Go!®
New Jersey ASK
Mathematics
Grade 4

Printed in the United States of America

Library of Congress Control Number 2009940390

ISBN-13: 978-0-7386-0816-7
ISBN-10: 0-7386-0816-5

L09

About Research & Education Association

Founded in 1959, Research & Education Association (REA) is dedicated to publishing the finest and most effective educational materials—including software, study guides, and test preps—for students in elementary school, middle school, high school, college, graduate school, and beyond.

Today REA's wide-ranging catalog is a leading resource for teachers, students, and professionals.

We invite you to visit us at *www.rea.com* to find out how "REA is making the world smarter."

Acknowledgments

We would like to thank REA's Larry B. Kling, Vice President, Editorial, for supervising development; Pam Weston, Vice President, Publishing, for setting the quality standards for production integrity and managing the publication to completion; Alice Leonard, Senior Editor, for project management, editorial guidance, and preflight editorial review; Senior Editor Diane Goldschmidt, for post-production quality assurance; Rachel DiMatteo, Graphic Artist, for her design contributions; and Christine Saul, Senior Graphic Artist, for cover design.

We also gratefully acknowledge Senior Math Editor, Mel Friedman, for technical review of the new edition and the writers, educators, and editors of REA and Northeast Editing for content development, editorial guidance, and final review. Thanks to Matrix Publishing for page design and typesetting and to Kathy Caratozzolo of Caragraphics for setting revisions to this edition.

Contents

Introduction

Welcome to an Educational Adventure

The New Jersey Assessment of Skills and Knowledge, or NJ ASK, is the Garden State's answer to the federal No Child Left Behind Act, which requires that states use standards-based testing to ensure that students are picking up the skills and knowledge necessary for academic success.

We at REA believe that a friendly, hands-on introduction and preparation for the test are keys to creating a successful testing experience. REA's NJ ASK books offer these key features:

- ✓ Clearly identified book activities
- ✓ Contextual illustrations
- ✓ Easy-to-follow lessons
- ✓ Step-by-step examples
- ✓ Tips for solving problems tailored for the proper grade level
- ✓ Exercises to sharpen skills
- ✓ Real practice

Below is helpful information for students, parents, and teachers concerning the NJ ASK and test taking in general. Organized practice is itself a prime skill for young students to master, because it will help set the tone for success long into the future as their educational adventure continues. It is REA's sincere hope that this book—by providing relevant, standards-based practice—can become an integral part of that adventure.

What is the NJ ASK?

The New Jersey Assessment of Skills and Knowledge is a standards-based assessment used in New Jersey's public schools. Performance on the NJ ASK test equates not with the grades students receives for teacher-assigned work but rather with proficiency measures pegged to how well students are acquiring the knowledge and skills outlined in the state's Core Curriculum Content Standards. Those proficiency measures fall into three broad categories, or bands: "partially proficient," "proficient," and "advanced proficient."

When is the NJ ASK given?

The test is administered in early spring. Grade 4 students take the NJ ASK Mathematics on two days. Testing on Day One is 63 minutes; on Day Two testing is 68 minutes. This does not include time to distribute materials, read directions, and take breaks.

What is the format of the NJ ASK?

The NJ ASK has two types of questions: multiple-choice and open ended. With multiple choice, students are asked to choose the correct answer out of four. With open-ended questions, children answer with written responses in their own words. Each test section is timed, and students may not proceed to the next section until time for the current section has expired. If students have not finished a section when time runs out, they must stop and put down their pencils. There are clear directions throughout the test.

Understanding the NJ ASK and This Book

Students:

This book was specially written and designed to make test practice easy and fruitful for you. Our practice tests are very much like the actual NJ ASK tests, and our review is filled with illustrations, drills, exercises, and practice questions to help you become familiar with the testing environment and to retain information about key topics.

Parents:

The NJ ASK and other state assessment tests are designed to give you and the school information about how well your children are achieving in the areas required by New Jersey's Core Curriculum Content Standards, which describe what students should know at the end of certain grades. This book helps your children to review and prepare effectively and positively for the NJ ASK in Mathematics.

Teachers:

When you introduce your students to the test-taking environment and the demands of the NJ ASK tests, you can use our authoritative book in your classroom for planned, guided instruction and practice testing. Effective preparation means better test scores!

Where can I obtain more information about the NJ ASK?

For more information about the NJ ASK, contact the State Department of Education or Measurement, Inc.:

www.state.nj.us/education/assessment

www.measinc.com/njask

Office of Evaluation and Assessment
Telephone: 609-292-4469
Mailing address:
New Jersey Department of Education
PO Box 500
Trenton, NJ 08625-0500

For more information on the National Assessment of Educational Process:

(NAEP) Mathematics Frameworks:

http://nagb.org/publications/frameworks.htm

Test Accommodations and Special Situations

Every effort is made to provide a level playing field for students with disabilities who are taking the NJ ASK. Most students with educational disabilities and most students whose English language skills are limited take the standard NJ ASK. Students with disabilities will be working toward achieving the standards at whatever level is appropriate for them. Supports such as large-print type are available for students who have a current Individualized Education Program (IEP) or who have plans required under Section 504 or who use these supports and accommodations during other classroom testing.

If the IEP team decides that a student will not take the NJ ASK in Language Arts Literacy, Mathematics, and/or Science, the child will take the Alternate Proficiency Assessment (APA).

Tips for Test Taking

- **Do your homework.** From the first assignment of the year, organize the day so there is always time to study and keep up with homework.
- **Communicate.** If there are any questions, doubts, or concerns about anything relating to school, study, or tests, speak up. This goes for teachers and parents, as well as students.
- **Get some rest.** Getting a good night's sleep the night before the test is essential to waking up sharp and focused.
- **Eat right.** Having a good breakfast—nothing very heavy—the morning of the test is what the body and mind need. Comfortable clothes, plenty of time to get to school, and the confidence of having prepared properly are all any student needs.
- **Test smart.** Read the questions carefully. Make sure answers are written correctly in the proper place on the answer sheet. Don't rush, and don't go too slow. If there is time, go back and check questions that you weren't sure about.

Format and Scoring of the NJ ASK Mathematics Test

The questions on the NJ ASK can contain items and concepts learned in earlier grades. The tests are administered in March so that schools and parents receive the reports by mid-June.

The NJ ASK Mathematics test for Grade 4 contains a total of 55 test items. Forty-three of these items are multiple-choice, eight of which are "use calculator" multiple-choice items. The test also contains four open-ended questions and eight short constructed-response questions.

Core Curriculum Content Standards in Mathematics

The NJ ASK is not diagnostic, but is designed to measure how well students are achieving the NJ CCCS. The NJ CCCS determine what students should know and be able to do at a certain grade level.

The distribution of standards in the test is as follows:

- 20 of the points on the NJ ASK 4 assess Number and Numerical Operations (Standard 1)
- 11 of the points on the NJ ASK 4 assess Geometry and Measurement (Standard 3)
- 11 of the points on the NJ ASK 4 assess Patterns and Algebra (Standard 3)
- 8 of the points on the NJ ASK 4 assess Data Analysis, Probability, and Discrete Mathematics (Standard 4)

Open-ended questions are scored by trained personnel. Each standard of the CCCS has strands (see the following table) and Cumulative Progress Indicators (CPIs). All strands are tested on the NJ ASK, but not all CPIs are. The CPIs that coordinate with each strand are included here. For more information about the CPIs, access *www.nj.gov/njded/frameworks/math*.

CCCS Strands on the NJ ASK 4 Mathematics Component

Standard	CCCS Strand	CPI	Chapter in This Book
Number and Numerical Operations	Number Sense	4.1.4.A.1-7	Chapter 1: Number Sense
	Numerical Operations	4.1.4.B.1-10	Chapter 2: Numerical Operations
	Estimation	4.1.4.C.1-4	Chapter 3: Estimation
Geometry and Measurement	Geometric Properties	4.2.4.A.1-5	Chapter 4: All about Lines and Shapes
	Transforming Shapes	4.2.4.B.1-3	Chapter 4: All about Lines and Shapes
	Coordinates of Geometry	4.2.4.C.1-2	Chapter 4: All about Lines and Shapes
	Units of Measurement	4.2.4.D.1-5	Chapter 5: Measurement
	Measuring Geometric Objects	4.2.4.E.1-3	Chapter 5: Measurement
Patterns and Algebra	Patterns	4.3.4.A.1	Chapter 6: Understanding Patterns
	Functions and Relationships	4.3.4.B.1	Chapter 6: Understanding Patterns
	Modeling	4.3.4.C.1-2	Chapter 6: Understanding Patterns

	Procedures	4.3.4.D.1-2	Chapter 6: Understanding Patterns
Data Analysis, Probability, and Discrete Mathematics	Data Analysis (statistics)	4.4.4.A.1-2	Chapter 7: Data Analysis and Probability
	Probability	4.4.4.B.1-3	Chapter 7: Data Analysis and Probability
	Discrete Mathematics—systematic listing and counting	4.4.4.C.1-2	Chapter 8: More About Analyzing Data
	Discrete Mathematics—vertex-edge graphs and algorithms	4.4.4.D.1-4	Chapter 8: More About Analyzing Data
Mathematical Processes	Problem Solving	4.5.4.A.1-5	Note: These standards pertain to the application of mathematics, not to mathematic principles. They are not independently assessed, but rather incorporated into test questions which assess the other four mathematics standards.
	Communication	4.5.4.B.1-4	
	Connections	4.5.4.C.1-6	
	Reasoning	4.5.4.D.1-6	
	Representations	4.5.4.E.1-3	
	Technology	4.5.4.F.1-6	

The standards presented in this book were created by the New Jersey State Department of Education. Source: New Jersey Assessment of Skills and Knowledge, 2009 *Score Interpretation Manual, Grades 3-8*: October 2009: Copyright © New Jersey Department of Education. For more information, visit the department's website at http://www.state.nj.us/education/aps/cccs/math/.

Chapter 1

Number Sense

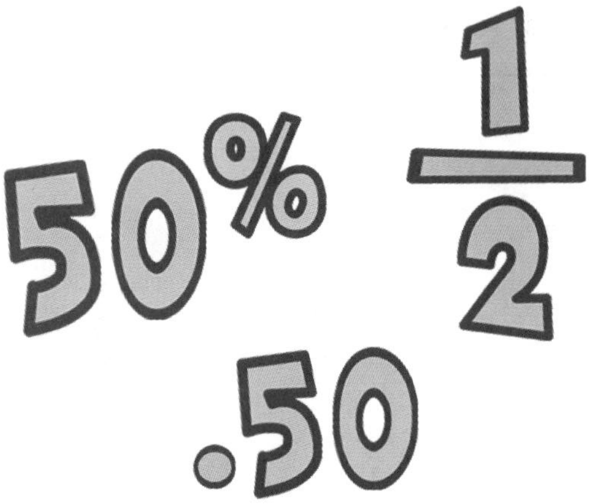

Numbers are everywhere. You see numbers when you look in the telephone book. You use numbers to tell time. Your height and weight are given in numbers. Each number represents a value. For example, the number 10,000 is less than the number 100,000. This chapter will help you to understand the value of very small numbers and numbers greater than one million. It will also show you how to compare numbers and put them in a certain order, such as from least to greatest.

To understand numbers, you should also know the **value** of decimals and fractions and the meaning of negative numbers. You need to know, for example, that –1 is less than 1. In this chapter, you will also learn about those concepts.

Whole Numbers

A **whole number** is an integer. An **integer** is a number on a number line. Zero is a whole number. Positive numbers are whole numbers. The numbers 1, 2, 3, 4, and 5 are positive numbers. Negative numbers are also integers. The numbers −1, −2, −3, −4, and −5 are negative numbers. The digits in whole numbers have a value, called a **place value**. The diagram below shows the place values for the number 100,000—one hundred thousand.

hundred thousand	ten thousand	thousand	hundred	ten	one
↓	↓	↓	↓	↓	↓
1	0	0,	0	0	0

Notice the use of commas to help you determine the value of a large number. The commas divide the number, from right to left, into groups of three. The three numbers in each group have ones, tens, and hundreds places, but the second group from the right is thousands, so they are thousands, ten thousands, and hundred thousands. Look at this number:

3,285

In this number, the 3 is in the one thousands place, the 2 is in the hundreds place, the 8 is in the tens place, and the 5 is in the ones place. So you would read it as "three thousand, two hundred eighty-five."

Now look at this number:

32,850

In this number, the 3 is in the ten thousands place, the 2 is in the one thousands place, the 8 is in the hundreds place, the 5 is in the tens place, and the 0 is in the ones place. So you would read it as "thirty-two thousand, eight hundred fifty."

Now let's look at a much larger number. The next group of three to the left of thousands is millions, and it follows the same pattern.

3,285,000

In this number, the 3 is in the millions place, the 2 is in the hundred thousands place, the 8 is in the ten thousands place, and the 5 is in the thousands place. There are zeros in the hundreds, tens, and ones places. You would read this number as "three million, two hundred eighty-five thousand."

Look at the chart below. Notice that each time a zero is added to the end of the number, the number moves up in place value and gets larger.

1 one

10 ten

100 one hundred

1,000 one thousand

10,000 ten thousand

100,000 one hundred thousand

1,000,000 one million

Practice Questions

Practice 1: Whole Numbers and Place Value

DIRECTIONS:

Choose the best of the answer choices given for each of the following problems. Fill in the circle next to your choice.

1. During the summer, about 250,000 people visit the beach in Wildwood, New Jersey. What is the value of the 5 in the number 250,000?

Ⓐ 5 hundreds

Ⓑ 5 thousands

● 5 ten thousands

Ⓓ 5 hundred thousands

HINT

Look back at the place values for the number 100,000 in the beginning of this chapter if you're not sure of the place value of the digit 5 in 250,000.

2. **The population of the state of New Jersey is about 8,717,925. What is the value of the 8 in the number 8,717,925?**

Ⓐ 8 thousands

Ⓑ 8 ten thousands

Ⓒ 8 hundred thousands

Ⓓ 8 millions

HINT

What is the place value of the 1 in the number 1,000,000 on page 3?

Fractions

You just learned about whole numbers. A fraction is not a whole number. It is part of a number. A fraction tells how many parts of something you have. The *total* number of parts goes on the bottom. This is the **denominator**. The number of parts *you* have goes on the top. This is the **numerator**. An easy way to remember this is to remember that the **d**enominator goes **d**own at the bottom of the fraction.

Suppose your family ordered a pizza with six slices.

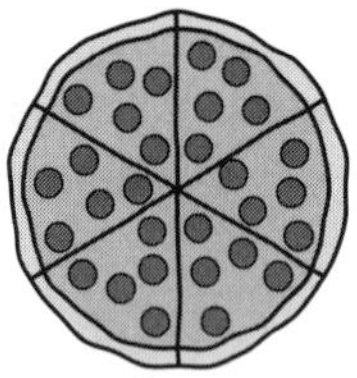

The pizza has six slices, so six is the denominator. In this case, the denominator tells how many slices of pizza make up the whole pizza. Now imagine that you eat one slice of pizza. This means that you eat one part of the pizza. The fraction showing how much of the pizza you eat is $\frac{1}{6}$.

Circle the numerator in each of the fractions below.

$$\frac{1}{2} \quad \frac{1}{3} \quad \frac{8}{13} \quad \frac{5}{16}$$

If you circled the 1, 1, 8, and 5, you are correct. If you missed any, review what a numerator is in the discussion on fractions.

Fractions appear on the number line between whole numbers. Look at this number line:

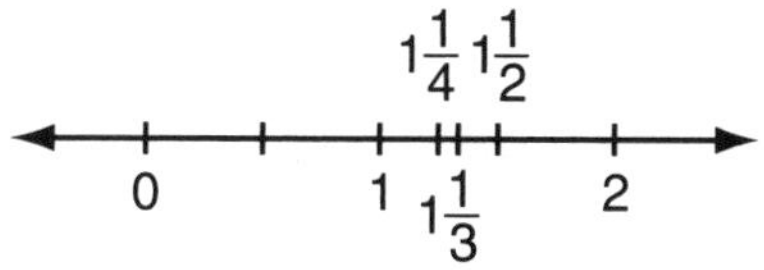

Notice that $1\frac{1}{2}$ is between 1 and 2, and $1\frac{1}{3}$ is also between 1 and 2.

Which Is Greater?

If you want to know which of two fractions is greater, and the denominators are the same, this is easy to do. The fraction with the larger numerator is greater. For example, $\frac{5}{7}$ is greater than $\frac{4}{7}$.

If the denominators are different, however, it is harder to tell which fraction is larger. If you have a diagram with the fractional parts shaded, you can usually see which fraction is larger.

As an example, look at the **shaded** circles below.

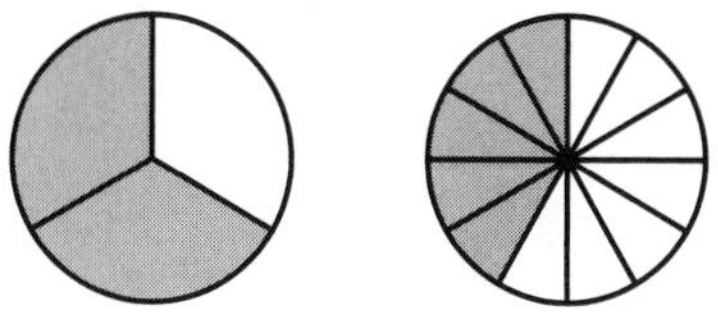

By looking at the circles, you can see that $\frac{2}{3}$ is definitely greater than $\frac{5}{12}$.

Look at the fractions below. On the line below the fractions, write them in order from GREATEST to LEAST. Use the shaded diagrams to help you.

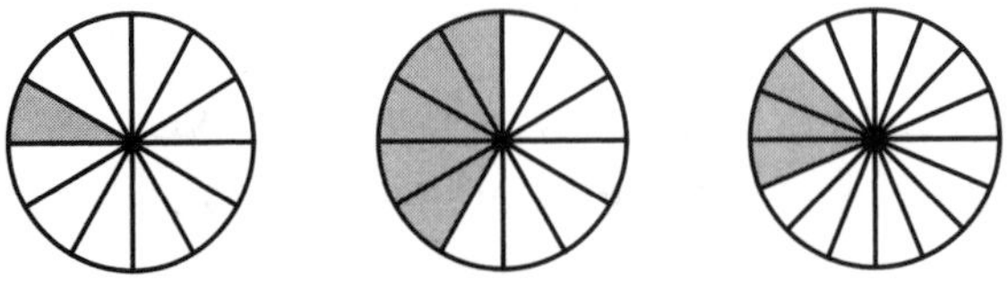

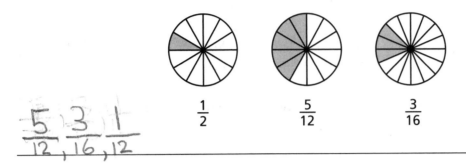

$\frac{1}{2}$ $\frac{5}{12}$ $\frac{3}{16}$

$\frac{5}{12}$, $\frac{3}{16}$, $\frac{1}{12}$

If you wrote $\frac{5}{12}$, $\frac{3}{16}$, $\frac{1}{12}$, you are right. Look carefully at the shaded parts of the circles if you didn't get this right.

Equivalent Fractions

Some fractions stand for the same amount, even though they have different numerators and denominators. These are called **equivalent fractions**. Look at these fractions.

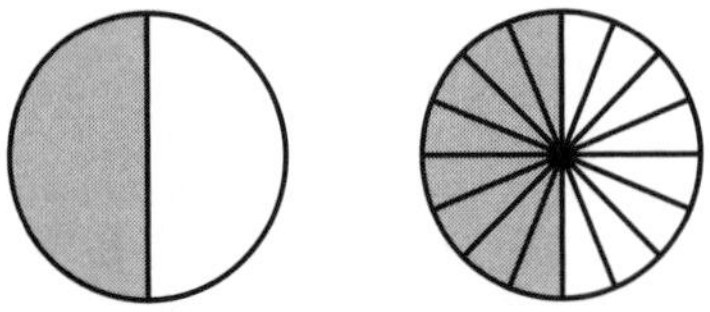

$\frac{1}{2}$ and $\frac{8}{16}$

From the shaded parts of the circles, you can see that the fractions $\frac{1}{2}$ and $\frac{8}{16}$ have the same value, even though they are written in different ways.

Compare the fractions below. Write < (less than), > (greater than), or = for each pair of fractions. Use the shaded circles to help you choose the right answer.

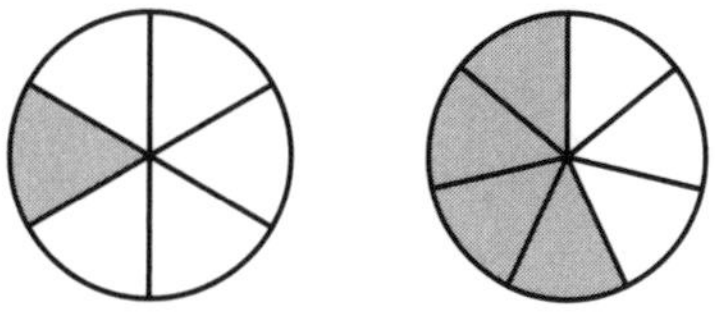

1. $\frac{1}{6} \boxed{<} \frac{4}{7}$

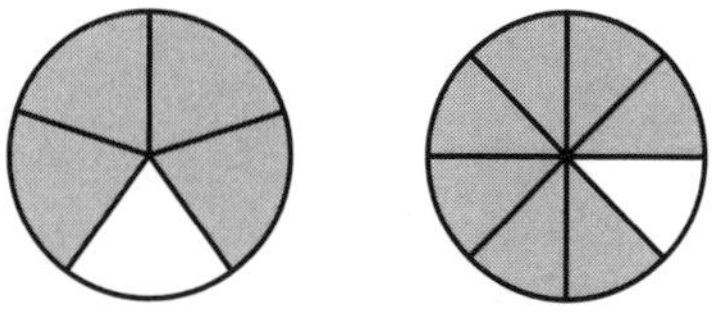

2. $\frac{4}{5} \boxed{<} \frac{7}{8}$

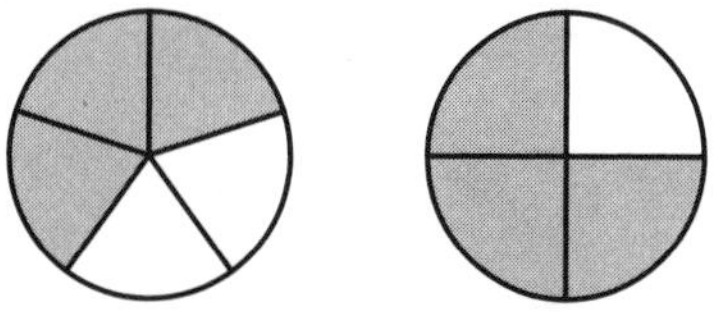

3. $\frac{3}{5} \boxed{<} \frac{3}{4}$

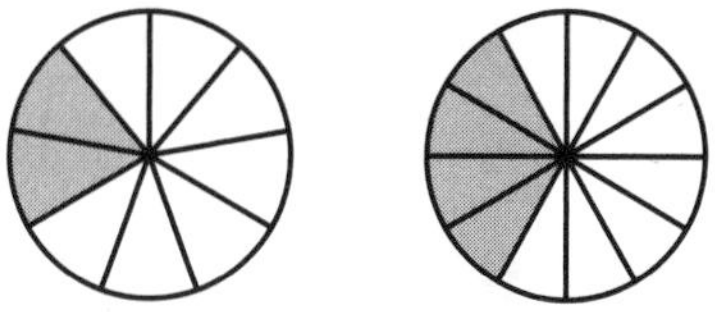

4. $\frac{2}{9} \boxed{<} \frac{4}{12}$

You are correct if your answers are

1. $\frac{1}{6} < \frac{4}{7}$
2. $\frac{4}{5} < \frac{7}{8}$
3. $\frac{3}{5} < \frac{3}{4}$
4. $\frac{2}{9} < \frac{4}{12}$

If you missed one or more, review the section on fractions.

Practice Questions

Practice 2: Fractions

DIRECTIONS:

Choose the best of the answer choices given for each of the following problems. Fill in the circle next to your choice.

1. Compare the shaded regions. Which symbol belongs in the box?

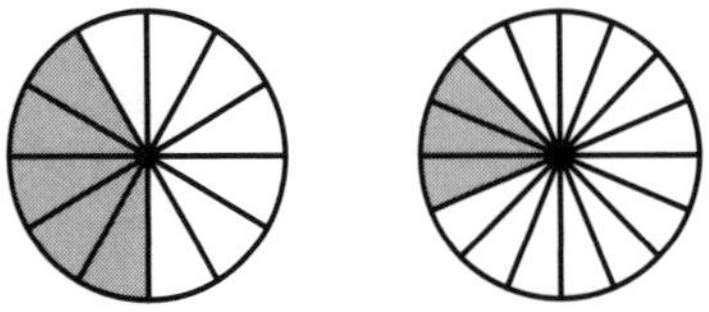

$$\frac{5}{12} \square \frac{3}{16}$$

Ⓐ <

Ⓑ >

Ⓒ =

Ⓓ None of the above

First, see whether the shaded area in the first circle is bigger than the shaded area in the second circle. If it is, choose the answer option with the greater than > sign.

2. Compare the shaded regions. Which symbol belongs in the box?

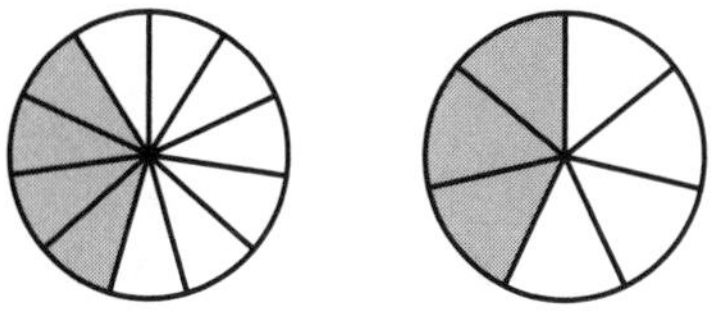

$$\frac{4}{11} \square \frac{3}{7}$$

Ⓐ $<$

Ⓑ $>$

Ⓒ $=$

Ⓓ None of the above

HINT

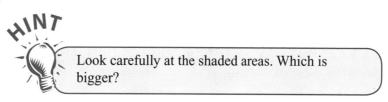

Look carefully at the shaded areas. Which is bigger?

Decimals

Like whole numbers, decimals have **place values**. Look at the diagram below for 0.62.

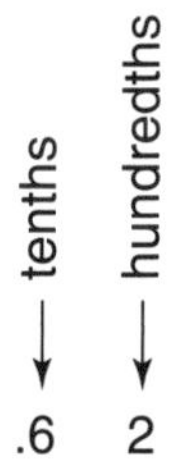

Notice that the place value for decimals is similar to that of whole numbers—but the place value moves to the right, and the place value gets *smaller* rather than larger, so that "hundredths" is larger than "thousandths." Notice that "th" is added to the end of each value for decimals, and there is no place value for "one-ths."

Look at this decimal:

.34

In this decimal, the 3 is in the tenths place and the 4 is in the hundredths place. If you add a zero after the decimal point and before the 3, the number is .034, which is smaller than .34, because 0 tenths (in .034) is smaller than 3 tenths (in .34).

A mixed decimal has a whole number and a decimal. A mixed decimal is always greater than a decimal. Look at these numbers:

$$1.25 > 0.25$$

But what if two numbers are both mixed decimals? If they have different whole number parts, the one with the greater whole number is greater. If they have the same whole number part, the one with the greater decimal is greater. For example,

$$3.27 > 2.74$$

$$1.25 > 1.15$$

Practice Questions

Practice 3: Decimals

DIRECTIONS:

Choose the best of the answer choices given for each of the following problems. Fill in the circle next to your choice.

1. Which group of numbers is in order from least to greatest?

Ⓐ .34 1.24 1.0

Ⓑ .34 1.0 1.24

Ⓒ 1.24 1.0 .34

Ⓓ 1.0 .34 1.24

HINT

Remember that a whole number is greater than a decimal, and if you have two mixed decimals with the same whole number part, choose the one with the greater decimal.

2. Which group of numbers is in order from least to greatest?

Ⓐ 1.50 .99 1.23

Ⓑ .99 1.50 1.23

Ⓒ 1.23 1.50 .99

Ⓓ .99 1.23 1.50

HINT

The number with only the decimal is the smallest.

Negative Numbers

The **number line** you looked at in the last section had only **positive** numbers. The number line can also extend to the left of zero to include **negative** numbers. This number line contains both positive and negative numbers:

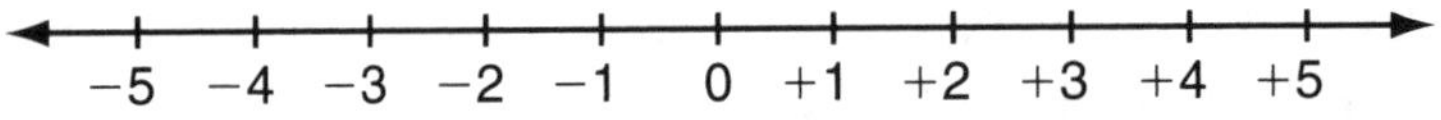

Negative numbers have lower values than positive numbers. For example,

$$-2 < 2$$

$$-10 < 1$$

Think about temperature. If it is 10 degrees outside, it is very cold. But if the temperature drops into the negative numbers, it is very, very cold. Look at each pair of numbers below. Write $<$ or $>$ in the box.

1. $-8 \boxed{<} 0$
2. $2 \boxed{>} -1$
3. $-10 \boxed{<} 1$
4. $5 \boxed{>} -5$

You are correct if your answers are

1. $-8 < 0$
2. $2 > -1$
3. $-10 < 1$
4. $5 > -5$

If you missed any of the answers, go back to review the section on negative numbers.

Practice Questions

Practice 4: Negative Numbers

DIRECTIONS:

Choose the best of the answer choices given for each of the following problems. Fill in the circle next to your choice.

1. **Which group of numbers is in order from least to greatest?**

   (A) −10 10 9

   (B) 10 −10 9

   (C) 9 −10 10

   (D) −10 9 10

HINT

Remember that a positive number is always greater than a negative number.

2. **Which group of numbers is in order from least to greatest?**

   (A) −5 −3 0

   (B) −3 −5 0

   (C) 0 −5 −3

   (D) −5 3 0

HINT

Remember that negative numbers get smaller as the digits increase. The higher negative number is smaller than the lower negative number.

Practice Questions

End-of-Chapter Practice Problems

DIRECTIONS:

Choose the best of the answer choices given for each of the following problems. Fill in the circle next to your choice.

1. Which group of numbers is in order from least to greatest?

Ⓐ 2.0 .90 2.09

Ⓑ .90 2.0 2.09

Ⓒ 2.09 .90 2.0

Ⓓ 2.0 2.09 .90

HINT: In a decimal, .0 is less than .09.

2. Compare the shaded regions. Which symbol belongs in the box?

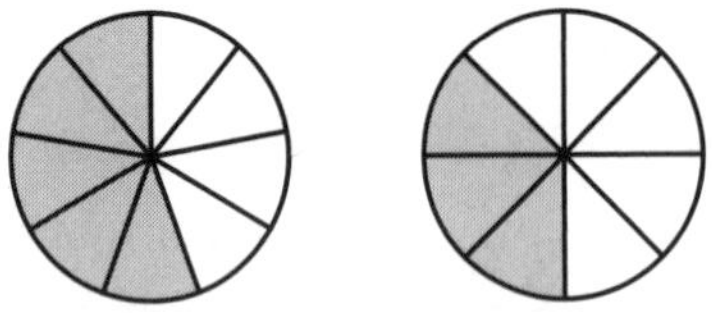

$\frac{5}{9} \square \frac{3}{8}$

Ⓐ <

Ⓑ >

Ⓒ =

Ⓓ None of the above

HINT: Compare the shaded portions of the two circles.

3. **The lottery prize in the state of New Jersey is worth 9,125,000 dollars. What is the value of 1 in the number 9,125,000?**

Ⓐ 1 thousand

Ⓑ 1 ten thousand

Ⓒ 1 hundred thousand

Ⓓ 1 million

HINT

If you can't figure out the value of 1, go back and look at the place values in the number 1,000,000 found toward the beginning of the chapter.

4. **Which group of numbers is in order from least to greatest?**

Ⓐ .45 1.01 2.43

Ⓑ 1.01 .45 2.43

Ⓒ 2.43 .45 1.01

Ⓓ .45 2.43 1.01

HINT

Remember that a decimal is smaller than a mixed decimal, and when comparing mixed decimals, compare the whole number parts first.

5. **About 6,234,000 schoolchildren wear eyeglasses. What is the value of 4 in the number 6,234,000?**

Ⓐ 4 hundreds

Ⓑ 4 thousands

Ⓒ 4 ten thousands

Ⓓ 4 hundred thousands

HINT The 4 is in the second grouping of three numbers.

6. **Compare the shaded regions. Which symbol belongs in the box?**

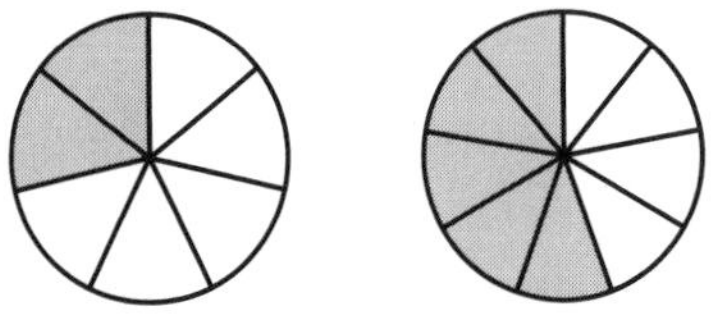

$\frac{2}{7} \square \frac{5}{9}$

Ⓐ $<$

Ⓑ $>$

Ⓒ $=$

Ⓓ None of the above

HINT Look carefully at the shaded regions.

7. **Which group of numbers is in order from least to greatest?**

Ⓐ −4 −5 −9

Ⓑ −9 −5 −4

Ⓒ −5 −9 −4

Ⓓ −4 −9 −5

HINT

Remember from the number line that for negative numbers, as the numeral gets larger, the value of the negative number gets smaller.

Chapter 2

Numerical Operations

In Chapter 1, you learned that a number's place value determines how large or small it is. You learned that fractions and decimals stand for parts of numbers. You compared numbers in different forms and put them in order from least to greatest.

This chapter shows how to solve problems for which you have to add, subtract, multiply, and divide numbers. You'll notice that some of these problems are easier to answer than others. Usually, you can answer the easier questions by using **mental math**. When you use mental math, you figure out the answer in your head. For other questions, you'll have to use pencil and paper to figure out the answer.

Do you like to count money? This chapter reviews counting money—adding and subtracting dollars and cents.

The NJ ASK test is given in sessions. For one part, you will be allowed to use a calculator. For other sessions, you are not allowed to use a calculator. In this chapter, you'll practice answering questions both ways.

Adding and Subtracting Numbers

You can usually use mental math to solve easier problems. For example, look at this problem:

Find the exact answer: 200 + 500

Ⓐ 300

Ⓑ 600

Ⓒ 700

Ⓓ 800

You should be able to answer this question quickly by using mental math. You know that 2 + 5 = 7, so 200 + 500 = 700. Answer choice C is the correct answer.

Let's try another.

Find the exact answer: 700 – 400

Ⓐ 300

Ⓑ 400

Ⓒ 500

Ⓓ 1,100

This question can also be solved easily by using mental math. You should know right away that 7 – 4 = 3, so 700 – 400 = 300.

Not all problems can be solved this quickly, however. Try to solve this problem:

Find the exact answer: 582 + 145

Ⓐ 349

Ⓑ 437

Ⓒ 727

Ⓓ 737

You probably can't solve this problem in your head. If you are not allowed to use a calculator, you'll need to use a pencil and paper. Set up the problem like this:

$$\begin{array}{r} 582 \\ +\ 145 \\ \hline \end{array}$$

When you set up the problem this way, it's easy to add the numbers. You can tell that the correct answer choice is C, 727.

Let's try another.

Find the exact answer: 703 − 256

Ⓐ 347

Ⓑ 349

Ⓒ 447

Ⓓ 459

You need a pencil and paper to answer this problem, too. If you use a pencil and paper, set up the problem this way:

$$\begin{array}{r} 703 \\ -\ 256 \\ \hline \end{array}$$

If you set up the problem this way, you can easily subtract the numbers and get 447 (answer choice C). Now practice using a calculator to solve the problem. Press the keys for 7 0 3 and then press the minus sign. Then press the keys for 2 5 6 and press the = sign.

Now let's try a **word problem**.

Karen has sold 210 tickets to raise money for her school. Her family bought 120 of these tickets. How many tickets did Karen sell to people other than her family?

Ⓐ 80

Ⓑ 90

Ⓒ 110

Ⓓ 120

To find out how many tickets Karen sold to people other than her family, you need to subtract 120 from 210. If you use a pencil and paper to solve this problem, set it up like this:

$$\begin{array}{r} 210 \\ -\ 120 \\ \hline \end{array}$$

When you subtract these numbers, you'll see that Karen sold 90 tickets to people other than her family. Answer choice B is correct.

Practice Questions

Practice 5: Adding and Subtracting Numbers

DIRECTIONS:

Choose the best of the answer choices given for each of the following problems. Fill in the circle next to your choice. You may NOT use a calculator.

1. Find the exact answer: 324 + 548

Ⓐ 762

Ⓑ 772

Ⓒ 862

Ⓓ 872

HINT

Use a pencil and paper to line up the numbers. Then add the numbers.

2. Find the exact answer: 809 − 310

Ⓐ 399

Ⓑ 401

Ⓒ 499

Ⓓ 501

HINT

Use a pencil and paper to line up the numbers so that 809 is on the top and 310 is on the bottom. Then subtract the numbers.

3. **Find the exact answer: 210 + 679**

Ⓐ 789

Ⓑ 799

Ⓒ 879

Ⓓ 889

210
+679
889

HINT

Set up the problem correctly and then add the numbers.

4. **Michelle has a comic book collection. She had 125 comic books, and her grandmother gave her 98 more. How many comic books does she have in all?**

Ⓐ 122

Ⓑ 123

Ⓒ 222

Ⓓ 223

11
125
+98
223

HINT

You need to add the two numbers to get the right answer.

Directions for the Open-Ended Question

The following question is an open-ended question. Remember to:

Read the question carefully and think about the answer.

Answer all the parts of the question.

Show your work or explain your answer.

You can answer the question by using words, tables, diagrams, OR pictures. You may use your calculator, ruler, and colored shapes.

5. William has a stamp collection. He had 210 stamps, and his sister gave him 30 more. Then William gave 53 stamps to his friend. How many stamps does William have now?

Show your work.

You have to show how you got your answer to this problem. It involves both addition and subtraction.

Multiplying and Dividing Numbers

For some problems on the NJ ASK, you'll be allowed to use a calculator. For others, you'll need to use a pencil and paper or mental math.

Find the exact answer: 848 ÷ 4

Ⓐ 212

Ⓑ 222

Ⓒ 301

Ⓓ 312

To solve this problem by using a calculator, press the keys for 848 and then press ÷ and 4, and then the = sign. The answer is 212, so answer choice A is correct.

If you are not allowed to use a calculator, you can set up the problem using pencil and paper like this:

$$4\overline{)848}$$

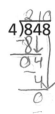

Let's try another one:

Find the exact answer: 42 × 15

Ⓐ 210

Ⓑ 620

Ⓒ 630

Ⓓ 740

To solve this question by using a calculator, press the keys for 42 and then the × sign. Then press 15 and the = sign. The answer is 630, so answer choice C is the correct answer. To solve this problem by using a pencil and paper, set it up like this:

$$\begin{array}{r} 42 \\ \times\ 15 \\ \hline \end{array}$$

Let's try one more:

Mrs. Harris bought juice boxes in packs of 6 for her students. Which of these could be the total number of juice boxes that she bought without having any left over?

Ⓐ 22

Ⓑ 24

Ⓒ 28

Ⓓ 32

To answer this question, you have to choose the answer choice into which 6 can be divided evenly. If you divide 6 into 22, you get 3.6666, so this is not the correct answer. If you divide 6 into 24, you get 4. The number 6 does not divide evenly into 28 and 32, so answer choice B, 24, is the only correct answer.

Practice Questions

Practice 6: Multiplying and Dividing Numbers

DIRECTIONS:

Choose the best of the answer choices given for each of the following problems. Fill in the circle next to your choice. You may NOT use a calculator.

1. Find the exact answer: 360 ÷ 2

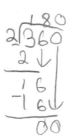

Ⓐ 130

Ⓑ 170

Ⓒ 180

Ⓓ 190

HINT

You might be able to solve this problem by using mental math. If not, set up the problem like this: $2\overline{)360}$

2. **Find the exact answer: 38 × 24**

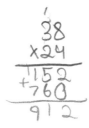

Ⓐ 228

Ⓑ 812

Ⓒ 822

Ⓓ 912

38
×24
152
+760
912

HINT

Set up the problem like this: $\begin{array}{r} 38 \\ \times\ 24 \\ \hline \end{array}$

Directions for the Open-Ended Question

The following question is an open-ended question. Remember to:

Read the question carefully and think about the answer.

Answer all the parts of the question.

Show your work or explain your answer.

You can answer the question by using words, tables, diagrams, OR pictures. You may use your calculator for this question.

3. **Jeremy has 168 stickers to give to 8 friends. He wants to give an equal number of stickers to each friend. How many stickers will he give to each friend?**

Show your work.

HINT

Set up the problem like this: $8\overline{)168}$. Then divide.

Counting Money

Some questions ask about money. You need to know the value of these coins and bills to answer these questions.

5¢

10¢

25¢

$1.00

$5.00

$10.00

Let's try a money problem:

A juice machine charges $0.85 (85¢) for a can of juice and accepts only nickels, dimes, and quarters. The machine requires exact change. What combination of coins could you put in the juice machine to get a can of juice?

Ⓐ 

Ⓑ 

Ⓒ 

Ⓓ 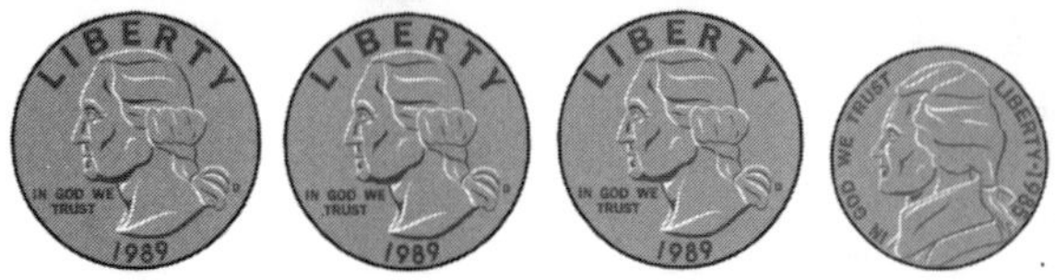

To answer this problem, count the coins in each answer choice. You need to choose the combination of coins that adds up to $0.85. The coins in answer choice A add up to $0.65, so this is not the correct answer. The coins in answer choice B add up to $0.70, so this is also not the correct answer. The coins in answer choice C add up to $0.85. This is the correct answer. The coins in answer choice D add up to $0.80, so this is not correct.

Let's try another one.

Bailey bought a goldfish for $0.75 and goldfish food for $1.25. She gave the clerk $2.00. How much change did she receive?

Ⓐ $0.0

Ⓑ $0.25

Ⓒ $0.30

Ⓓ $0.50

To solve this problem, you need to add $0.75 and $1.25. Then subtract this number from $2.00. The answer is zero. Bailey did not receive any change.

Let's try one more counting money problem:

Rick made a display for his science fair project. He spent $1.25 on a poster board and $3.40 on a package of construction paper. He gave the clerk a $5 bill. How much change did he receive?

Show your work.

You need to show your work for this question. First, add $1.25 and $3.40 to see how much Rick spent. When you add these numbers, you get $4.65. Next, subtract this number from $5.00 to see how much change Rick got. The answer is $0.35. Rick received $0.35 change.

Practice Questions

Practice 7: Counting Money

DIRECTIONS:

Choose the best of the answer choices given for each the following problems. Fill in the circle next to your choice. You are allowed to use a calculator to answer these items.

1. To ride on a carousel at a mall, you have to pay 95¢. The ride accepts only nickels, dimes, and quarters, and you must have exact change. Which combination of coins do you need?

Ⓐ 

Ⓑ 

Ⓒ 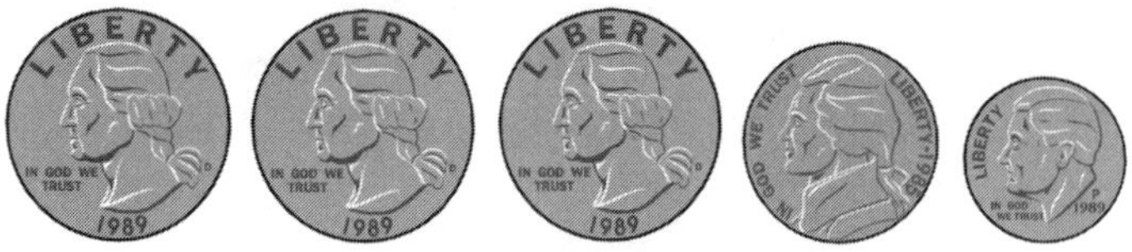

Ⓓ 

HINT

Remember to add up the value of the coins in each answer choice.

Directions for the Open-Ended Question

The following question is an open-ended question. Remember to:

Read the question carefully and think about the answer.

Answer all the parts of the question.

Show your work or explain your answer.

You can answer the question by using words, tables, diagrams, OR pictures. You may use your calculator for this question.

2. A pinball machine charges 70¢ to play a game and accepts only nickels, dimes, and quarters. What combination of coins could you put in the machine to play a game?

Show your work or explain your answer.

I'll put 2 quarters and two dimes and a nickel.

HINT

Remember that a quarter has a value of 25¢, a dime has a value of 10¢, and a nickel has a value of 5¢.

DIRECTIONS:

Choose the best of the answer choices given for each the following problems. Fill in the circle next to your choice. You are allowed to use a calculator to answer these items.

3. Mark spent $2.75 to mail a package to his brother and $0.50 to mail an envelope to his friend. He gave the clerk $5.00. How much change did he receive?

Ⓐ $1.25

Ⓑ $1.75

Ⓒ $2.25

Ⓓ $3.25

HINT

Remember to add what Mark spent and then subtract this amount from $5.00 to get his change.

Practice Questions

End-of-Chapter Practice Problems

DIRECTIONS:

Choose the best of the answer choices given for each of the following problems. Fill in the circle next to your choice. You may NOT use a calculator.

1. Find the exact number: 251 + 300

Ⓐ 451

Ⓑ 551

Ⓒ 651

Ⓓ 751

251
+300
551

HINT

You can probably solve this problem by using mental math. What is 2 + 3?

2. Mr. Renfer bought markers in packs of 12 for his art students. Which of these could be the total number of markers that he bought without having any markers left over?

Ⓐ 14

Ⓑ 26

Ⓒ 36

Ⓓ 40

HINT

You will be able to divide 12 exactly into the correct answer choice.

3. Find the exact answer: 242 ÷ 2

(A) 120

(B) 121

(C) 122

(D) 142

HINT

You might be able to do this problem by using mental math. Divide 2 into each digit in 242.

4. A machine charges 65¢ for a package of crackers and accepts only nickels, dimes, and quarters. Which combination of coins could you put into the machine to get a package of crackers?

(A) 

(B) 

(C) 

(D) 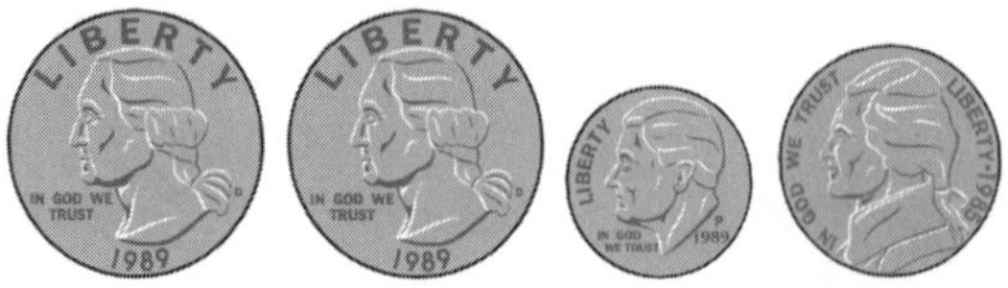

HINT

Add the coin values in each answer choice.

5. **Find the exact answer: 592 − 356**

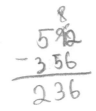

Ⓐ 144

Ⓑ 236

Ⓒ 244

Ⓓ 336

HINT

Set up the problem correctly and then subtract.

Directions for the Open-Ended Question

The following question is an open-ended question. Remember to:

Read the question carefully and think about the answer.

Answer all the parts of the question.

Show your work or explain your answer.

You can answer the question by using words, tables, diagrams, OR pictures.
You may NOT use your calculator.

6. **Miguel has 124 coins in his coin collection. He gives 86 of his coins to the library. How many coins does he have left?**

   Show your work or explain your answer.

HINT

The number of coins Miguel has left is the difference between what he had and what he gave away.

DIRECTIONS:

Choose the best of the answer choices given for each of the following problems. Fill in the circle next to your choice. You may NOT use a calculator.

7. Find the exact answer: 67 × 19

- Ⓐ 670
- Ⓑ 770
- Ⓒ 1,273
- Ⓓ 1,274

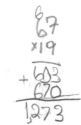

HINT

Set up the numbers correctly, and carefully multiply.

8. A farmer sells apples for \$0.35 each. Martina buys 4 apples and gives the farmer \$2.00. How much change will she receive?

- Ⓐ \$0.35
- Ⓑ \$0.60
- Ⓒ \$0.65
- Ⓓ \$1.40

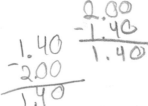

HINT

Begin by multiplying \$0.35 by 4. Then subtract this amount from \$2.00.

Chapter 3

Estimation

How long do you think it will take you to finish reading this chapter? You don't know for sure, since you just started. But you could probably **estimate**—or guess—how long it would take. Do you think it might take an hour? That's a good estimate.

For questions that ask you to estimate, you can usually figure out a **range of values** that includes the exact answer. Many of the questions in Chapter 2 asked you to find the exact answer, but sometimes all that is needed is an answer choice that is close to the exact answer, as you will learn in this chapter. You will NOT be allowed to use a calculator for estimation questions on the NJ ASK test.

Rounding

You can use mental math to answer some estimation questions. Remember that when you use mental math, you figure out the answer in your head without using a pencil and paper or a calculator.

For most questions, the best way to estimate is to **round** numbers. You can round numbers to the nearest 10 or the nearest 100, for example. When you round to the nearest 10, you look closely at the number in the ones place. If the number in the ones place is 5 or more, you round up, and if the number is 4 or less, you round down.

The numbers below are rounded to the nearest 10.

Number	Rounded to Nearest 10
23	20
34	30
67	70
78	80
91	90

For the number 23, 3 is in the ones place. The number 3 is less than 4, so you round down to 20 rather than up to 30. So the number 23 rounded to the nearest 10 is 20. See how it works?

Round each of these numbers to the nearest 10.

Number	Rounded to Nearest 10
11	10
15	20
24	20
37	40
42	40
59	60
65	70

You are correct if your answers are:

Number	Rounded to Nearest 10
11	10
15	20
24	20
37	40
42	40
59	60
65	70

If you missed any of these answers, go back to check the digit in the ones place. Remember that a 5 gets rounded up, not down.

When you round to the nearest 100, you look closely at the number in the tens place and ignore the number in the ones place. Just as with in rounding to the nearest 10, if the number in the tens place is 5 or greater, you round up, and if this number is 4 or less, you round down. These numbers are rounded to the nearest 100:

Number	Rounded to Nearest 100
123	100
182	200
214	200
356	400
479	500
591	600

Now you try it.

Round each of these numbers to the nearest 100.

Number	Rounded to Nearest 100
115	100
179	200
234	200
390	400
450	500
625	600

You are correct if your answers are:

Number	Rounded to Nearest 100
115	100
179	200
234	200
390	400
450	500
625	600

If you missed any of these, go back to check the number in the tens place. Remember that if the number in the tens place is 5, the number gets rounded up, not down. Also, the numbers in the ones place are not used when rounding to the nearest 100.

Estimating Addition

When you estimate addition problems, the answer options usually give you a **range**. A range has two numbers, and the exact answer is somewhere between these two numbers. For addition, you estimate the **sum**, which is the number you get when you add two numbers together. Look at the problem below:

Estimate 813 + 279. The sum is between which numbers?

- Ⓐ 50 and 400
- Ⓑ 450 and 700
- Ⓒ 750 and 1,000
- Ⓓ 1,050 and 1,300

To answer this problem, you need to round 813 to the nearest 100. So 813 is rounded to 800. Then round 279 to the nearest 100. That's 300. Now add these numbers together. You get 1,100. The number 1,100 is between 1,050 and 1,300, so answer choice D is correct.

Let's try another one.

Estimate 311 + 297. The sum is between which numbers?

- Ⓐ 50 and 400
- Ⓑ 450 and 700
- Ⓒ 750 and 1,000
- Ⓓ 1,050 and 1,300

The number 311 rounded to the nearest 100 is 300. The number 297 rounded to the nearest 100 is 300. Add these two numbers together: 300 + 300 = 600. Answer choice B gives a range of between 450 and 700. The number 600 is in this range, so this is the correct answer choice.

Practice Questions

Practice 8: Estimating Addition

DIRECTIONS:

Choose the best of the answer choices given for each of the following problems. Fill in the circle next to your choice. You may NOT use a calculator.

1. Estimate 720 + 292. The sum is between which numbers?

   Ⓐ 400 and 600

   Ⓑ 700 and 900

   Ⓒ 1,000 and 1,200

   Ⓓ 1,300 and 1,500

HINT

Round 720 and 292 to the nearest 100. Then add those two numbers together.

2. Estimate 109 + 258. The sum is between which numbers?

   Ⓐ 100 and 200

   Ⓑ 300 and 600

   Ⓒ 600 and 800

   Ⓓ 800 and 1,000

HINT

Round 109 and 258 to the nearest 100. Then add those two numbers together.

Estimating Subtraction

Questions that ask you to estimate subtraction are set up just like questions that ask you to estimate addition. They ask you to choose the correct range of numbers. For subtraction, however, you'll look for the **difference** instead of the sum. Let's try this one:

Estimate 678 − 214. The difference is between which numbers?

Ⓐ 50 and 400

Ⓑ 450 and 700

Ⓒ 750 and 1,000

Ⓓ 1,050 and 1,300

To answer this question, round 678 to 700 and 214 to 200. Then subtract 200 from 700. The answer is 500, so answer choice B is correct.

Let's try another problem.

Estimate 685 − 497. The difference is between which numbers?

Ⓐ 100 and 300

Ⓑ 400 and 600

Ⓒ 700 and 900

Ⓓ 1,000 and 1,200

Round 685 and 497 to the nearest 100. The number 685 rounded to the nearest 100 is 700, and the number 497 rounded to the nearest 100 is 500. When you subtract 500 from 700, the answer is 200. Answer choice A is correct.

Practice Questions

Practice 9: Estimating Subtraction

DIRECTIONS:

Choose the best of the answer choices given for each of the following problems. Fill in the circle next to your choice. You may NOT use a calculator.

1. Estimate 780 − 349. The difference is between which numbers?

   Ⓐ 100 and 299

   Ⓑ 300 and 399

   Ⓒ 400 and 599

   Ⓓ 600 and 899

HINT

Round 780 and 349 to the nearest 100. Then subtract the smaller number from the larger number and choose the correct answer choice.

2. Estimate 836 − 432. The difference is between which numbers?

   Ⓐ 1,200 and 1,500

   Ⓑ 1,000 and 1,100

   Ⓒ 700 and 900

   Ⓓ 200 and 500

HINT

Begin by rounding both numbers to the nearest 100. Then subtract the second number from the first, and choose the right range.

Estimating Multiplication

For multiplication problems, you estimate the **product**, which is the number you get when you multiply two numbers together. Rounding will help you to estimate the product. Look at this problem:

Estimate 38 × 22. The product is between which numbers?

- Ⓐ 30 and 70
- Ⓑ 80 and 150
- Ⓒ 300 and 700
- Ⓓ 800 and 1,500

To estimate the answer to this problem, round 38 to the nearest 10, which is 40. Round 22 to the nearest 10, which is 20. When you multiply 40 × 20, the answer is 800. Answer choice D is the correct answer.

Let's try one more.

Estimate 48 × 25. The product is between which numbers?

- Ⓐ 30 and 80
- Ⓑ 100 and 150
- Ⓒ 300 and 800
- Ⓓ 1,000 and 1,500

To estimate the answer to this problem, round 48 to the nearest 10, which is 50. Then round 25 to the nearest 10, which is 30. Multiply these numbers. Your estimated answer is 1,500. Answer choice D is correct.

Practice Questions

Practice 10: Estimating Multiplication

DIRECTIONS:

Choose the best of the answer choices given for each of the following problems. Fill in the circle next to your choice. You may NOT use a calculator.

1. Estimate 43 × 18. The product is between which numbers?

Ⓐ 30 and 80

Ⓑ 100 and 150

Ⓒ 300 and 800

Ⓓ 1,000 and 1,500

HINT

Round 43 and 18 to the nearest 10 and multiply.

2. Estimate 29 × 11. The product is between which numbers?

Ⓐ 30 and 80

Ⓑ 100 and 150

Ⓒ 300 and 800

Ⓓ 1,000 and 1,500

HINT

Round both numbers to the nearest 10. Then use mental math to estimate the answer.

Estimating Division

You can also use rounding to estimate division. Note that when you divide one number into another, the number you get is called the **quotient**. Look at this problem:

Estimate 117 ÷ 9. The quotient is between which numbers?

- Ⓐ 0 and 5
- Ⓑ 5 and 10
- Ⓒ 10 and 20
- Ⓓ 20 and 30

To solve this problem, round 117 to 100. For this problem, it also helps to round 9 to 10. You know that 10 goes into 100 ten times, so answer choice C is correct.

Let's try another.

Estimate 550 ÷ 5. The quotient is between which numbers?

- Ⓐ 5 and 30
- Ⓑ 50 and 300
- Ⓒ 500 and 1,000
- Ⓓ 1,000 and 6,000

To estimate the quotient to this problem, round 550 to 600. Then divide 600 by 5 to get 120. Answer choice B is correct. Note that if you rounded 5 up to 10 before you divided, you would get the same range for your answer, which is 60. Finally, you might have been able to find the actual answer (110) by mental math, and that would help you to find the range, but usually estimation problems aren't easy to do by using mental math.

Practice Questions

Practice 11: Estimating Division

DIRECTIONS:

Choose the best of the answer choices given for each of the following problems. Fill in the circle next to your choice. You may NOT use a calculator.

1. Estimate 148 ÷ 4. The quotient is between which numbers?

Ⓐ 0 and 5

Ⓑ 5 and 20

Ⓒ 20 and 40

● 40 and 60

HINT

Round 148 to 100. Then divide 100 by 4.

2. Estimate 246 ÷ 6. The quotient is between which numbers?

Ⓐ 30 and 50

Ⓑ 10 and 20

● 5 and 10

Ⓓ 0 and 5

HINT

Round 246 to 200. About how many times does 6 go into 200? If you don't know, try rounding 6 to 5 and dividing.

Practice Questions

End-of-Chapter Practice Problems

DIRECTIONS:

Choose the best of the answer choices given for each of the following problems. Fill in the circle next to your choice. You may NOT use a calculator.

1. Estimate 795 + 116. The sum is between which numbers?

Ⓐ 50 and 400

Ⓑ 450 and 700

Ⓒ 750 and 1,000

Ⓓ 1,050 and 1,300

HINT

Round 795 and 116 to the nearest 100 and add.

2. Estimate 85 × 12. The product is between which numbers?

Ⓐ 30 and 80

Ⓑ 100 and 150

Ⓒ 300 and 800

Ⓓ 900 and 1,500

HINT

Round both 85 and 12 to the nearest 10.

3. **Estimate 252 ÷ 2. The quotient is between which numbers?**

Ⓐ 10 and 30

Ⓑ 100 and 300

Ⓒ 1,000 and 3,000

Ⓓ 10,000 and 30,000

HINT

Round 252 to the nearest 100 and divide by 2.

4. **Estimate 925 − 347. The difference is between which numbers?**

Ⓐ 100 and 299

Ⓑ 300 and 499

Ⓒ 500 and 699

Ⓓ 700 and 899

HINT

Round 925 and 347 to the nearest 100 and subtract.

5. **Estimate 372 + 108. The sum is between which numbers?**

Ⓐ 50 and 400

Ⓑ 450 and 700

Ⓒ 750 and 1,000

Ⓓ 1,050 and 1,300

HINT

Round 372 and 108 to the nearest 100 and add.

6. **Estimate 87 × 12. The product is between which numbers?**

Ⓐ 30 and 80

Ⓑ 100 and 150

Ⓒ 300 and 800

Ⓓ 900 and 1,200

HINT: Round 87 and 12 to the nearest 10 and multiply.

7. **Estimate 114 ÷ 6. The quotient is between which numbers?**

Ⓐ 30 and 50

Ⓑ 10 and 20

Ⓒ 5 and 9

Ⓓ 0 and 5

HINT: Round 114 to the nearest 100 and 6 to the nearest 10 and divide.

Chapter 4

All About Lines and Shapes

Shapes are formed by lines, and there are many different types of shapes. Shapes can be two- or three-dimensional. In this chapter, you'll learn about lines and shapes.

Lines

A **line** is straight and goes in two directions. To show that it continues in two different directions, a line has an arrow at each end. You can see a line below:

A **line segment** is part of a line. It is different from a line, because it has a beginning and an end. A point is used to show where a line segment begins and ends. This point is called an **endpoint**. Look at the line segment shown below. It has two endpoints.

A **ray** is also part of a line, but it is different from a line segment, because it has only one endpoint and one arrow. The arrow means that it keeps on going in one direction, and the endpoint means that it stops in the other direction. You can see a ray below. Notice that it has one endpoint and one arrow.

Parallel lines run in the **same direction**. They can be **vertical** (up and down), **horizontal** (side to side), or even at an angle (such as corner to corner), but they never cross each other.

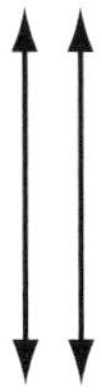

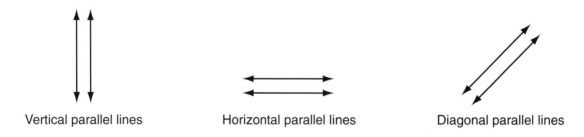

Vertical parallel lines

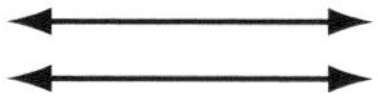

Horizontal parallel lines

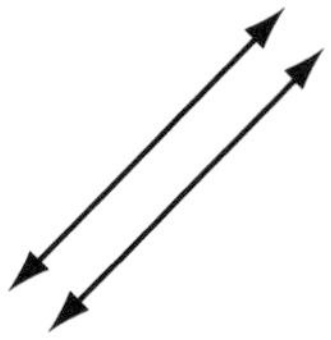

Diagonal parallel lines

Perpendicular lines cross each other like the lines in a plus sign (+). They meet at a 90° angle. When lines cross, they are said to **intersect**. The place where lines intersect is called the **point of intersection**. Look at the perpendicular lines shown here:

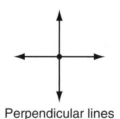

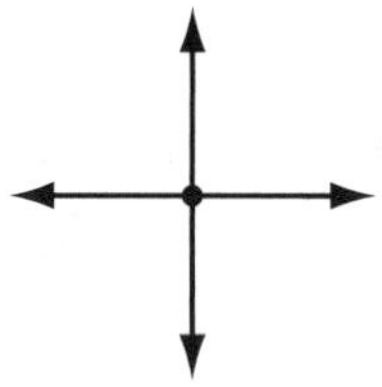

Perpendicular lines

Can you name each of the figures below? Write the name of the figure on the line beneath it.

1. 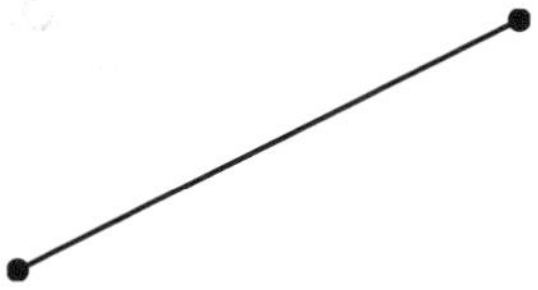

line segment

2. 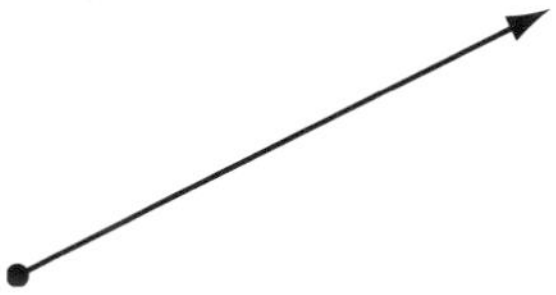

ray

3. 

line

4. 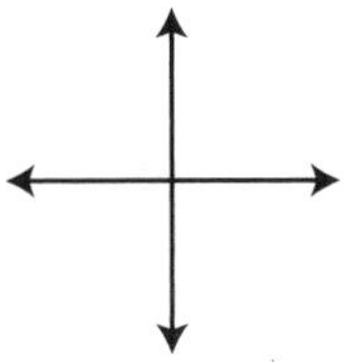

Perpendicular lines

5. 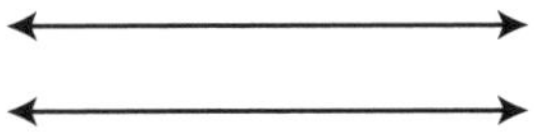

Horizontal parallel lines

Now fill in the blanks with the correct words.

6. The points that show where a line segment begins and ends are called end points.

7. A line **has an arrow at each end.**

8. The point where two lines intersect is called the point of intersection **.**

You are correct if your answers are

1. a line segment
2. a ray
3. a line
4. perpendicular lines
5. parallel lines
6. endpoints
7. line
8. point of intersection

If you missed any of these, go back to the discussion of lines at the beginning of this chapter.

Practice Questions

Practice 12: Lines

DIRECTIONS:

Choose the best of the answer choices given for each of the following problems. Fill in the circle next to your choice.

1. Which of these is a ray?

(A) 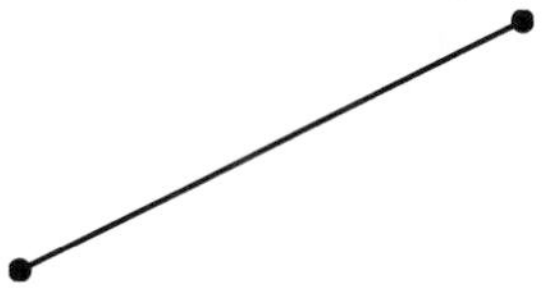

(B) 

(C) 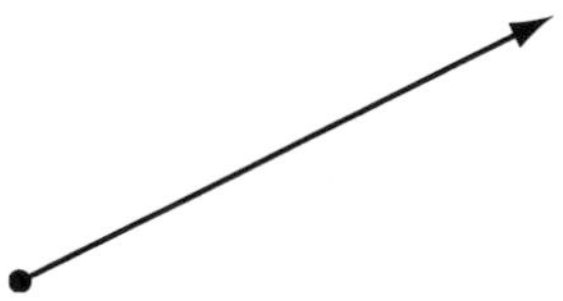

(D) 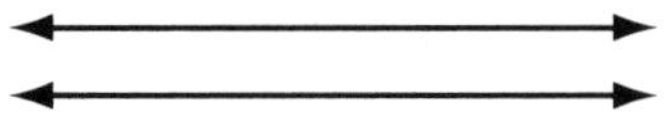

Remember that a ray does not have two arrows or two endpoints.

2. **What is point *A* called on the line segment *AB*?**

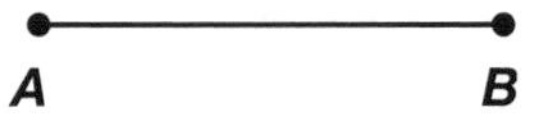

Ⓐ point of intersection

Ⓑ segment

Ⓒ endpoint

Ⓓ side

HINT

Review the section of the chapter on lines if you're not sure.

3. **What kind of lines are below?**

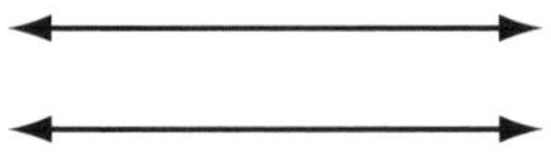

Ⓐ rays

Ⓑ parallel

Ⓒ perpendicular

Ⓓ endpoints

HINT

Review the section of the chapter on lines if you're not sure.

Angles

Two rays can make an **angle**. Look at the angle below. Each of the rays has an arrow at one end. The point where the rays meet is called the **vertex** of the angle. Each ray is called a **side** of the angle.

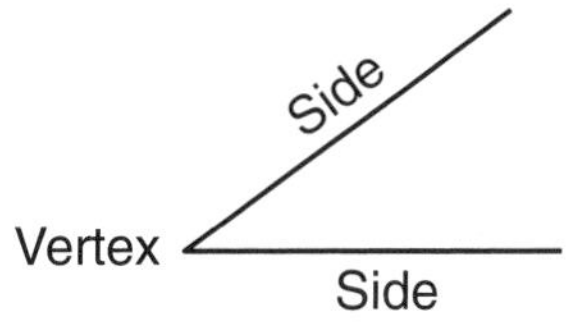

Angles are measured in **degrees**. A **protractor** is used to measure degrees. It is a lot like a ruler.

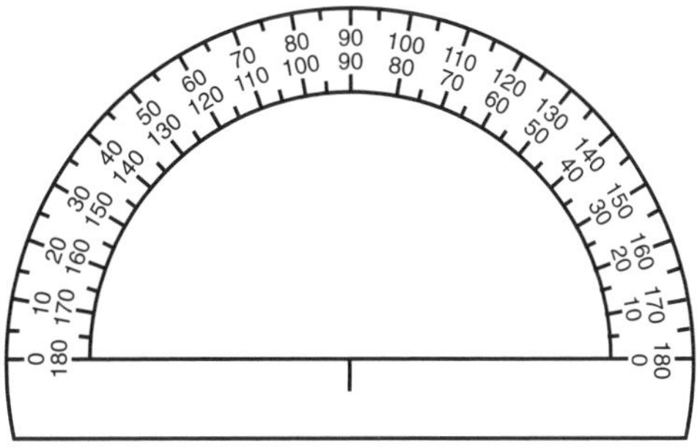

Angles have different names, depending on their measurement. A **right angle** measures exactly 90°. Look at the right angle below.

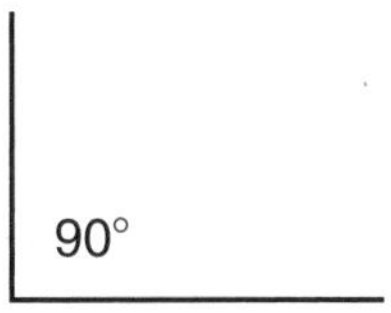

An **acute angle** measures less than 90°. It looks as if it is not open as much as a right angle. See the acute angle below? It measures 45°.

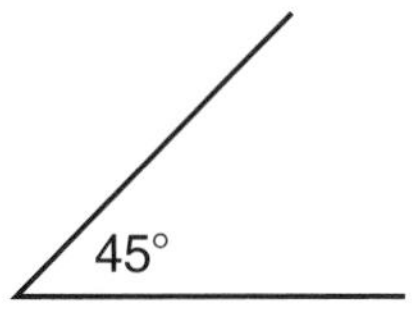

An **obtuse angle** measures more than 90°. It looks as if it is open more than a right angle. See the obtuse angle below? It measures 135°.

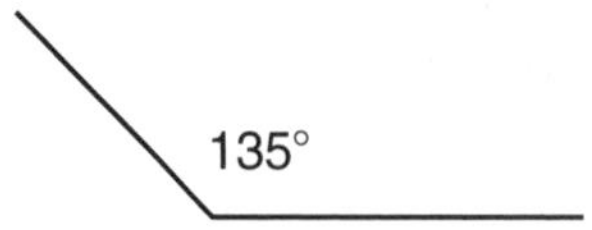

Can you name each of the angles below?

1. An ___obtuse___ **angle has more than 90°.**

2. An angle measuring less than 90° is called an ___acute___ **angle.**

3. A ___right___ **angle measures exactly 90°.**

4. The point where two rays meet to form an angle is called the ______________.

You are correct if your answers are:

1. obtuse
2. acute
3. right
4. vertex

If you missed any of these, review the section on angles in this chapter.

Practice Questions

Practice 13: Angles

DIRECTIONS:

Choose the best of the answer choices given for each of the following problems. Fill in the circle next to your choice.

1. Which of the following shows an acute angle?

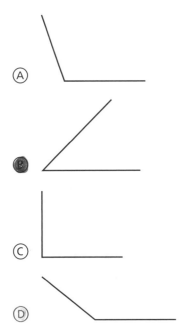

Ⓐ 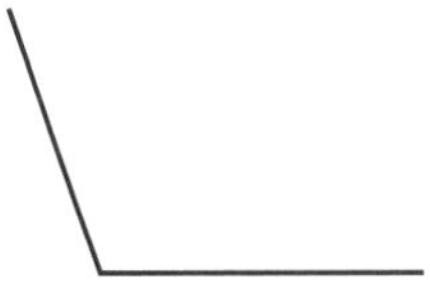

Ⓑ 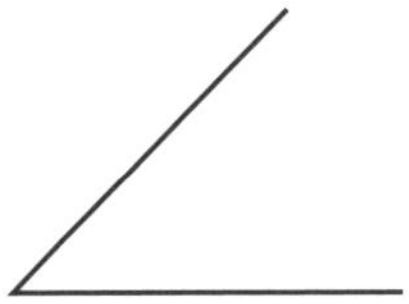

Ⓒ 

Ⓓ 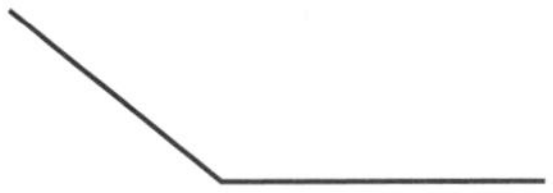

HINT

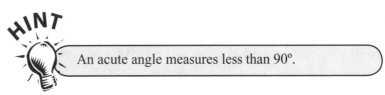

An acute angle measures less than 90°.

2. Which of the following shows a right angle?

(A) 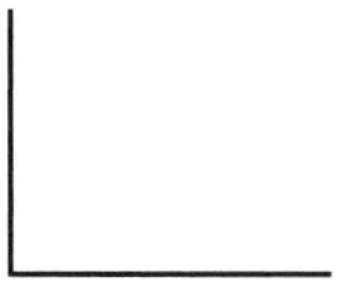

(B) 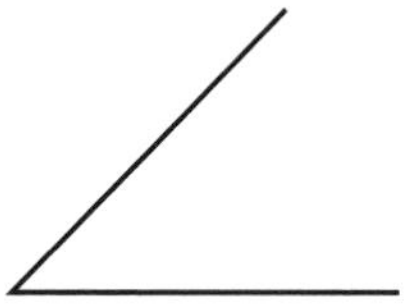

(C) 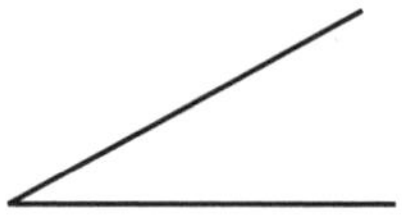

(D) 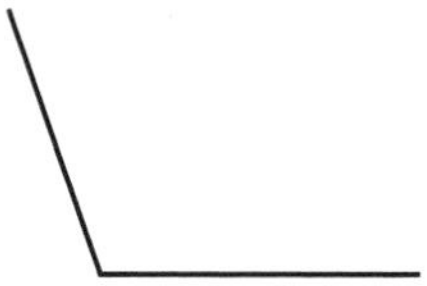

Remember that a right angle measures exactly 90°.

Two-Dimensional Shapes

Two-dimensional shapes are flat. They have a **length** and a **height**, but they don't have **depth**. Let's look at some typical two-dimensional shapes.

Circles

A **circle** is a round shape. All of the **points** on a circle are exactly the same distance from the **center** of the circle.

The **distance** around a circle is called the **circumference**. It is the length of the outside of the circle.

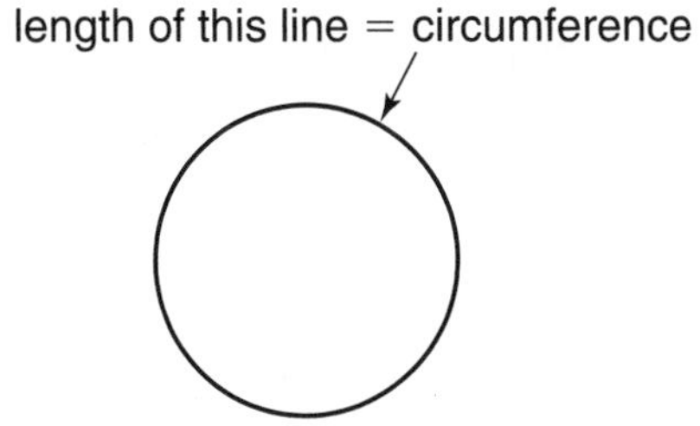

The distance across a circle—from one side to the other and going through the **center**—is called the **diameter**. The diameter of a circle is shown here.

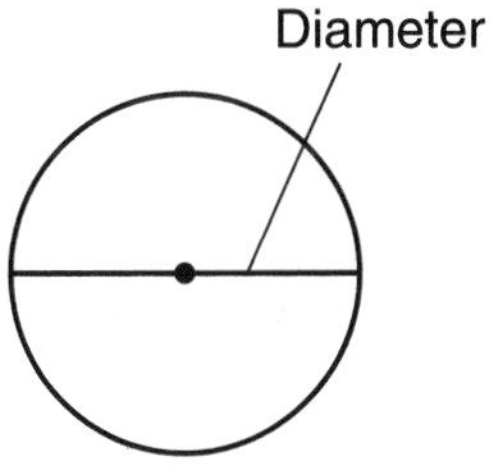

The distance from the center of the circle to any point on the circle is called the **radius**. The radius is one-half the length of the diameter.

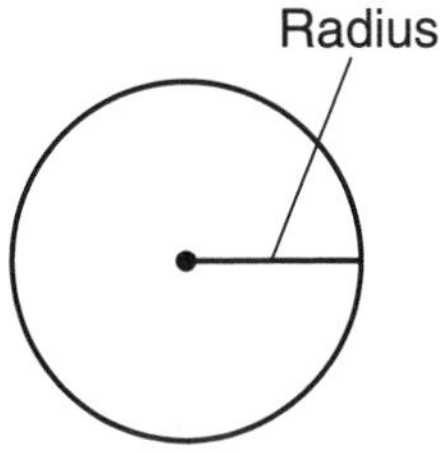

Triangles

A **triangle** is a figure with three sides. Triangles come in different shapes and sizes. Their sides can be equal, but they don't have to be.

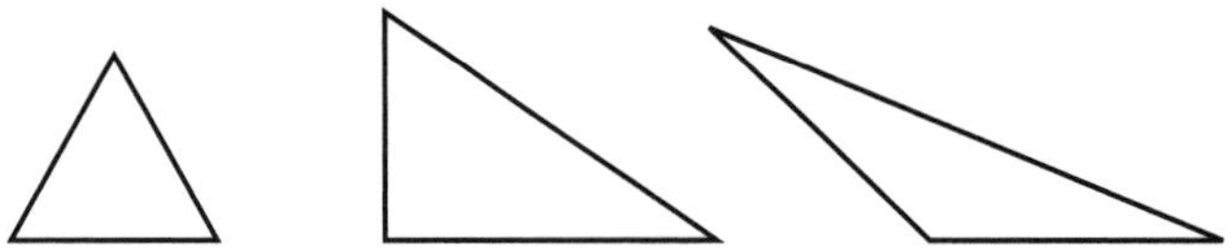

All triangles contain angles. A right triangle has one right angle:

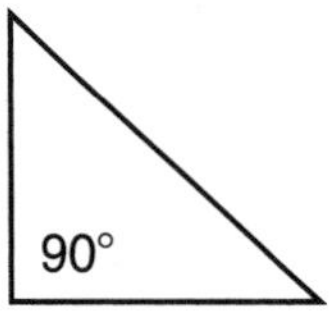

Some triangles have one obtuse angle, which you learned is an angle larger than a right angle. These triangles are called obtuse triangles.

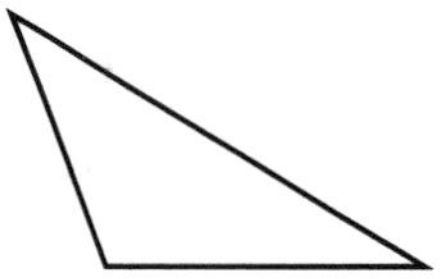

Quadrilaterals

A **quadrilateral** has four sides. Circles and triangles are not quadrilaterals. Rectangles and squares are quadrilaterals, because they have four sides.

A **rectangle** has two pairs of equal sides, and all angles are 90°. Rectangles can be different sizes, but two pairs of sides will always be equal.

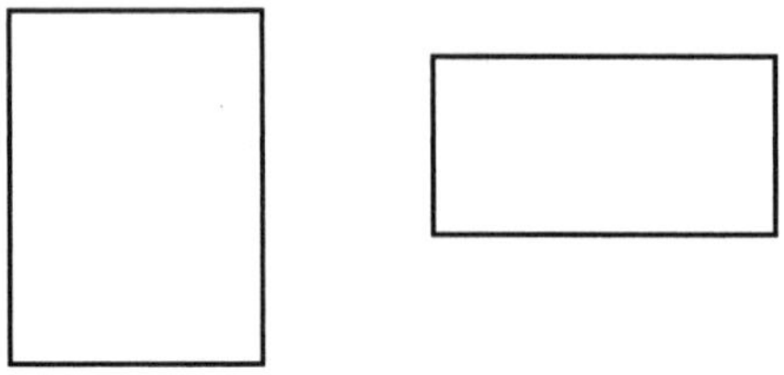

A **square** is a rectangle, with all four sides equal. Squares can be different sizes, but the sides are always equal.

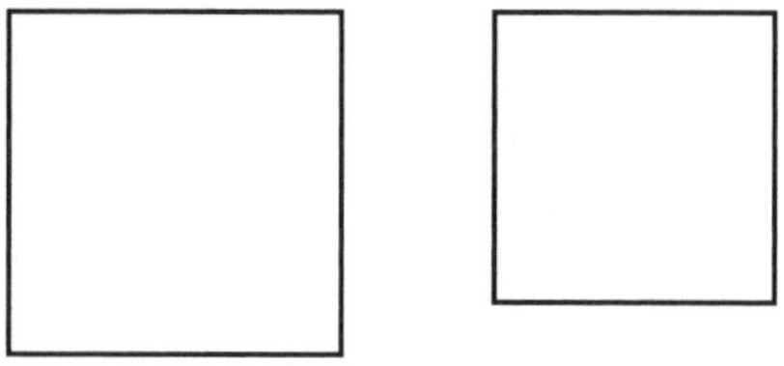

Other Two-Dimensional Shapes

A **pentagon** is a shape with five sides. These sides do not have to be equal.

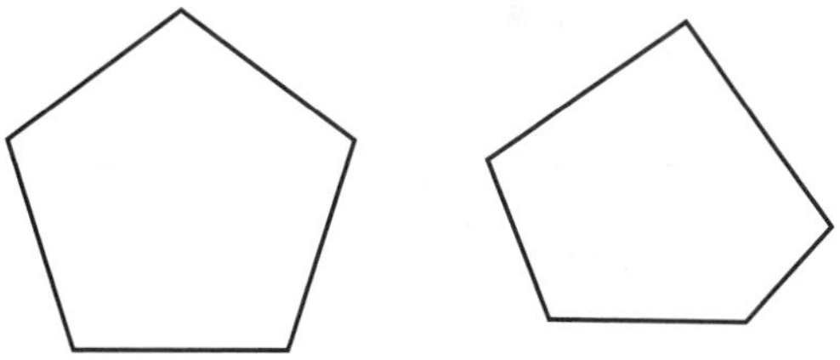

A **hexagon** is a shape with six sides. These sides do not have to be equal.

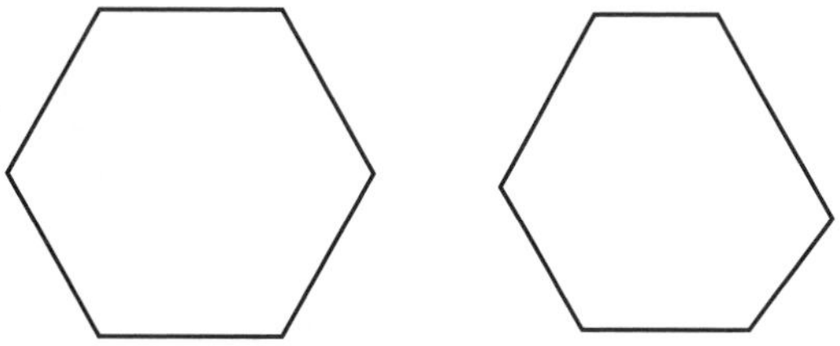

An **octagon** has eight sides. These sides do not have to be equal.

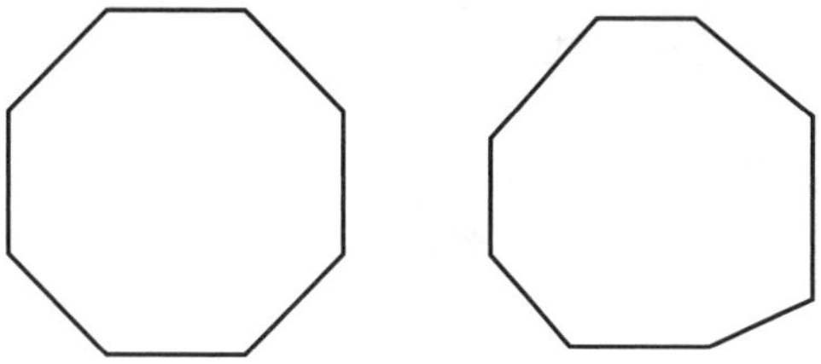

Look at the following two-dimensional shapes. Write what kind of shape each is on the line below it.

1. 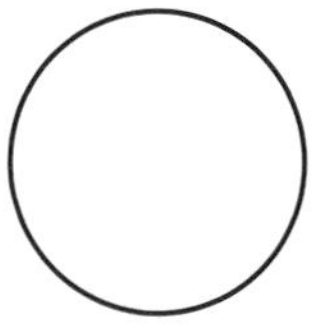

circle

2. 

square

3. 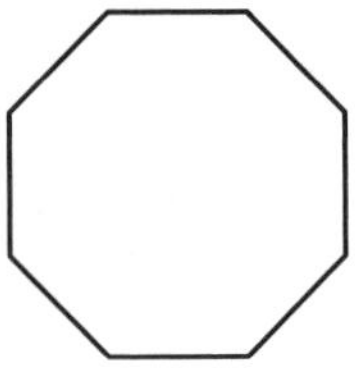

octangon

4. 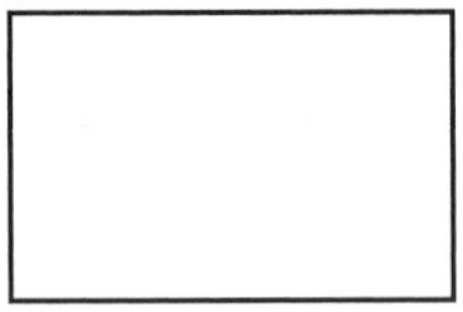

rectangle

5. 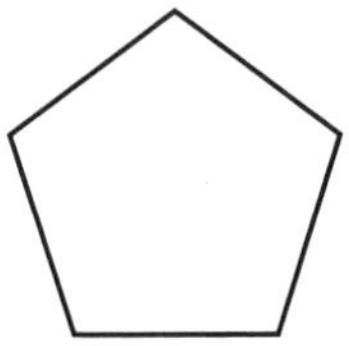

pentagon

Now fill in the blanks with the correct words.

6. The ______________________________ is the distance around a circle.

7. A ______________________________ is a shape with six sides, and these sides do not have to be equal.

8. A ______________________________ has four sides that are the same length, and all angles are 90°.

9. A ______________________________ is a line going from one side of a circle to the other and passing through the center.

10. A ______________________________ has four sides, four 90° angles, and the opposite sides are equal.

11. A ______________________________ is a line drawn from the center of a circle to a point on the circle.

12. A ______________________________ has three sides, and these sides do not have to be equal.

13. An ______________________________ has eight sides, and these sides do not have to be equal.

14. A ______________________________ has five sides, and these sides do not have to be equal.

You are correct if your answers are:

1. circle
2. square
3. octagon
4. rectangle
5. pentagon
6. circumference
7. hexagon
8. square
9. diameter
10. rectangle
11. radius
12. triangle
13. octagon
14. pentagon

If you missed one or more answers, review the section on two-dimensional shapes in this chapter.

Practice Questions

Practice 14: Two-Dimensional Shapes

DIRECTIONS:

Choose the best of the answer choices given for each of the following problems. Fill in the circle next to your choice.

1. Which shape below is an octagon?

Ⓐ 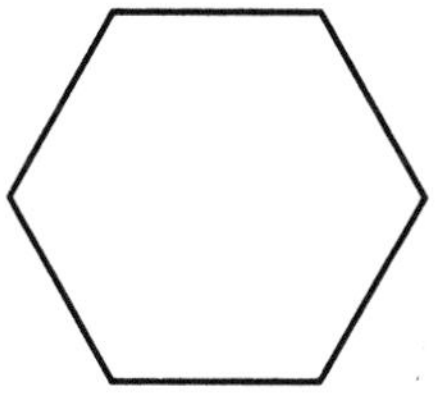

Ⓑ 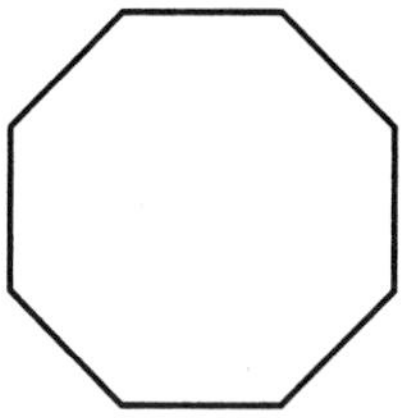

Ⓒ 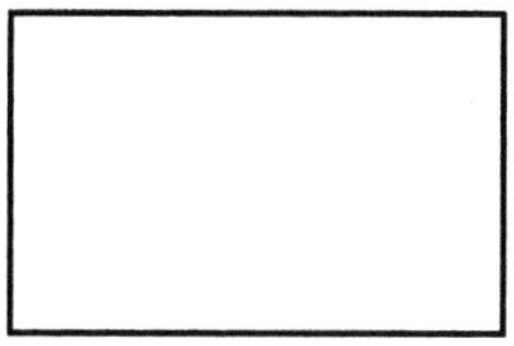

Ⓓ 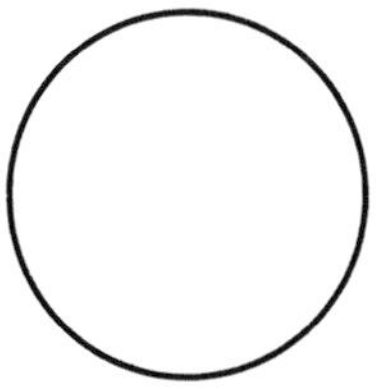

HINT

An octagon has eight sides that do not have to be equal.

2. **Michi wrote the following riddle to her friend:**

   The distance between the point in my center and any point on my outline is equal. What am I?

   What is the answer to the riddle?

   Ⓐ triangle

   Ⓑ octagon

   Ⓒ circle

   Ⓓ square

HINT

If you're not sure of this answer, go back and reread the section of this chapter that describes different kinds of shapes.

3. **Which of the following is a quadrilateral?**

   Ⓐ circle

   Ⓑ triangle

   Ⓒ hexagon

   Ⓓ rectangle

HINT

Remember that a quadrilateral has four sides.

Three-Dimensional Shapes

Three-dimensional shapes look different from two-dimensional shapes, because they have **depth**, or a **width**. Three-dimensional shapes are sometimes called **solids**.

Look at the three-dimensional shape shown here. It is a **cube**. It looks like a square, but it has width. A cube looks like a block.

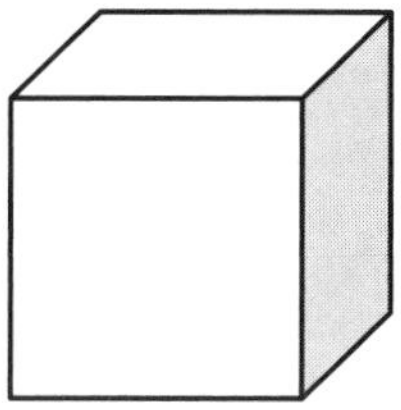

Notice that there are special names for parts of three-dimensional shapes. Each flat part on a three-dimensional shape is called a **face**. The lines in the shape are called **edges**, and the edges meet at **vertices**. (Vertices is the plural of **vertex**, or corner.) Each face on the cube is a shaped like a square. A cube has six faces and eight vertices.

Look at the **rectangular prism** below. It looks a lot like a box. Note that it also looks like a rectangle, except it has width. Like a square, a rectangular prism has six faces and eight vertices.

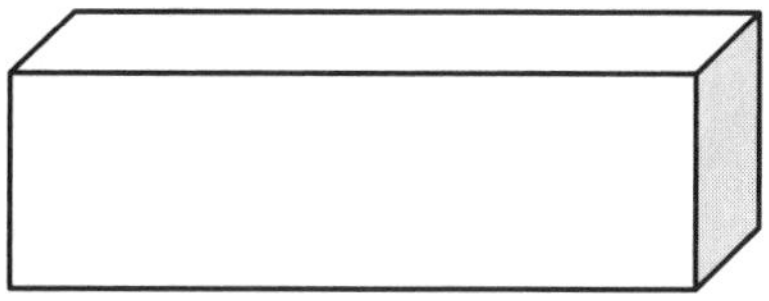

A **pyramid** looks a lot like a triangle. Its base can be a triangle or a quadrilateral, and it is often a square, as shown here. This pyramid has five faces and five vertices.

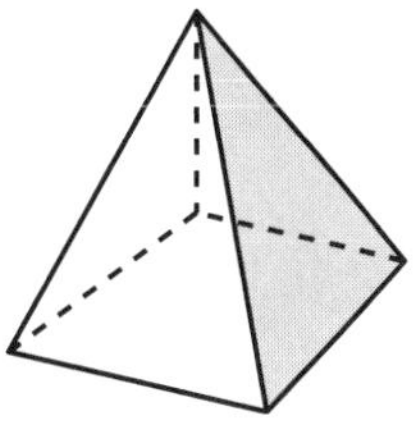

A **sphere** has no faces and no vertices. A sphere is a circle with depth. You can see from the figure below that it looks like a ball.

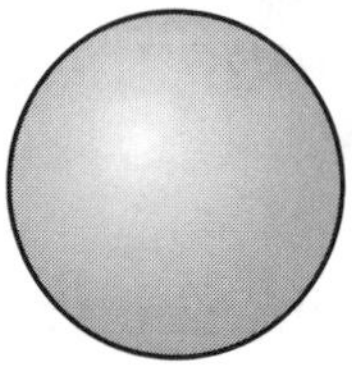

A **cone** looks just like an ice cream cone (see below). It has only one face and one vertex. The face is a circle.

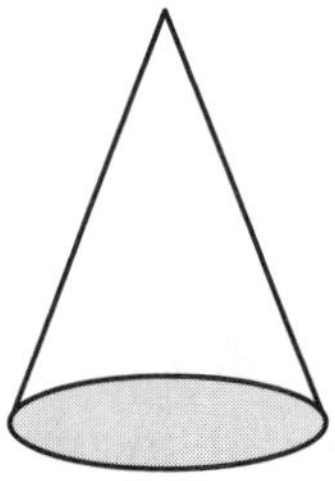

A **cylinder** has a top face and a bottom face and no vertices. Both of its faces are circles. A can is an example of a cylinder, as can be seen below.

Look at each of the three-dimensional shapes below. Write what kind of shape each is on the line below it. Turn to the end of this exercise to check your answers.

1. 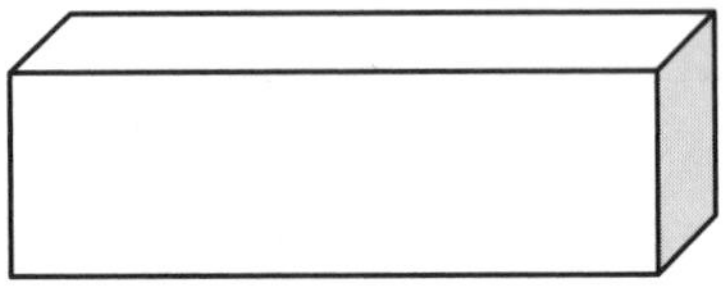

rectangular prism
____

2. 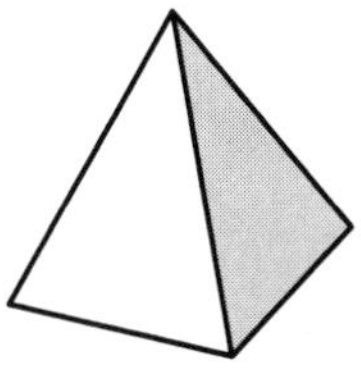

pyramid

3. 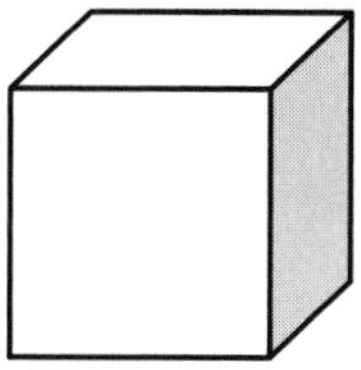

cube

4. 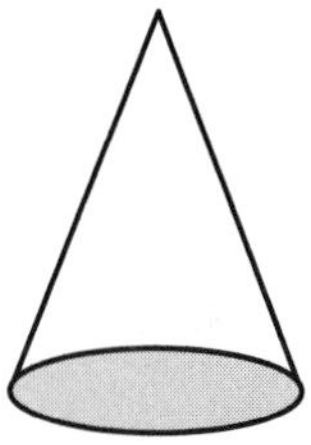

cone

5. 

cylinder

Now fill in the blanks with the correct words.

6. The flat part of a three-dimensional shape is called the face ____________________.

7. The edges of a three-dimensional shape meet at corners, or, vertics ________________.

8. A sphere ________________ is a three-dimensional shape with no faces.

9. A cone ________________ looks like an ice cream cone.

10. The base of a pyramid ________________ is often a square.

11. A rectangular prism ________________ looks like a box.

Draw a line from each three-dimensional shape on the left to the two-dimensional shape it is most like on the right.

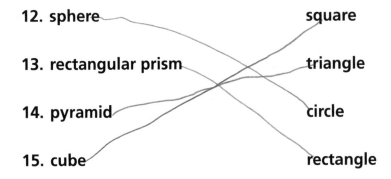

12. sphere	square
13. rectangular prism	triangle
14. pyramid	circle
15. cube	rectangle

You are correct if your answers are:

1. rectangular prism
2. pyramid
3. cube
4. cone
5. cylinder
6. face
7. corners, or vertices
8. sphere
9. cone
10. pyramid
11. rectangular prism (can be a cube but doesn't have to be)
12. sphere (circle)
13. rectangular prism (rectangle)
14. pyramid (triangle)
15. cube (square)

Practice Questions

Practice 15: Three-Dimensional Shapes

DIRECTIONS:

Choose the best of the answer choices given for each of the following problems. Fill in the circle next to your choice.

1. Which shape below is a sphere?

Ⓐ 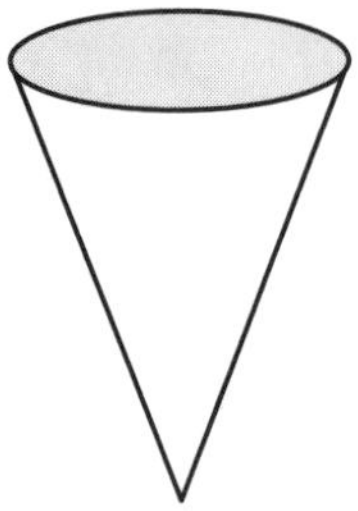

Ⓑ 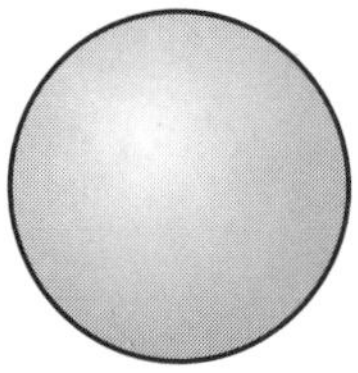

Ⓒ 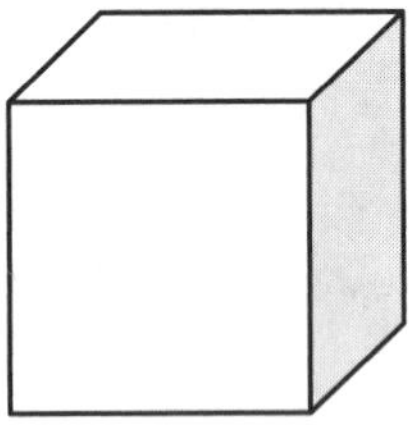

Ⓓ 

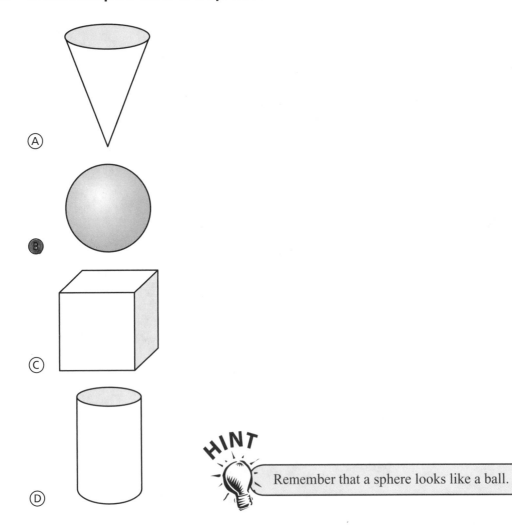

HINT: Remember that a sphere looks like a ball.

2. Juan wrote the following riddle on the chalkboard:

I have 5 faces and 5 vertices, and I look like a triangle that has a square on the bottom. What am I?

What is the answer to the riddle?

- Ⓐ cone
- Ⓑ cylinder
- Ⓒ triangular pyramid
- Ⓓ sphere

HINT

Think about a figure that looks like a triangle with a square on the bottom. What is this three-dimensional shape called? If you're not sure, turn back and review this section.

Lines of Symmetry

If you cut some shapes in half, the two **halves** will look exactly the same. Such shapes are said to have a **line of symmetry**. This line is imaginary. If you fold the shape over the line of symmetry, the two halves match up exactly. They are **mirror images**, or **reflections**, of each other.

Look at the shapes below. Each shape has a line of symmetry. In these figures, this line is down the center of the shape.

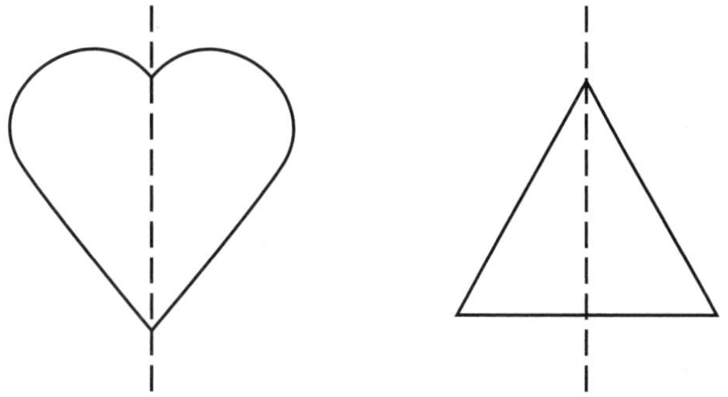

Now look at these shapes. They have a dotted line down the center, but they are not the same on both sides. These shapes do *not* have a line of symmetry.

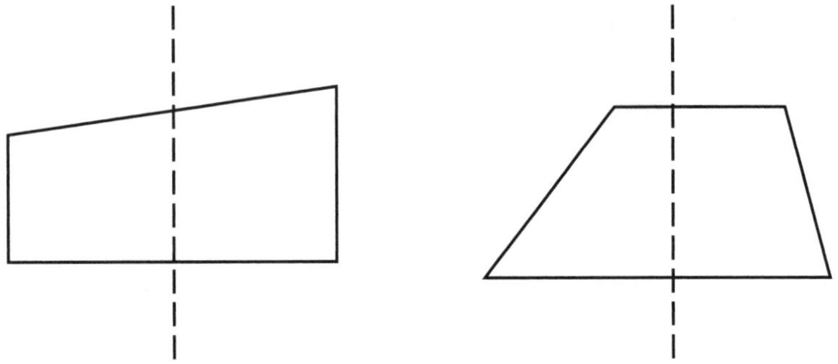

Shapes can have a **vertical** (up and down), **horizontal** (left to right), or **diagonal** line of symmetry. The shapes you have looked at so far have a vertical line of symmetry. The letters below have a horizontal line of symmetry.

Some shapes have more than one line of symmetry.

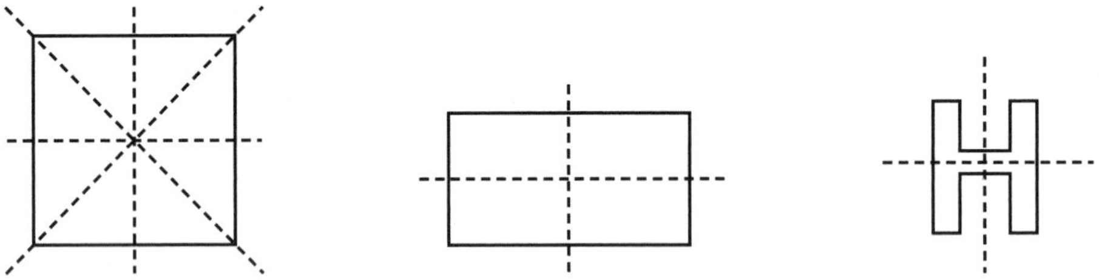

Put a check in the box for each shape that has at least one line of symmetry.

1. ☑ 

2. ☑ 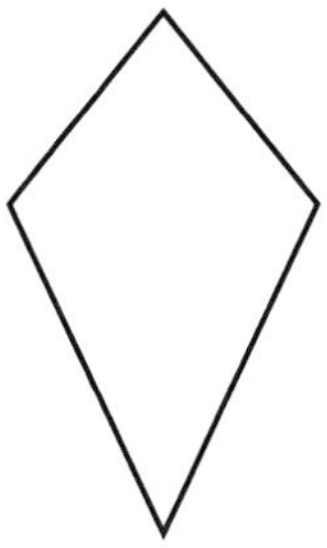

3. ☐ 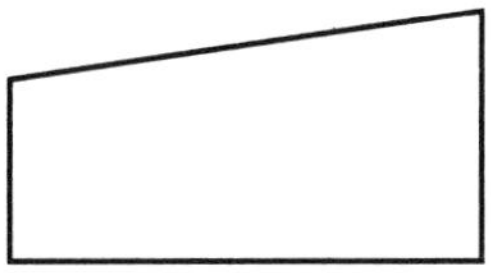

Only the first two of these three shapes have a line of symmetry, and the diamond actually has more than one.

Let's look at some more shapes.

On the line below each shape, tell how many lines of symmetry it has.

1. 

five

2. 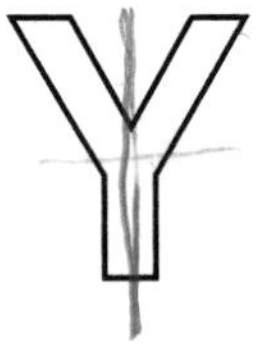

one

3. 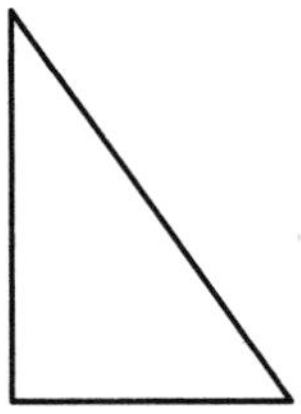

none

The star has five lines of symmetry; the letter Y has only one; and the triangle has none.

Practice Questions

Practice 16: Lines of Symmetry

DIRECTIONS:

Choose the best of the answer choices given for each of the following problems. Fill in the circle next to your choice.

1. Melissa made these cutouts for a mobile. Which cutout has more than one line of symmetry?

Ⓐ 

(B) 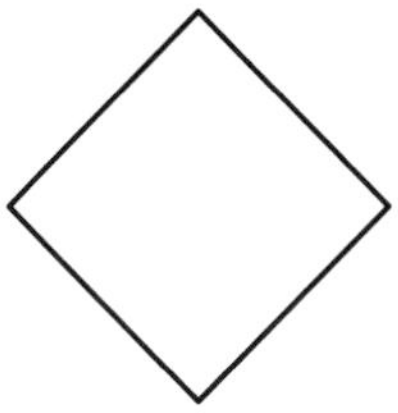

Ⓒ 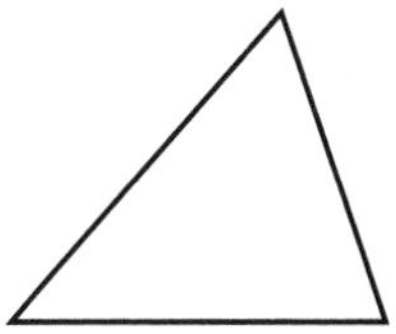

Ⓓ 

HINT

If you're not sure, draw a vertical, a horizontal, and a diagonal line on each shape. Choose the shape that can be divided in half with mirror images more than once.

2. **Which of these letters has a line of symmetry?**

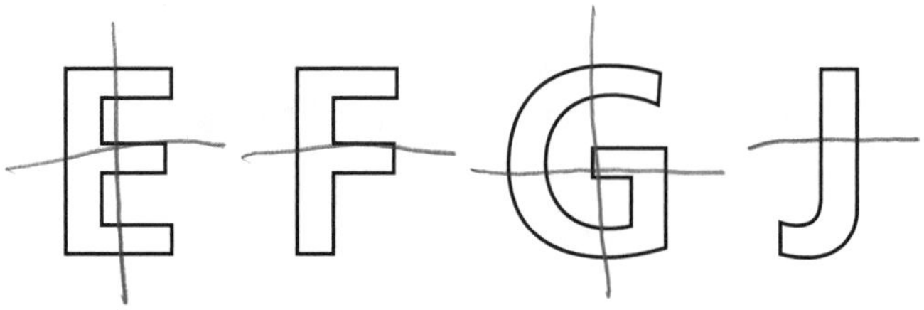

(A) **E**

(B) **F**

(C) **G**

(D) **J**

HINT

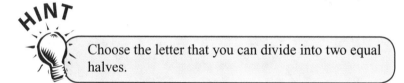

Choose the letter that you can divide into two equal halves.

Congruent Shapes

Shapes that are the same size and same shape are called **congruent shapes**. Look at the rectangles below. These rectangles are congruent, because they are the same shape and size.

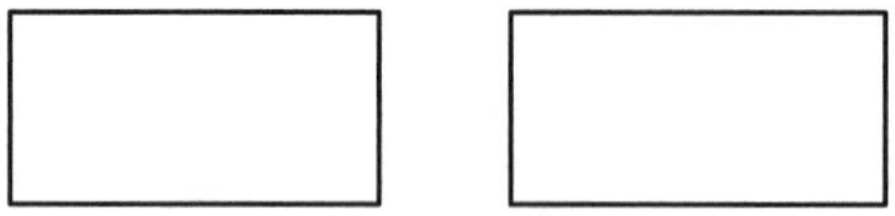

Now look at these triangles. They are not congruent.

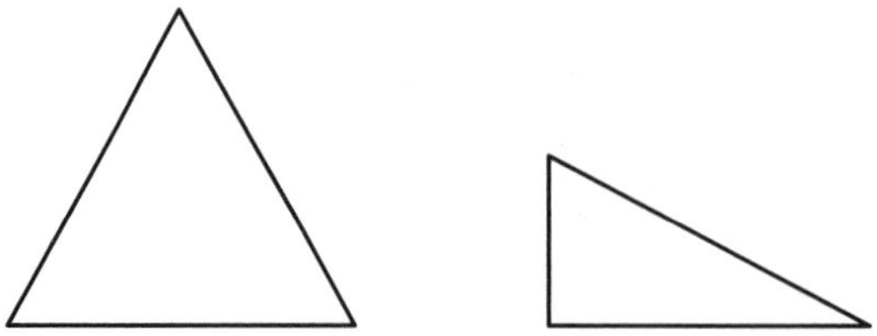

Practice Questions

Practice 17: Congruent Shapes

DIRECTIONS:

Choose the best of the answer choices given for each of the following problems. Fill in the circle next to your choice.

1. Which of the following shows a pair of congruent figures?

Ⓐ 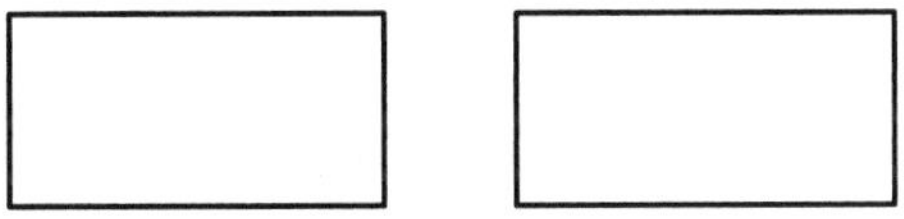

Ⓑ 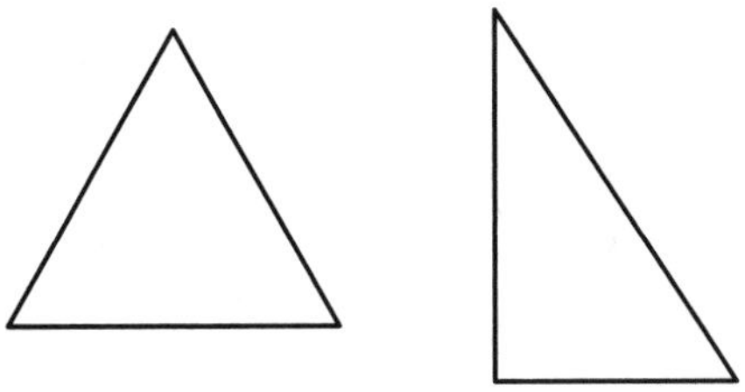

Ⓒ 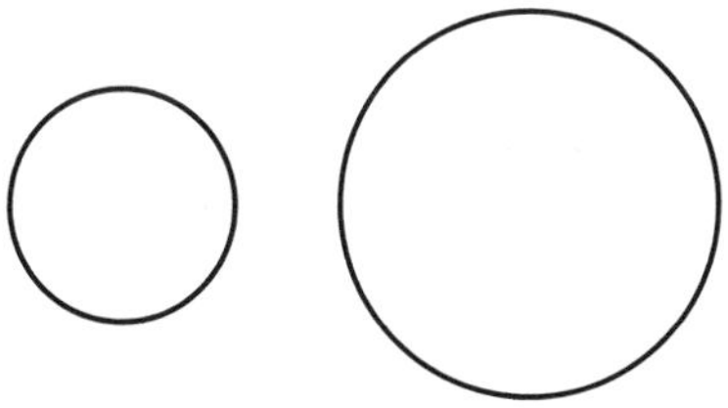

Ⓓ 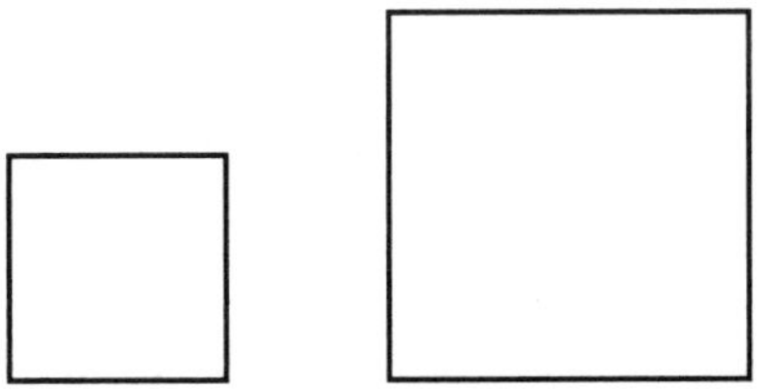

HINT

Choose the pair of shapes that is exactly the same.

2. **Which of the following shows a pair of figures that is NOT congruent?**

Ⓐ 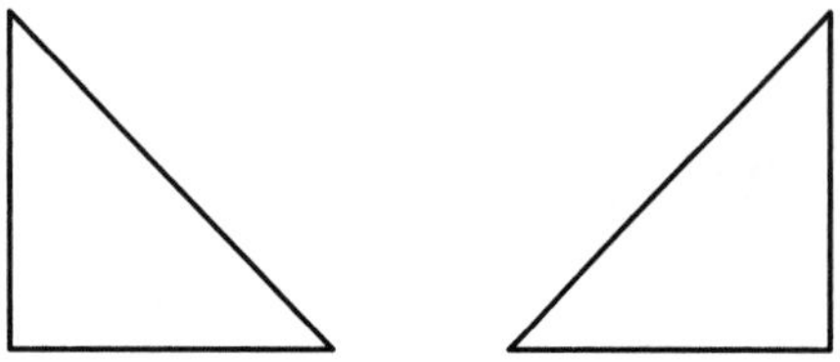

Ⓑ 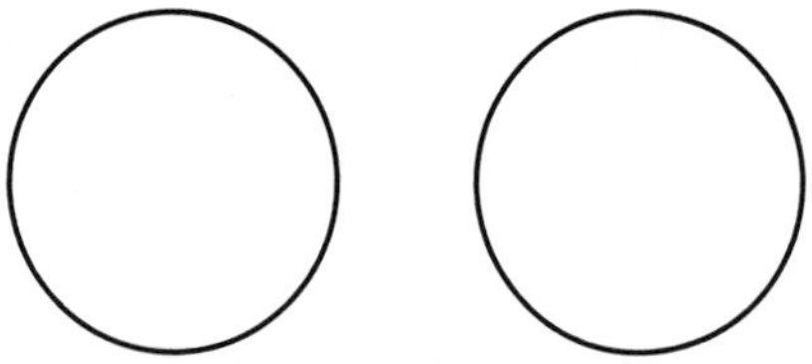

Ⓒ 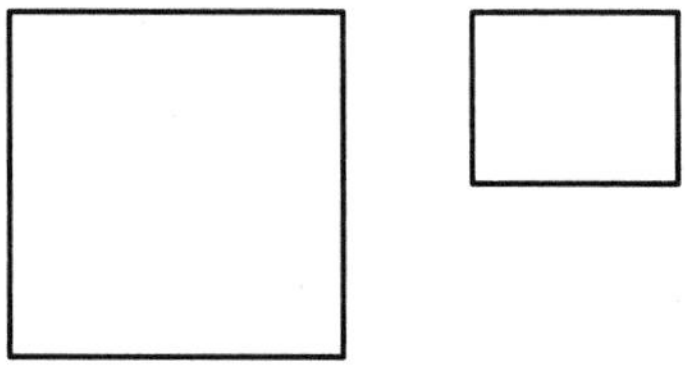

Ⓓ 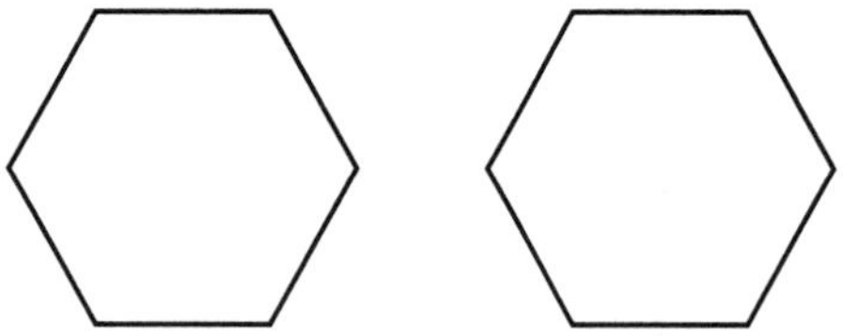

HINT

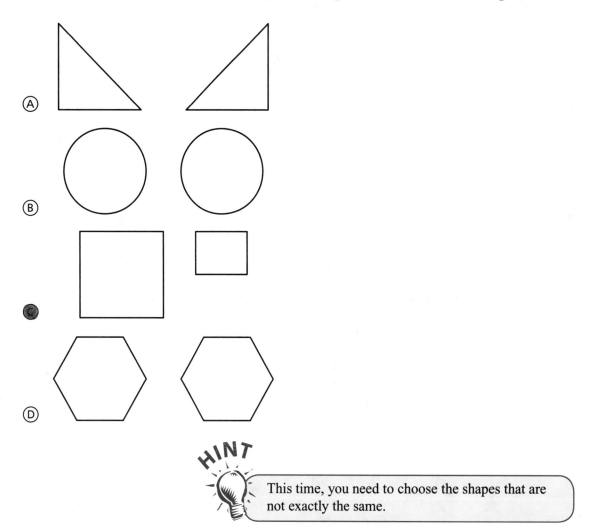

This time, you need to choose the shapes that are not exactly the same.

Moving Shapes

A shape can be moved in three basic ways: a slide, a flip, and a turn. Look at this figure:

Slide

If you **slide** the figure above, you move it in one direction without turning it. The shape looks as if it is has actually been slid. You can slide a shape in any direction, and as long as you don't turn it or flip it over, it's called a slide. Here are some ways you can slide a shape:

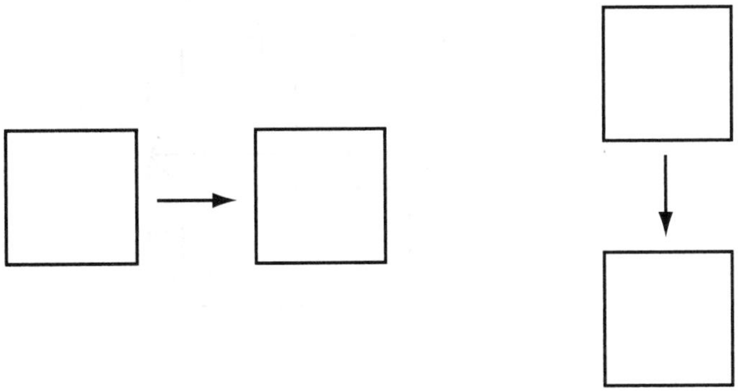

Flip

A shape that is flipped looks as if it is a mirror image, which is why a flip is sometimes called a **reflection**. The shape is flipped across a line, but often it is an imaginary line. The shapes below are flipped across dotted lines.

Turn

When you **turn** a shape, you move it so it looks as if it is tipping over or lying on its side. Look at the letter below to see how it is turned.

You can also turn a letter like this:

Tessellations

Tessellations (TESS-el-AY-shuns) are patterns of shapes joined together to cover a surface with no empty spaces between the shapes. Look at the tessellation below.

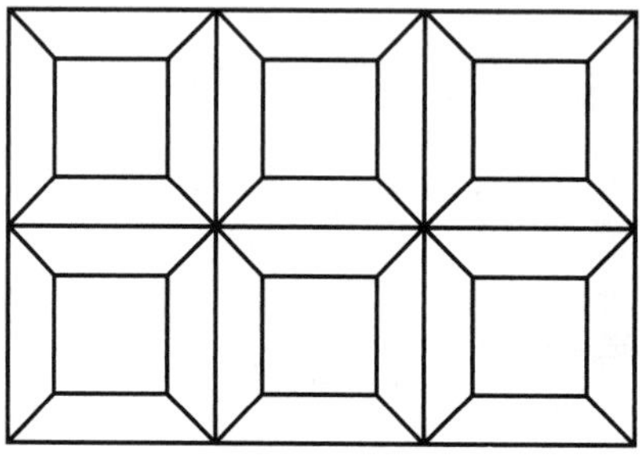

Look each of the following groups of shapes. Put a checkmark in the box if the group is a tessellation.

1. ☑ 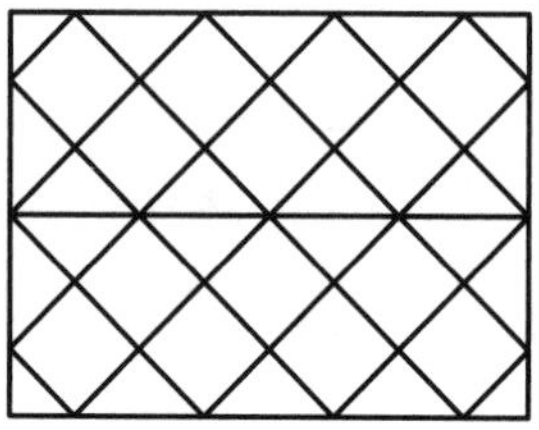

2. ☐ 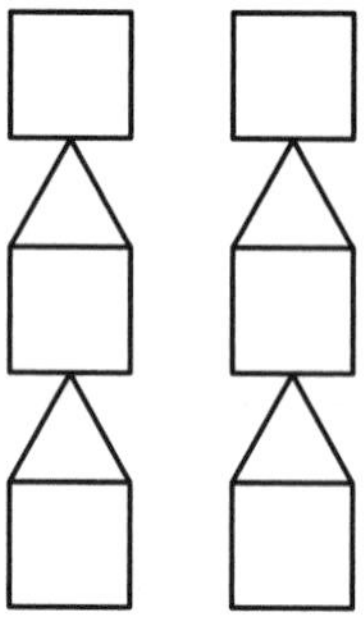

If you checked only the first group of shapes, you are correct. The second group is not a tessellation, because there is empty space between the shapes.

Practice Questions

Practice 18: Moving Shapes

DIRECTIONS:

Choose the best of the answer choices given for each of the following problems. Fill in the circle next to your choice.

1. Which picture shows only a slide?

Ⓐ 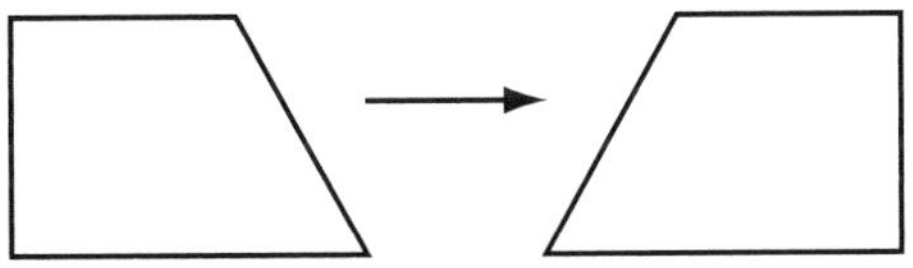

Ⓑ 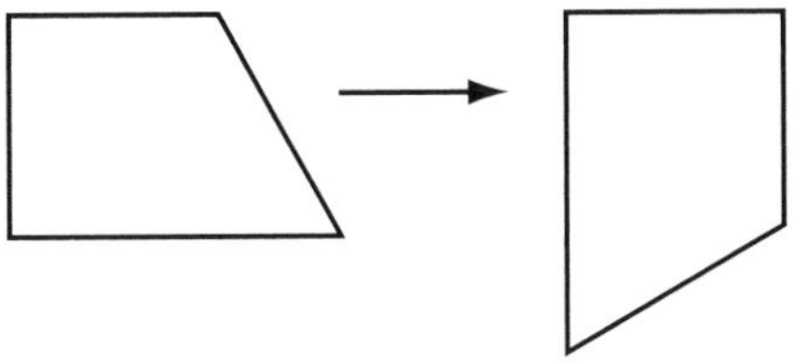

Ⓒ 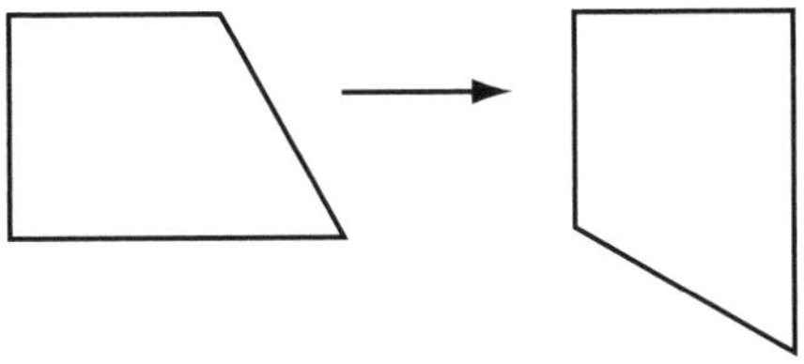

Ⓓ 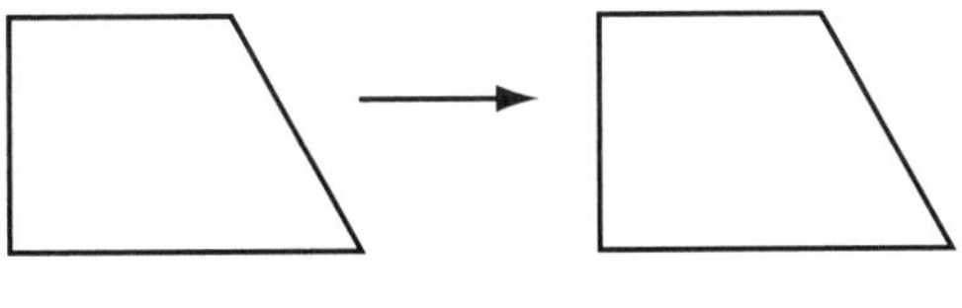

HINT

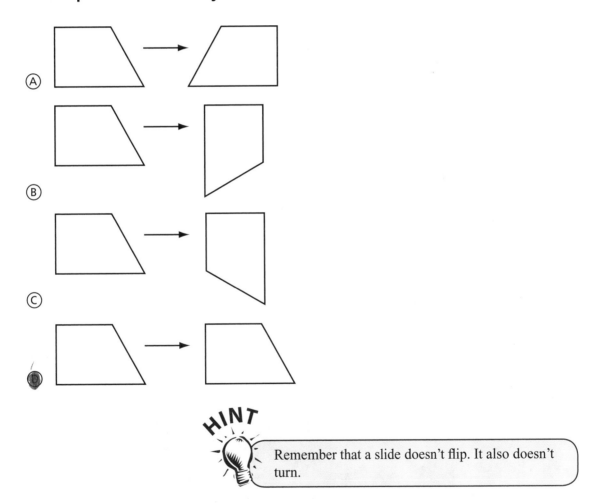

Remember that a slide doesn't flip. It also doesn't turn.

2. **Which of the following represents a flip of the figure shown over the line?**

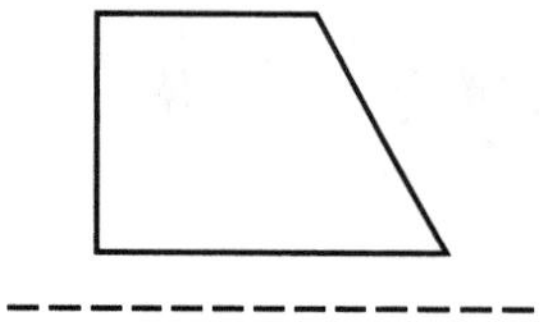

Ⓐ 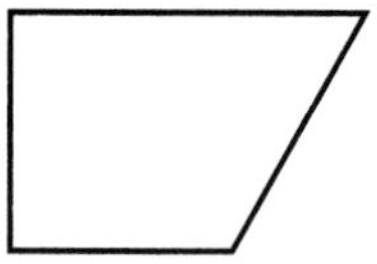

Ⓑ 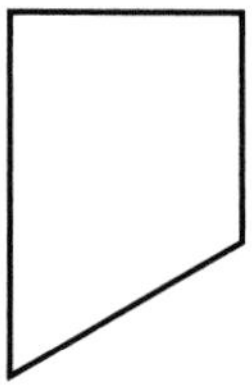

Ⓒ 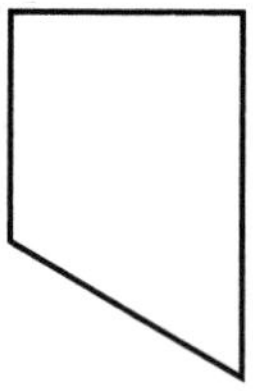

Ⓓ 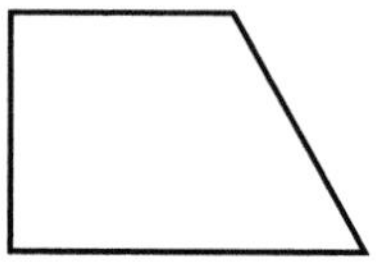

HINT

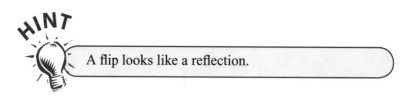

A flip looks like a reflection.

3. **Which of the following shows a turn of the figure below?**

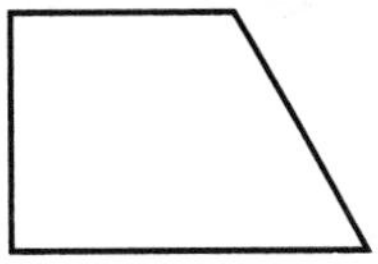

Ⓐ 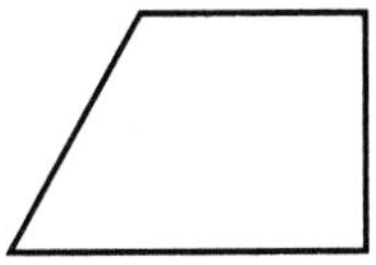

Ⓑ 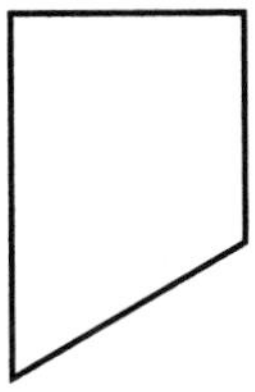

Ⓒ 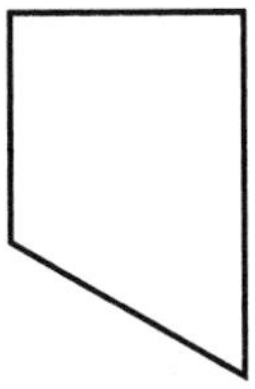

Ⓓ 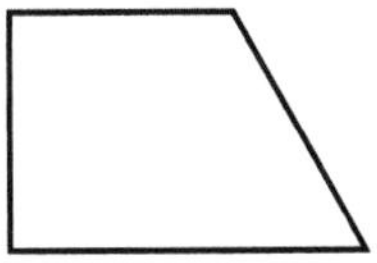

Remember that a turn doesn't flip. It just rotates.

4. **Which of the following belongs in the tessellation shown below?**

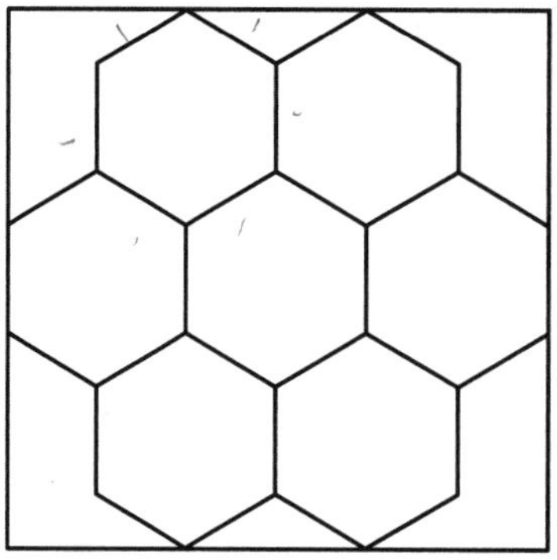

Ⓐ 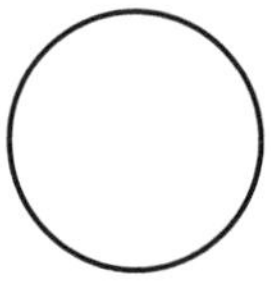

Ⓑ 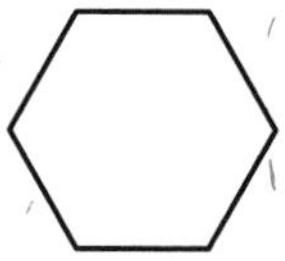

Ⓒ 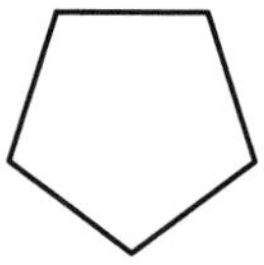

Ⓓ 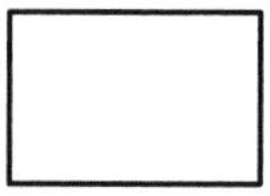

HINT

Choose the figure that would fit without leaving a gap.

Coordinate Grids

A **coordinate grid** looks like a lot of squares with two main lines, or **axes**. The ***x*-axis** runs across the bottom of the grid from left to right, and the ***y*-axis** runs along the side of the grid, from the bottom to the top. Each axis has an arrow at the end to show that it keeps on going, like a line. Look at the *x*-axis and *y*-axis on this grid. Notice that there are numbers on both of them.

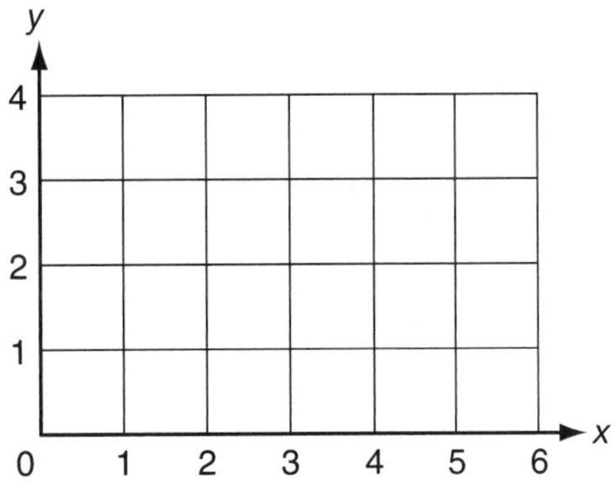

The places on the grid where any two lines cross are called **points**. Each point has an "address," just like a house or an apartment has an address. When you identify a point, you count across from zero on the *x*-axis and then count up the *y*-axis until you hit that point. This is the point's address, which is called its **coordinates**. Coordinates are written as two numbers in parentheses, with the *x* value first and the *y* value second.

Look at the point and its coordinates on this coordinate grid:

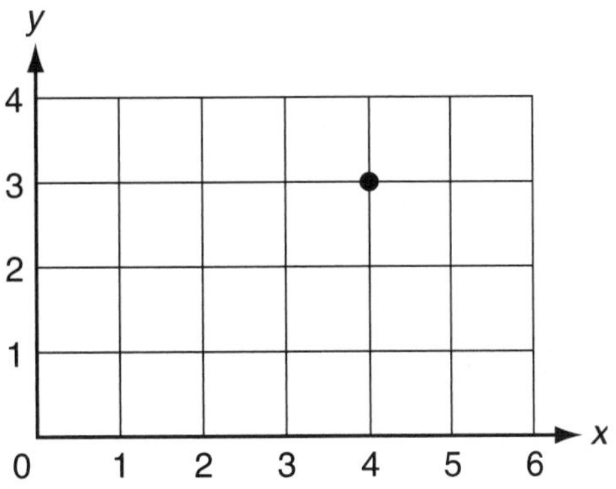

Its coordinates are (4, 3). This means its *x* value is 4 and its *y* value is 3.

Now you try one. Write the coordinates for points *A* and *B* shown on the grid below. Remember to begin counting on the *x*-axis. This is the number that comes first.

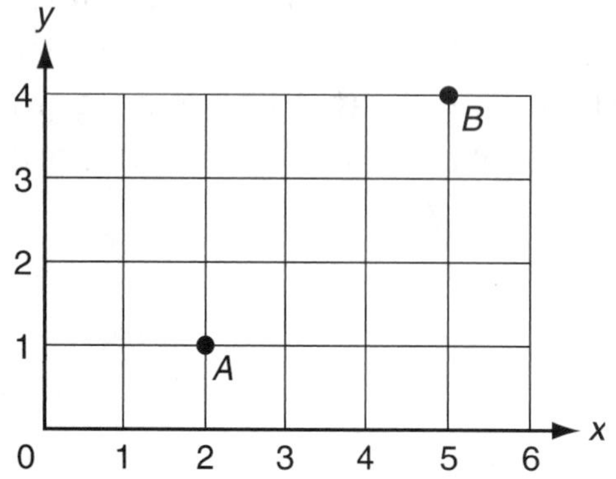

The coordinates for *A* are (2, 1), and the coordinates for *B* are (5, 4).

Practice Questions

Practice 19: Coordinate Grids

DIRECTIONS:

Choose the best of the answer choices given for each of the following problems. Fill in the circle next to your choice.

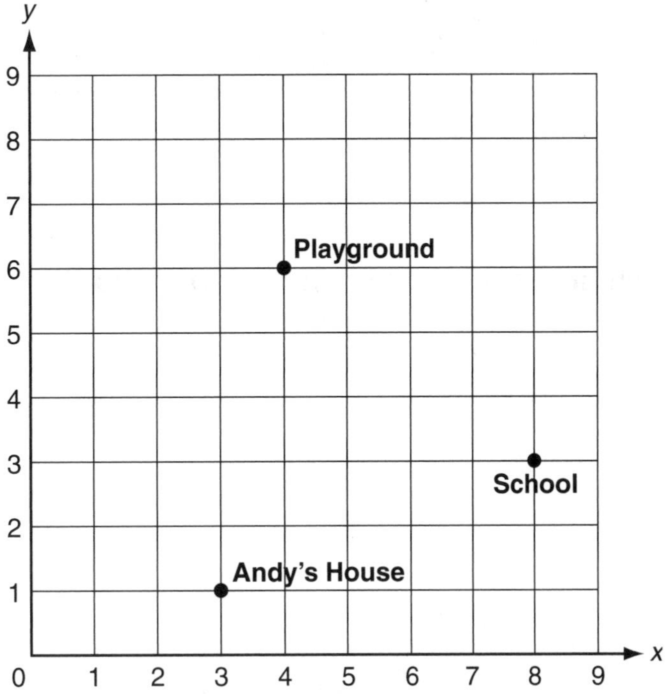

1. Which ordered pair shows the location of the playground?

- Ⓐ (3,1)
- Ⓑ (4, 6)
- Ⓒ (8, 3)
- Ⓓ (3, 6)

Find the playground on the grid. Count over along the x-axis, and then count up on the y-axis.

2. Which ordered pair shows the location of Andy's house?

- Ⓐ (3, 1)
- Ⓑ (1, 3)
- Ⓒ (8, 3)
- Ⓓ (0, 3)

HINT

Find Andy's house on the grid. Count over on the *x*-axis. Then count up on the *y*-axis.

3. Which ordered pair shows the location of the school?

- Ⓐ (3, 8)
- Ⓑ (8, 3)
- Ⓒ (1, 3)
- Ⓓ (4, 6)

HINT

Find the school on the grid. Count over on the *x*-axis. Then count up on the *y*-axis.

Practice Questions

End-of-Chapter Practice Problems

DIRECTIONS:

Choose the best of the answer choices given for each of the following problems. Fill in the circle next to your choice.

1. Bobby made these cutouts for a mobile. Which cutout has more than one line of symmetry?

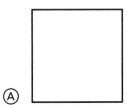

Ⓐ 

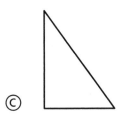

Ⓑ 

Ⓒ 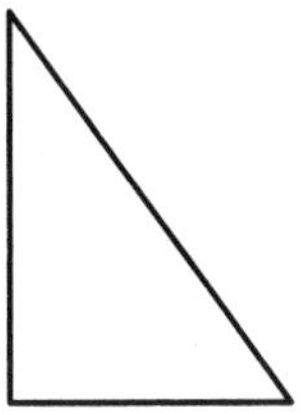

● 

HINT

Remember that a shape can be cut into two identical halves by lines of symmetry in more than one way.

2. **Which triangle has an angle larger than a right angle?**

Ⓐ 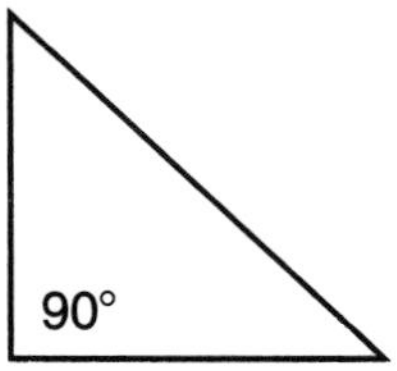

Ⓑ 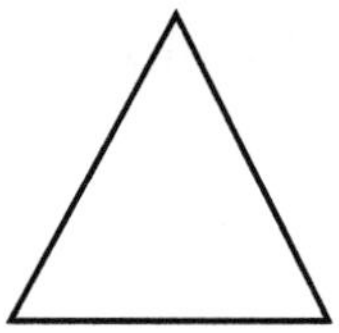

Ⓒ 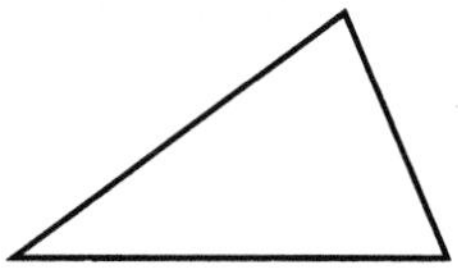

Ⓓ 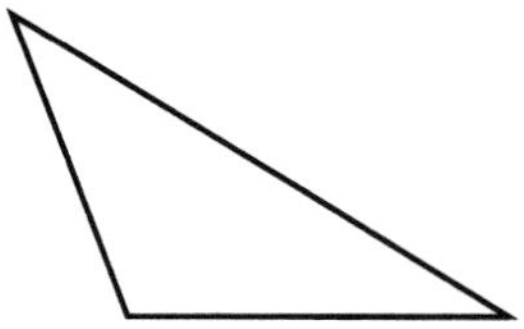

HINT

Look at the triangle with the 90° angle marked. Choose a triangle that has an angle larger than this.

3. Which of the following shows a pair of congruent figures?

(A) 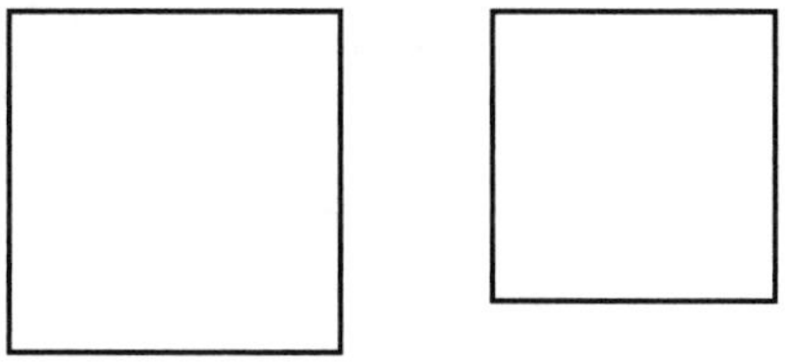

(B) 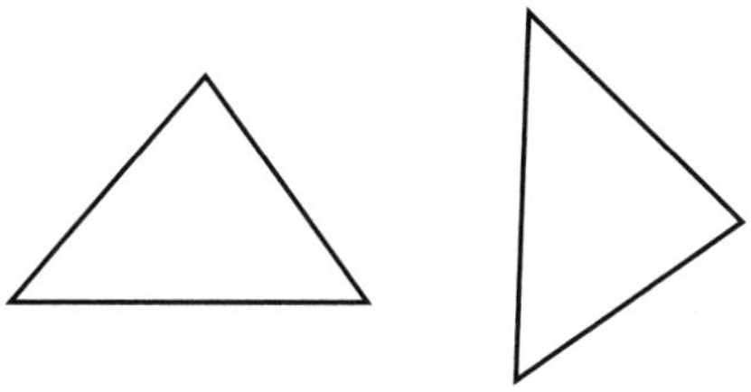

(C) 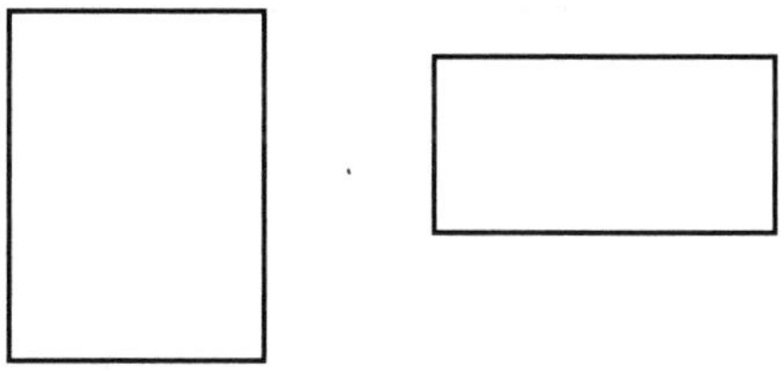

(D) 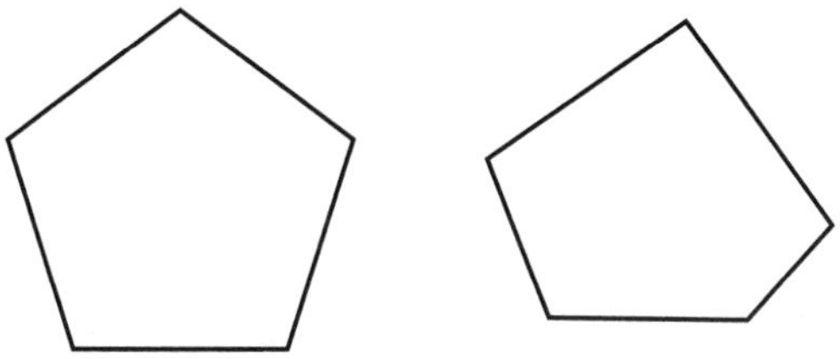

HINT

Remember that congruent figures are exactly alike.

4. **Max wrote the following riddle for his friend:**

I have 6 faces, 8 vertices, and I look like a box. What am I?

What is the answer to this riddle?

Ⓐ pyramid

Ⓑ cone

Ⓒ rectangular prism

Ⓓ sphere

HINT

Begin by eliminating answer choices that you know are incorrect.

5. **What angle below is an obtuse angle?**

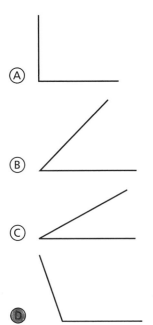

Ⓐ 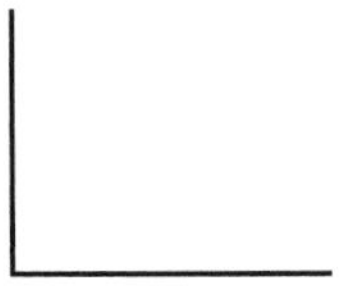

Ⓑ 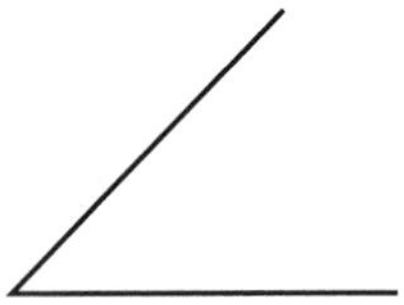

Ⓒ 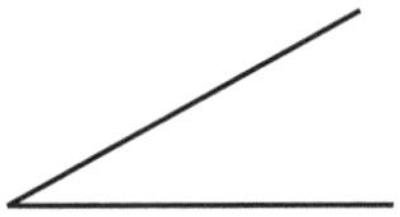

Ⓓ 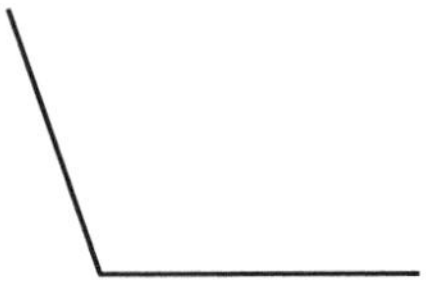

HINT

An obtuse angle is greater than 90°.

6. What is the name of the line segment inside the circle shown below?

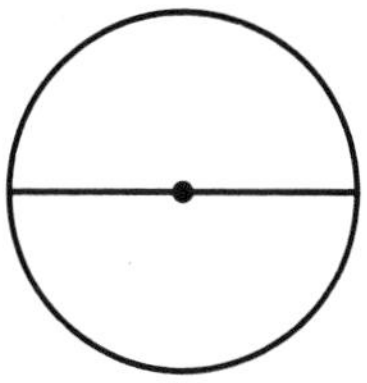

Ⓐ point

Ⓑ radius

Ⓒ diameter

Ⓓ circumference

HINT

Remember that a circumference goes around the circle and the radius is one-half of the diameter.

7. What are these lines called?

Ⓐ parallel lines

Ⓑ rays

Ⓒ line segments

Ⓓ perpendicular lines

HINT

If you can't remember what these lines are called, reread that part of the chapter.

8. **What is the point where two rays meet called?**

(A) angle

(B) vertex

(C) point of intersection

(D) endpoint

HINT

If you don't know this answer, reread the section of the chapter about angles.

9. **What is the name of a two-dimensional figure with six sides?**

(A) sphere

(B) pentagon

(C) hexagon

(D) rectangular prism

HINT

Eliminate answer choices that refer to three-dimensional figures.

Directions for the Open-Ended Question

The following question is an **open-ended** question. Remember to:

Read the question carefully and think about the answer.

Answer all the parts of the question.

Show your work or explain your answer.

You can answer the question by using words, tables, diagrams, OR pictures. You may use your calculator, ruler, and colored shapes.

10. Look at the figures below.

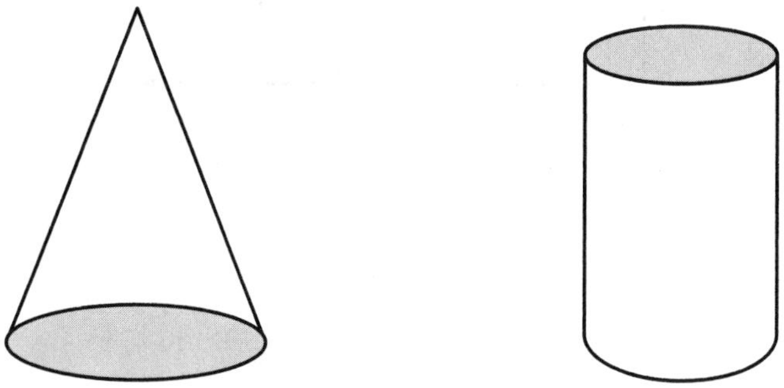

- **Name each figure.**
- **How many faces does each figure have?**
- **Write one way the figures are the same.**
- **Write one way the figures are different.**

DIRECTIONS:

Choose the best of the answer choices given for each of the following problems. Fill in the circle next to your choice.

11. What is the location of Point *A*?

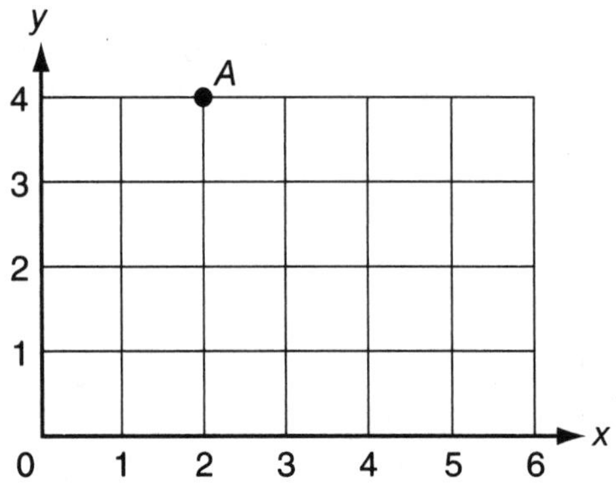

Ⓐ (2, 4)

Ⓑ (4, 2)

Ⓒ (3, 4)

Ⓓ (3, 2)

Move along the x-axis and then up on the y-axis until you reach Point A.

12. Which shows a flip of the arrow?

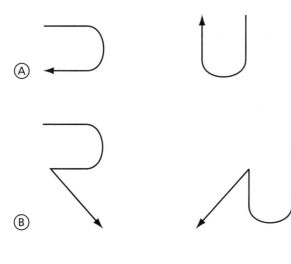

Ⓐ 

Ⓑ 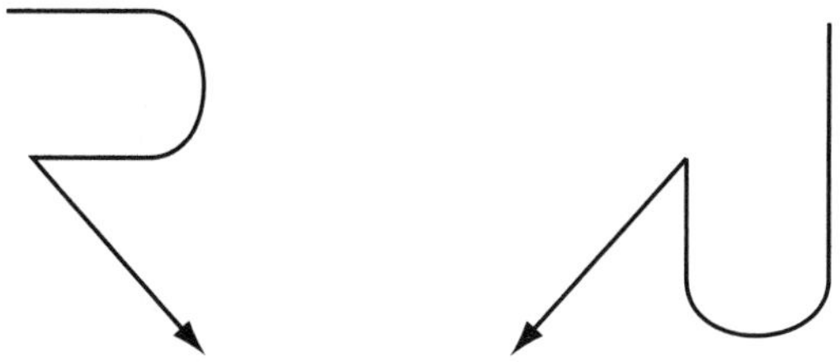

Ⓒ 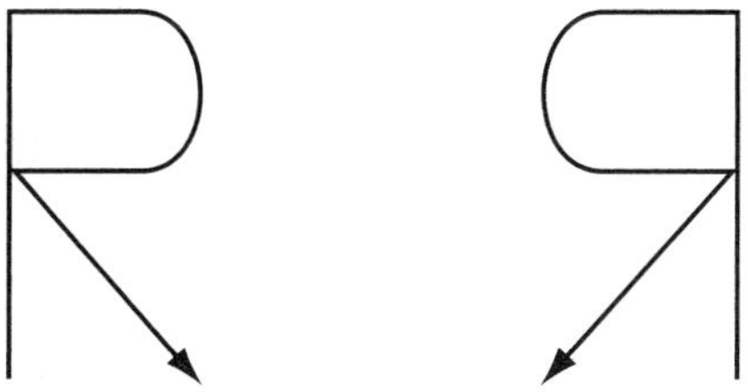

Ⓓ 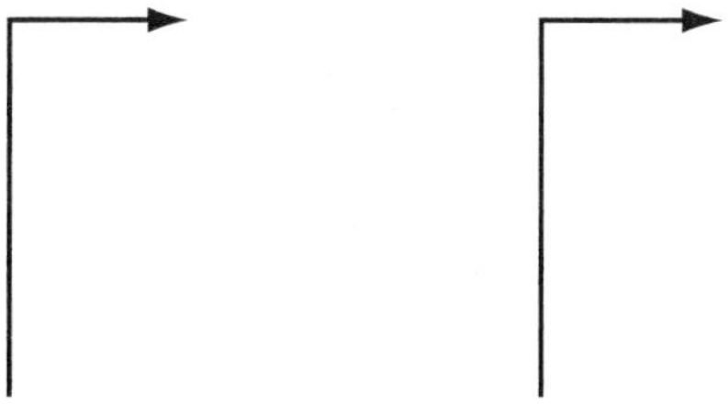

Chapter 5

Measurement

Do you know how tall you are? If you do, it's because someone measured your height. Do you know how much you weigh? If you do, it's because someone weighed you. We measure many different things. We measure the food we eat. Some kinds of food are priced by how much they weigh. Others are priced by their capacity. Milk is often measured in gallons.

We also measure distance—how far things are. How far is your school from your home? You would probably measure this distance in miles. (Unless, of course, you live next door to the school; then you might measure the distance in feet or yards.)

You'll learn about two units of measurement in this chapter: the United States (U.S.) Customary unit of measurement (inches, feet, miles, ounces, pounds, quarts, and so on) and the metric system (centimeters, meters, kilometers, grams, kilograms, liters, and so on).

In this chapter, you'll learn about the different ways in which things can be measured.

Length (U.S. Customary Units)

How far is it to your best friend's home? How tall is a doorway? How long is a caterpillar? All of these questions can be answered by measuring distance. In this section of this chapter, you'll learn the U.S. Customary units for **distance**, or length.

Length is a kind of distance that refers to how long something is. You measure small objects by using **inches**. Have you ever have used a **ruler** before? If you have, you have probably seen inches marked off on a ruler. A **fraction of an inch** is a part of an inch. The lines that mark off inches on a ruler are usually longer than the other lines on a ruler. The smaller lines are used to indicate fractions of inches.

You would use inches to measure these things:

- the length of a pen or pencil
- the length of your finger
- the length of a feather
- the length of anything shorter than 12 inches

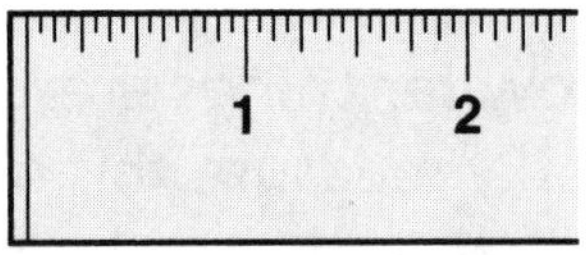

Most rulers measure up to 12 inches. Twelve inches equals one **foot**. A one-foot ruler is good to measure things like line segments. It is also good to measure anything that is just a few inches long.

But what do you use to measure things that are longer than 12 inches? If they aren't too long, you can use **feet** to do this. Do you know how tall you are? Your height is often measured in feet. Feet are also used to measure short distances. Longer rulers can have a few feet. For example, measuring tapes are many feet long.

You would use feet to measure these things:

- your height
- the length of a room
- the height of a doorway

You can also use yards to measure things that are longer than a couple of feet. People sometimes measure distances by using yards. There are three feet in a **yard**. Have you ever watched a football game? If you have, you might know that the distance the players run down the field is measured in yards. A U.S. football field is 100 yards long.

Yards can be used to measure these things:

- your street
- a swimming pool
- your classroom

Very large distances are measured in **miles**. There are 5,280 feet in every mile. Imagine that your school is 15 miles away. It is easier to say that your school is 15 miles away than to say it is 79,200 feet away!

Miles can be used to measure the distance between cities or faraway places.

Fill in the blank with the correct unit of measurement.

1. **The long lines on a ruler are used to measure** inches.

2. **Very long distances are measured in** miles.

3. **One yard equals three** feet.

4. **Twelve inches equals one** foot.

You are correct if your answers are:

1. inches
2. miles
3. feet
4. foot

If you missed one of these answers, go back to the last section, on U.S. Customary system for length.

Length (Metric System)

You read in the beginning of this chapter that the metric system is another method of measurement. Many people in other countries use the metric system to measure things. Some people in the United States also prefer to use the metric system.

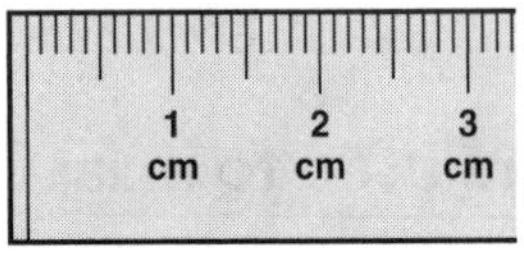

Centimeters are smaller than inches, so you would use them to measure small objects. Can you think of a small object that could be measured in centimeters? You could measure a leaf or a paper clip by using centimeters.

You could use centimeters to measure these things:

- your finger
- a feather
- a bee

Decimeters are the next largest unit of measurement. There are 10 centimeters in every decimeter. You might use decimeters to measure these things:

- wrapping paper
- cloth

There are 100 centimeters in a **meter**. A meter is a little longer than a yard (3 feet).

You might use meters to measure these things:

- your street
- a soccer field
- a swimming pool
- your classroom

To measure very long distances, you would use **kilometers**. There are 1,000 meters in one kilometer. If you wanted to measure the distance to your friend's house across town, you could measure it in kilometers.

Fill in the blank with the correct metric unit of measurement.

1. A meter **is a little longer than three feet.**

2. A centimeter **is a unit used to measure small objects.**

3. kilometers **are units used to measure very long distances.**

4. There are 10 centimeters in a decimeter **.**

You are correct if your answers are:

1. meter
2. centimeter
3. Kilometers
4. decimeter

If you missed any of these, review the section on metric units of length.

Practice Questions

Practice 20: Length

DIRECTIONS:

Choose the best of the answer choices given for each of the following problems. Fill in the circle next to your choice.

1. **What is the most reasonable estimate of the height of your bedroom ceiling?**

   Ⓐ 10 inches

   Ⓑ 8 feet

   Ⓒ 10 yards

   Ⓓ 8 miles

HINT

Think about the distance from your bedroom floor to the ceiling. Is it very small or very large? It is probably somewhere in the middle. Choose the answer that is somewhere in the middle that makes sense.

2. What is the most reasonable estimate of the length of a penny?

Ⓐ 1.5 centimeters

● 1 decimeter

Ⓒ 1.5 meters

Ⓓ 1 kilometer

HINT

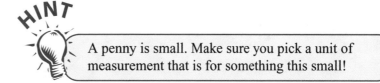

A penny is small. Make sure you pick a unit of measurement that is for something this small!

Weight (U.S. Customary Units)

When you go to the doctor, you get weighed on a scale. As you learned earlier, food is often sold according to how much it weighs. In this section of this chapter, you'll learn about units of measurement for weight.

To measure very small items, we use **ounces**. Think of a regular slice of bread. It weighs about one ounce. There are 16 ounces in every **pound**. That means that 16 slices of bread weigh 1 pound.

We can use ounces to measure these things:

- a slice of bread
- a piece of chicken
- a potato
- a pencil or pen
- your shoe

We can use pounds to measure these things:

- you!
- a sack of flour
- your desk
- a bag of topsoil

Tons are used to measure very large things. There are 2,000 pounds in one ton. Think of a car. An average car (not an SUV) weighs about $1\frac{1}{2}$ tons! That's really heavy!

You can use tons to measure these things:

- a boxcar of coal on a train
- a ship
- an elephant

Fill in the blank with the correct U.S. Customary unit of measurement.

1. **Your weight is measured in ______________________.**

2. **A slice of bread weighs about one ______________________.**

3. **There are 2,000 pounds in a ______________________.**

You are correct if your answers are:

1. pounds
2. ounce
3. ton

If you missed any of these, review the section on U.S. Customary units of weight.

Weight (Metric System)

Just like length, weight can also be measured by using metric units. **Grams** are used to tell the weight of tiny objects. A paperclip weighs about one gram. That's very light!

You would use grams to measure these things:

- a postcard
- a pencil or pen
- spices

Kilograms are used to measure bigger things. One kilogram weighs a little more than two pounds. There are 1,000 grams in every kilogram.

You would use kilograms to measure these things:

- you!
- a sack of flour
- your desk
- a piece of chicken

Metric tons are a lot like U.S. Customary tons. A metric ton is equal to 1,000 kilograms. You would use metric tons to measure these things:

- a car
- a ship
- an elephant

Complete this exercise about measuring weight by using metric units.

1. metric tons **are used to weigh very large objects.**

2. **There are 1,000 grams in every** kilogram.

3. grams **are used to weigh things that are very small.**

You are correct if your answers are:

1. Metric tons
2. kilogram
3. Grams

If you missed any of these, review the section on the metric system for weight.

Practice Questions

Practice 21: Weight

DIRECTIONS:

Choose the best of the answer choices given for each of the following problems. Fill in the circle next to your choice.

1. What is the most reasonable estimate of the weight of two cars?

Ⓐ 2 tons

Ⓑ 2 pounds

Ⓒ 2 ounces

Ⓓ 2 grams

HINT

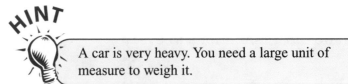

A car is very heavy. You need a large unit of measure to weigh it.

2. A scale is used to weigh an object. The scale reads 1 gram. What object is most likely being weighed?

Ⓐ a potato

Ⓑ a piece of lettuce

Ⓒ a magazine

Ⓓ a television

HINT

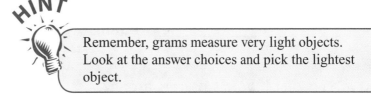

Remember, grams measure very light objects. Look at the answer choices and pick the lightest object.

Capacity (U.S. Customary Units)

The word **capacity** means how much substance, like a liquid, a container can hold. Capacity can also be measured by using U.S. Customary and metric units of measure.

Do you like to eat cereal with a teaspoon or a tablespoon? A **teaspoon** is a small spoon. There are 3 teaspoons in every **tablespoon**, which is a larger spoon.

A measuring **cup** holds 16 tablespoons of liquid. The next largest unit of measurement is a **pint**. There are two cups in every pint. The milk and juice cartons that come with most school lunches are measured in pints.

A **quart** is equal to 2 pints, or 4 cups, of liquid. Sometimes milk that you buy at a grocery store will come in a quart container.

Larger amounts of liquid, such as water, are usually measured in **gallons**. You can also buy a gallon of milk at the store, which equals 4 quarts.

Complete this exercise about measuring capacity.

1. A tablespoon **is bigger than a teaspoon.**

2. A cup **holds 16 tablespoons of liquid.**

3. Large amounts of liquid are measured in gallons**.**

4. A quart **equals 2 pints of liquid.**

You are correct if your answers are:

1. tablespoon
2. cup
3. gallons
4. quart

If you missed any of these, review U.S. Customary units of capacity.

Capacity (Metric System)

A **liter** is about the same size as a quart. You might see milk or soft drinks sold in liter or two-liter containers. A **milliliter** is a very small amount, a thousandth of a liter, and is commonly used by a pharmacist or a doctor for measuring liquid medicines.

Complete this exercise about measuring capacity.

1. milliliter **are used to measure very small amounts of a liquid.**

2. A liter **is about the same size as a quart.**

You are correct if your answers are:

1. milliliter
2. liter

Practice Questions

Practice 22: Capacity

DIRECTIONS:

Choose the best of the answer choices given for each of the following problems. Fill in the circle next to your choice.

1. What is the most reasonable estimate of the amount of liquid in a 2-cup thermos?

Ⓐ 1 pint

Ⓑ 1 milliliter

Ⓒ 1 quart

Ⓓ 1 liter

HINT

If you don't know the answer to the question, reread the section on capacity. Find the unit of measurement that is about the same as a cup.

2. What is the most reasonable estimate of the amount of water in a swimming pool?

Ⓐ 80,000 cups

Ⓑ 80,000 pints

Ⓒ 80,000 quarts

Ⓓ 80,000 gallons

HINT

A swimming pool is pretty big! Remember that you will need a larger unit to measure the amount of water in a pool.

Volume

Imagine that you are holding a shoe box. How much space do you think is inside of the shoe box? Suppose you wanted to fill the shoe box with confetti. How much confetti could it hold? **Volume** is the measure of the amount of space inside of something. In the U.S. Customary system of measurement, volume is often measured in cubic inches, written as in^3, or in cubic feet or cubic yards.

In the metric system, volume is often measured in cubic centimeters, written as cm^3, or cubic meters. Look at the figure below. It is a three-dimensional shape—a cube. Its volume is given in cubic inches.

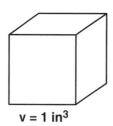

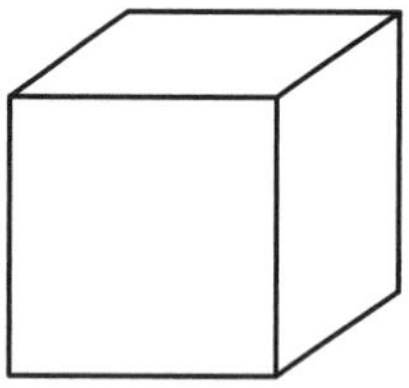

$v = 1\ in^3$

Perimeter

The **perimeter** of a two-dimensional shape is the **sum** of all of the sides. The perimeter measures the distance around the object. To find the perimeter of most objects, you need to add the lengths of all the sides together.

Let's shade in the blocks that go around a pool to make the perimeter easier to find.

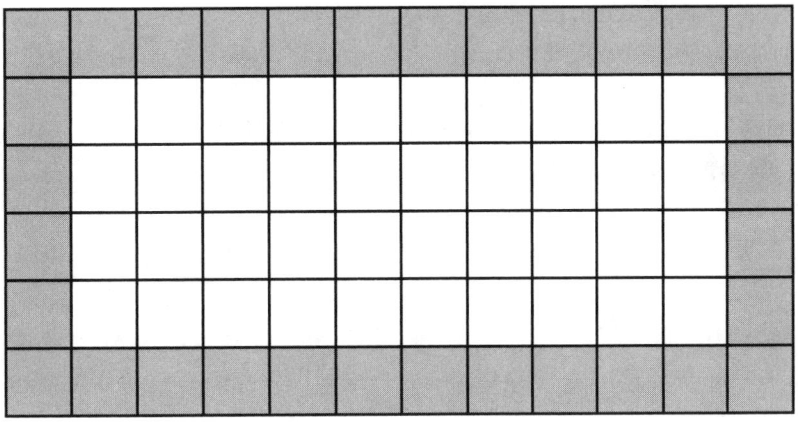

There are 12 block edges, or unit edges, on each of the two long sides of the pool. When you add them together, you get 24. There are unit edges along each of the two shorter sides of the pool. Adding those two together, you get 12. Now you need to add the sum of the two longer sides with the sum of the two shorter sides. 24 + 12 = 36. The perimeter of this pool is 36 units.

Now let's take a look at another object to find its perimeter. Suppose you have measured all of the sides of a triangle like the one below:

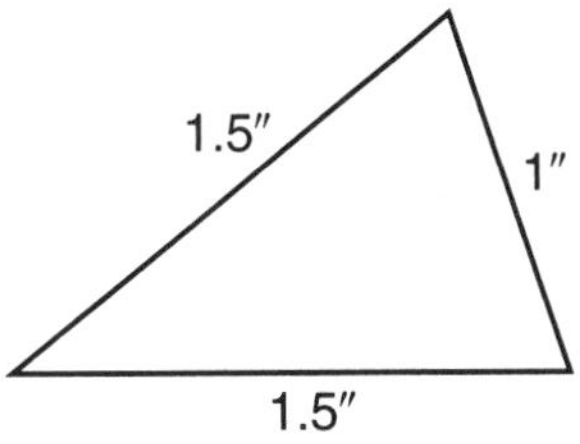

Using your ruler, you find that one side of the triangle measures 1 inches. Another side measures 1.5 inches. The last side also measures 1.5 inches.

To find the perimeter, you need to add all of these inches together as you did with the block edges around the pool. The perimeter of this triangle is 1 + 1 + 1.5 = 4 inches.

Sometimes you know the perimeter and either the length or width of an object, but you have to find the missing dimension.

For example, read this open-ended question:

Cindy has a rectangular garden. She plans to put a fence around the garden. She has 48 feet of fencing and wants the garden to be 14 feet long.

How wide will Cindy's garden be? Show you how got your answer.

If Cindy is going to put fences posts 4 feet apart around the garden, how many fence posts will she need? Show all your work and explain your answer.

It might help to draw a rectangle like the one shown here to answer this question.

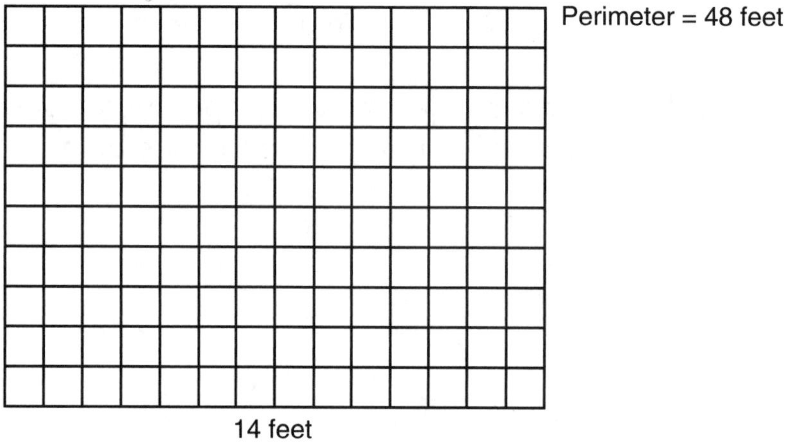

You know that the length of the garden is 14 feet. Label both sides of the rectangle 14. You also know that Cindy has 48 feet of fencing, which will go around her garden. This is the perimeter of the garden. When you add the two sides that make up the lengths and the two sides that make up the widths, the total will be 48 feet. So, you know the length—two sides of the rectangle—equals 28 feet. When you subtract 28 from 48, you get 20. This is the total for the two sides that are the widths of the rectangle. If you divide 20 by 2, you get 10. Cindy's garden is 10 feet wide.

To answer the second part of the problem, divide 48 by 4, since Cindy plans to put a fence post every 4 feet. The answer is 12. Cindy will need 12 fence posts.

Area

Area measures the amount of space covered by a whole object. You saw that the perimeter measures the distance around an object. The area measures the space the entire object covers.

You can figure out the area of an object by counting all the blocks needed to cover it.

Look at the square below:

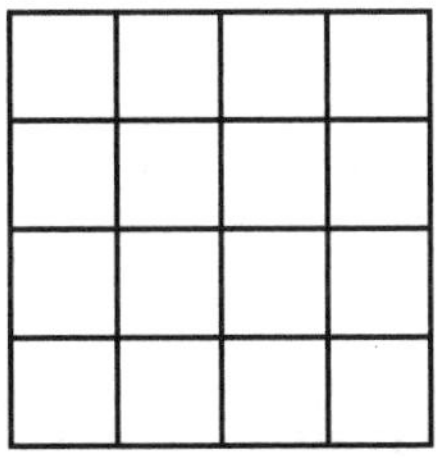

Count all of the blocks that cover the square. There are 16 blocks. So the amount of space that this square takes up is equal to 16 blocks.

Let's try another example. Take a look at the shaded triangle in the square:

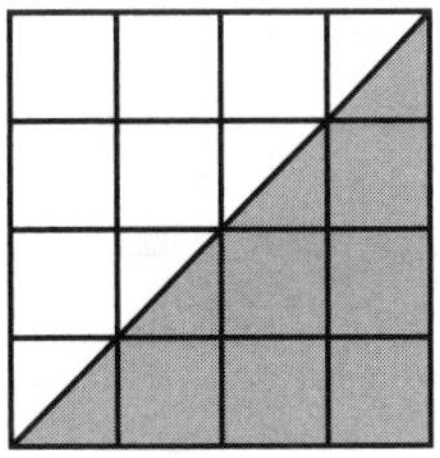

You already know that the square has an area of 16 blocks. What part of the square does the triangle cover?

Count the number of blocks that the triangle covers. Parts of the triangle cover only half of a block. When you have two halves, add them together to make one whole block.

When you are finished, you should come up with the number 8. The triangle covers 6 whole blocks and 4 half-blocks. When you add each of the four halves together, you get 2 whole blocks. $6 + 2 = 8$.

You can also figure out this problem another way.

You know that the square covers an area of 16 blocks. By looking at the shaded blocks, you can see that the triangle covers half of the square.

Can you figure out what half of 16 is? Half means to divide into two equal parts, so divide 16 by 2. The answer is 8!

Practice Questions

Practice 23: Perimeter and Area

DIRECTIONS:

Choose the best of the answer choices given for each of the following problems. Fill in the circle next to your choice.

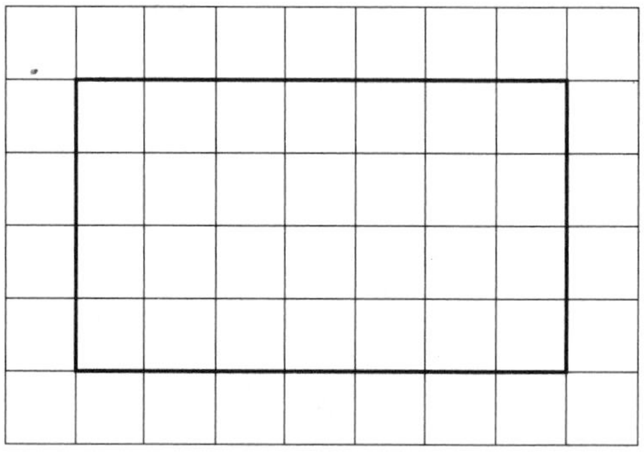

1. What is the perimeter of the rectangle shown above?

Ⓐ 4

Ⓑ 7

Ⓒ 22

Ⓓ 28

HINT

The perimeter is the distance around a shape. Use the block edges as an aid to count the distance around this rectangle. This is the perimeter. Remember to count the whole length and the whole width.

2. **What is the area of the rectangle in problem 1?**

Ⓐ 4

Ⓑ 7

Ⓒ 22

Ⓓ 28

HINT

When you are asked to find the area, count all the blocks.

3. **Mr. Harmon is putting a fence around a rectangular deck in his backyard. He plans to use 36 feet of fencing, and the deck is 10 feet long. How wide is his deck?**

36
−10
26

Ⓐ 2

Ⓑ 4

Ⓒ 6

Ⓓ 8

HINT

Add the two known sides of the deck. Subtract this number from the total length of fencing, and then divide that answer by 2.

Measuring Time

Measuring time involves telling the time it will be when something happens. For example, suppose it is 1:00 and you want to know what time it will be in two hours. It will be 3:00!

Most clocks have both a "big" hand a "little" hand. The big hand tells what minute it is, and the little hand tells what hour it is. Look at the clock below. The hours are printed on the inside of the clock, and the minutes are printed on the outside of the clock.

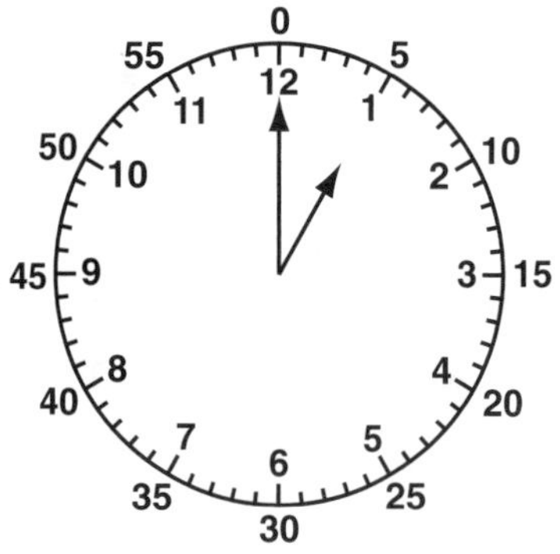

To tell the time, you look at the hour hand first and then the minute hand.

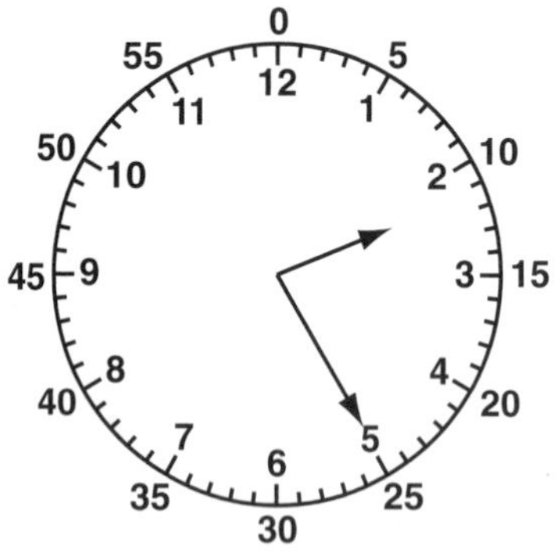

What time does this clock show? The hour hand, the little hand, is on the 2 and the minute hand, the big hand, is on the 25. It is 2:25.

Let's try another one.

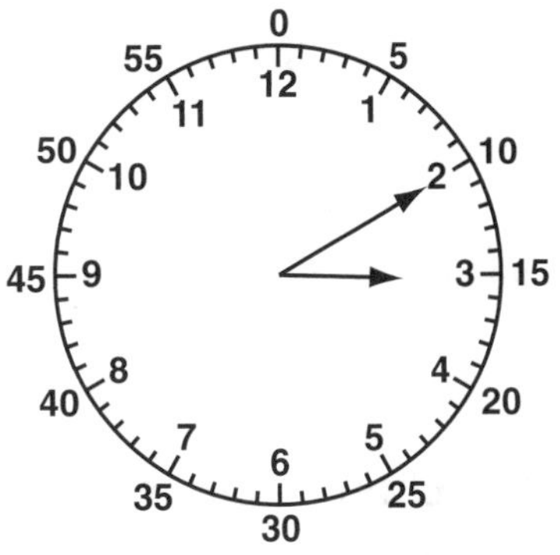

The hour hand, the little hand, is on the 3, and the minute hand, the big hand, is on the 10. It is 3:10.

The time from 12 noon until 11:59 at night is called P.M. The time from midnight until 11:59 in the morning is called A.M.

Read this problem.

Santina went to her friend's house at 3:00 P.M. Her mother told her to be home in 1 hour and 50 minutes. What time did Santina need to be home?

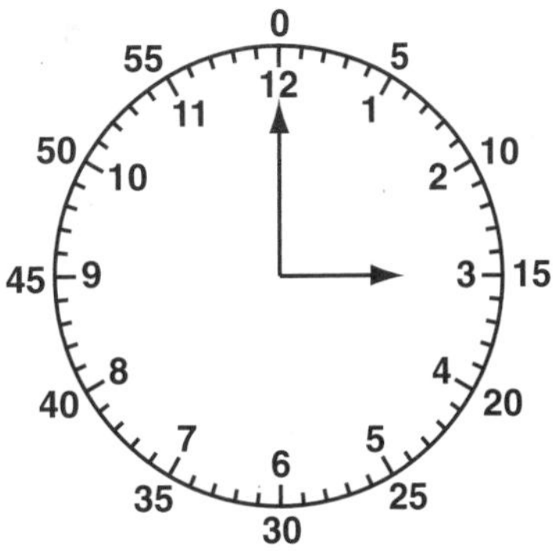

Ⓐ 3:50 P.M.

Ⓑ 4:40 P.M.

Ⓒ 4:50 P.M.

Ⓓ 5:00 P.M.

Did you get it right? If you add one hour to 3:00 P.M., it is 4:00 P.M. If you add another 50 minutes to this time, it is 4:50 P.M. Santina needed to be home by 4:50 P.M.

Practice Questions

Practice 24: Measuring Time

DIRECTIONS:

Choose the best of the answer choices given for each of the following problems. Fill in the circle next to your choice.

1. Zack gets out of school at 2:30 P.M., as shown on the clock below. Then he goes to track practice for 1 hour and 15 minutes. What time does track practice end?

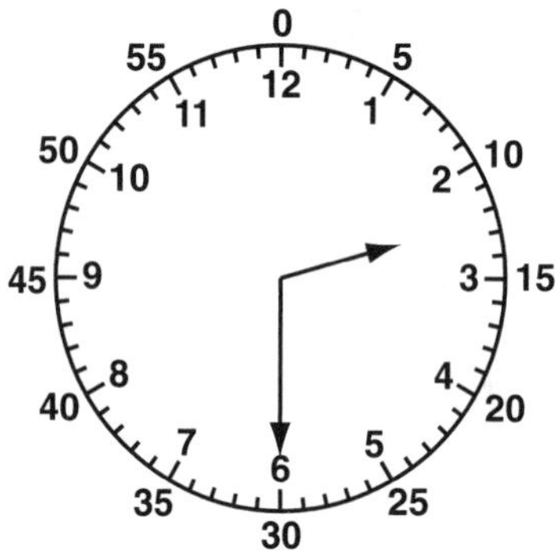

Ⓐ 2:45 P.M.

Ⓑ 3:00 P.M.

Ⓒ 3:15 P.M.

Ⓓ 3:45 P.M.

Add one hour to 2:30. Then add 15 minutes to this time.

2. **Christie has math class in the morning until 9:10 A.M., as shown on the clock below. After this, she goes to study hall for 30 minutes. What time does study hall end?**

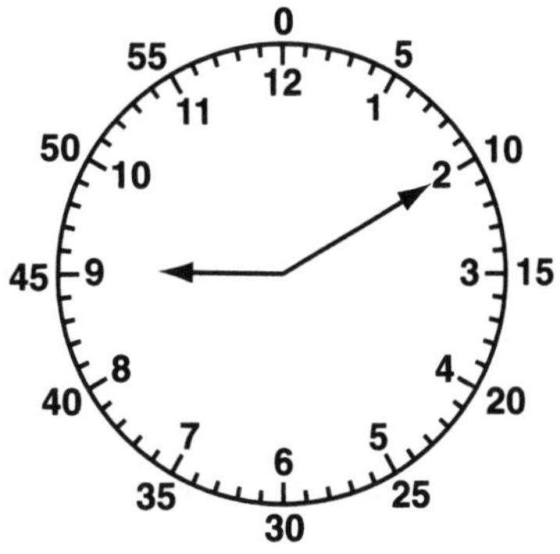

Ⓐ 9:20 A.M.

Ⓑ 9:30 A.M.

Ⓒ 9:40 A.M.

Ⓓ 9:50 A.M.

The hour doesn't change in this problem. Add 30 minutes to 10 minutes.

Practice Questions

End-of-Chapter Practice Problems

DIRECTIONS:

Choose the best of the answer choices given for each of the following problems. Fill in the circle next to your choice.

1. What is the most reasonable estimate of the weight of a truck?

Ⓐ 30 ounces

Ⓑ 30 pounds

Ⓒ 300 pounds

Ⓓ 3 tons

HINT

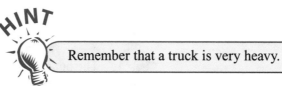

Remember that a truck is very heavy.

2. **What is the perimeter of the rectangle shown below?**

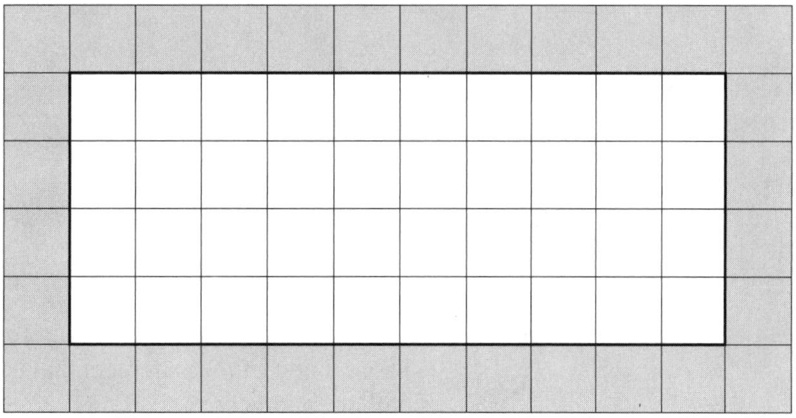

Ⓐ 20

Ⓑ 28

Ⓒ 30

Ⓓ 40

HINT

Add up the lengths of all the sides of the rectangle.

3. **Mrs. Garner wants to put up a wallpaper border in her living room. She needs 64 feet of border. The width of the room is 10 feet. What is the length of the room?**

Ⓐ 12 feet

Ⓑ 14 feet

Ⓒ 20 feet

Ⓓ 22 feet

HINT

Add the two widths of the room and subtract from 64 to get the total for the two lengths of the room. Remember to divide this by 2 to get the length.

4. What unit of measure would be best to measure the length of a sidewalk in front of a house?

Ⓐ inches

Ⓑ centimeters

Ⓒ meters

Ⓓ kilometers

HINT

Choose a unit of measurement that is not extremely small or extremely large.

5. On Saturday, Alicia finishes doing her chores at 9:30 A.M, as shown on the clock below. After this, she can go outside and play for 1 hour and 30 minutes. What time does she need to return home?

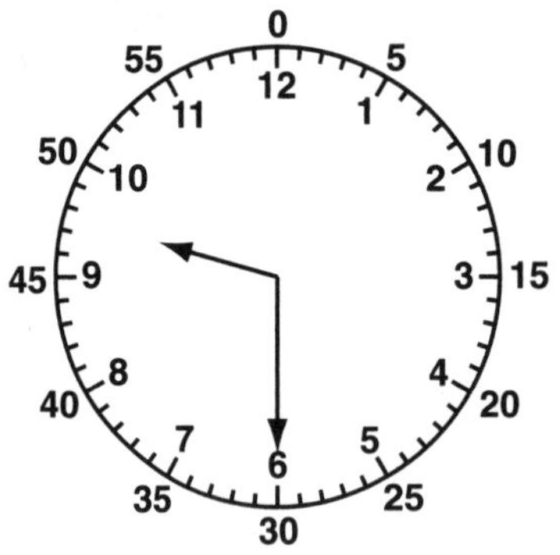

Ⓐ 10:00 A.M.

Ⓑ 10:30 A.M.

Ⓒ 11:00 A.M.

Ⓓ 11:30 A.M.

HINT

Remember that 30 minutes plus 30 minutes is 1 hour.

Chapter 6

Understanding Patterns

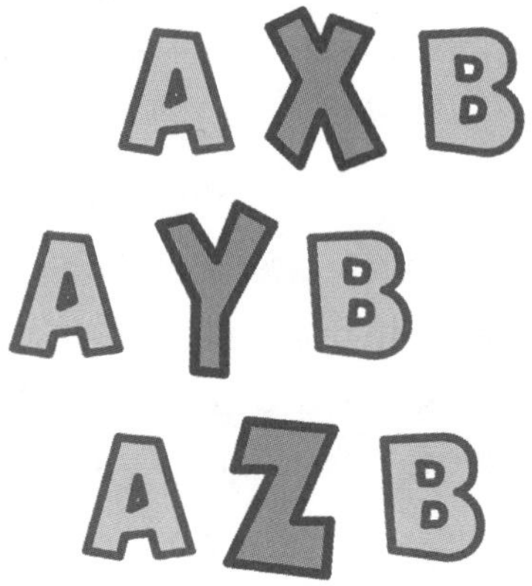

In mathematics, patterns are everywhere. If you count by twos—2, 4, 6, 8, and 10—you are using a pattern. If you count by threes or fours, you're also using a pattern. Some patterns stop eventually, and others keep on going, sometimes in more than one direction. You'll learn about patterns in this chapter.

You'll also learn about functions in this chapter. A **function** is a kind of pattern. Functions can be used to find the missing value in a number sentence—for example, to find what belongs in the box in a sentence such as $3 \times \square = 0$. The **associative** and **commutative properties** help to find missing values. You'll also learn about these properties in this chapter.

Patterns

If a group of numbers has a pattern, you can usually tell what number comes next. Patterns that keep on going are called continuous. These patterns usually have three dots at the end. These three dots are called ellipses (ee-LIP-seez). Look at the numbers on the next page.

1, 5, 9, 13, 17 . . .

The ellipses (series of dots) at the end mean that the pattern keeps on going. Look for a pattern in these numbers. Do they get larger or smaller? They get larger. What to you have to add to each number to get the next number?

$$1 + 4 = 5$$

$$5 + 4 = 9$$

$$9 + 4 = 13$$

$$13 + 4 = 17$$

You add 4 to each number to get the next number. So the next number is 21.

Now look at this pattern:

17, 13, 9, 5, 1 . . .

This means that this pattern continues for numbers less than one. Can you think of a number that is less than one? Zero is less than one. Negative numbers are also less than one, as you learned in an earlier chapter. For this pattern, you subtract 4 from each number to get the next number, so the next number is -3.

Now look at this group of numbers:

2, 4, 6, 8, 2, 4, 6, 8 . . .

These numbers are a **repeating pattern**. Can you see that the next number is a 2? In fact, can you see that the next five numbers are 2, 4, 6, 8, 2? So sometimes a pattern involves repetition, not just changing each number by some operation, such as addition, subtraction, multiplication, or division.

Look at the next group of numbers. Can you figure out what the next number is?

40, 34, 28, 22, 16, 10 . . .

Look for a pattern in these numbers. Do they get larger or smaller? They get smaller. What do you have to subtract from each number to get the next number?

$$40 - 6 = 34$$
$$34 - 6 = 28$$
$$28 - 6 = 22$$
$$22 - 6 = 16$$
$$16 - 6 = 10$$

You subtract 6 from each number to get the next number. So the next number in the pattern is 4.

Practice Questions

Practice 25: Patterns

DIRECTIONS:

Choose the best of the answer choices given for each of the following problems. Fill in the circle next to your choice.

1. Which rule is assigned to these numbers?

6, 14, 22, 30, 38, 46 . . .

Ⓐ Add 4

Ⓑ Add 6

Ⓒ Add 8

Ⓓ Add 10

HINT

Look at the numbers as they get larger. What is added to each number to get the next one?

2. **Which rule is assigned to these numbers?**

52, 49, 46, 43, 40, 37, 34, 31 . . .

Ⓐ Subtract 2

Ⓑ Subtract 3

Ⓒ Subtract 4

Ⓓ Subtract 5

HINT

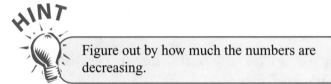

Figure out by how much the numbers are decreasing.

Function Machines

A **function** is a kind of pattern. A **function machine** is an imaginary machine you can use to help you determine a pattern. You put a number into the machine. Then another number is added to, subtracted from, multiplied by, or divided into this number, and a new number comes out of the machine. The numbers you put into the machine are called input. The numbers that come out of the machine are called output. A table of numbers under the function machine helps you to determine the pattern. Look at the function machine below:

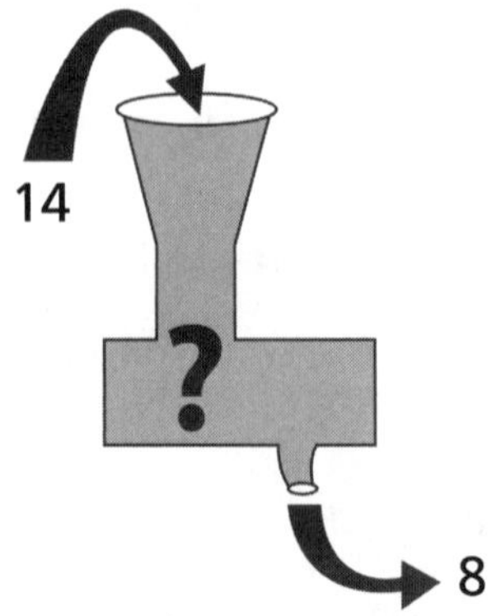

Input	14	8	10	12
Output	8	2	4	?

Can you figure out the missing number in the table? All of the numbers in the table have 6 subtracted from them. The number 6 subtracted from 12 is 6. The missing number is 6, because $12 - 6 = 6$.

Let's try another problem, but one that has two function machines.

When 7 is dropped into the first function machine, it comes out as 5. When 5 is dropped into the second function machine, it comes out as 10. The tables for both function machine are shown below. What happens to 11 if it goes through both function machines?

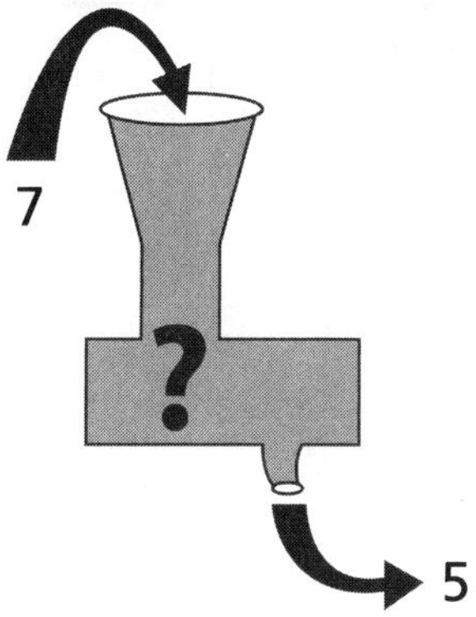

The following table shows some other input and output data for the first machine.

Input	7	10	6	11
Output	5	8	4	?9

The second function machine operates as follows:

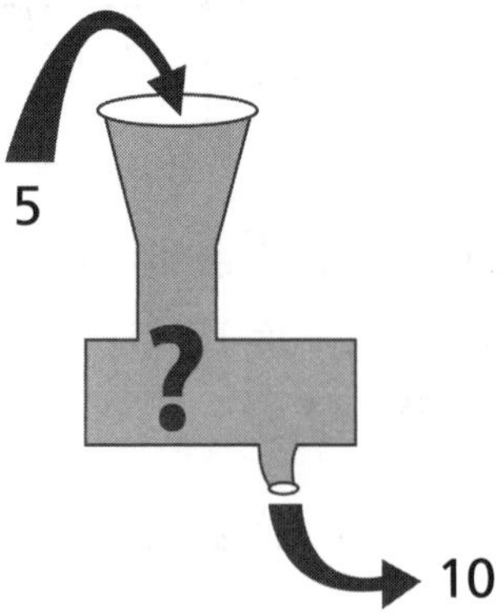

The table shows some other input and output data for the second machine.

Input	5	8	4	☐
Output	10	13	9	?

Ⓐ 14

Ⓑ 11

Ⓒ 9

Ⓓ 4

First you have to find the missing number in the first table so you can insert it into the second machine. Did you figure out the pattern for the first function machine? The number 2 is subtracted from each of the input numbers to get the output number. So if the number 11 is input, 9 will be the output number.

Now look at the second table. The output from the last table is now the input. What happens to the numbers in this table? They each get larger by 5. To find the missing number in this table, you have to add 5 to 9. The missing number is 14, so the correct answer choice is A.

Practice Questions

Practice 26: Function Machines

DIRECTIONS:

Choose the best of the answer choices given for each of the following problems. Fill in the circle next to your choice.

1. When 9 is dropped into this machine, it comes out as 18.

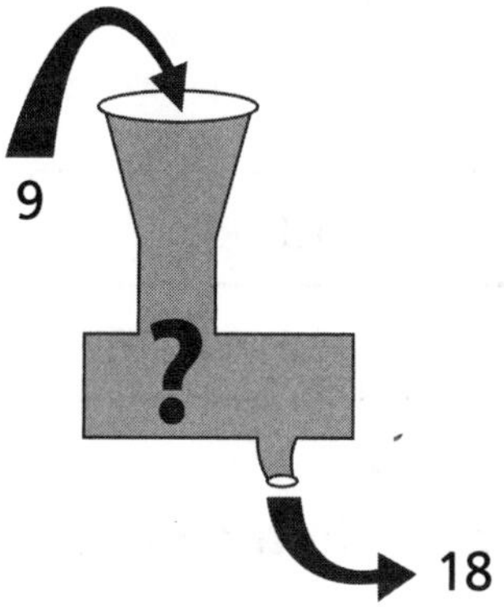

Input	9	7	11	12
Output	18	16	20	?

What does 12 come out as when it is dropped into the function machine?

Ⓐ 4

Ⓑ 21

Ⓒ 20

Ⓓ 22

HINT

Think about what is happening to each of the number. Are they getting larger. By how much?

2. When 13 is dropped into this function machine, it comes out as 10.

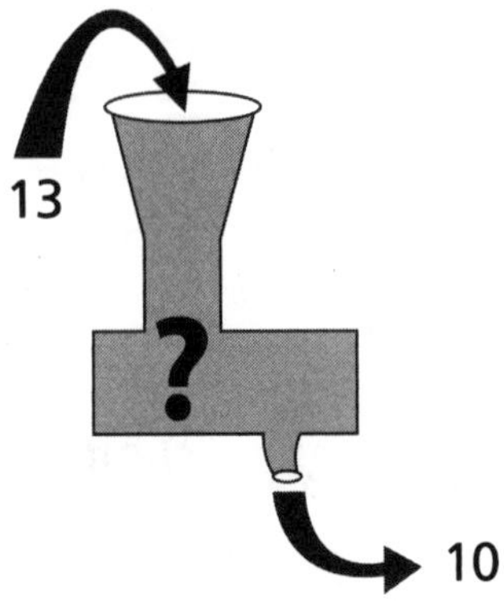

The following table shows some other input and output data for the machine.

Input	13	7	15	9
Output	10	4	12	?

What is the missing number in the table?

Ⓐ 5

Ⓑ 6

Ⓒ 7

Ⓓ 8

HINT

Figure out how much is subtracted from each of the numbers in the input row of the table to get the numbers in the output row.

3. When 4 is dropped into the first of two machines, it comes out as 9. When 9 is dropped into the second machine, it comes out as 12.

For the first machine:

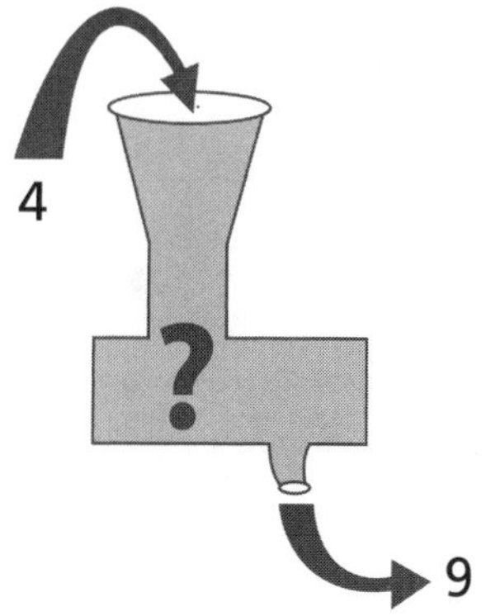

The table below shows some other input and output data for the first machine.

Input	4	6	3	7
Output	9	11	8	?

For the second machine:

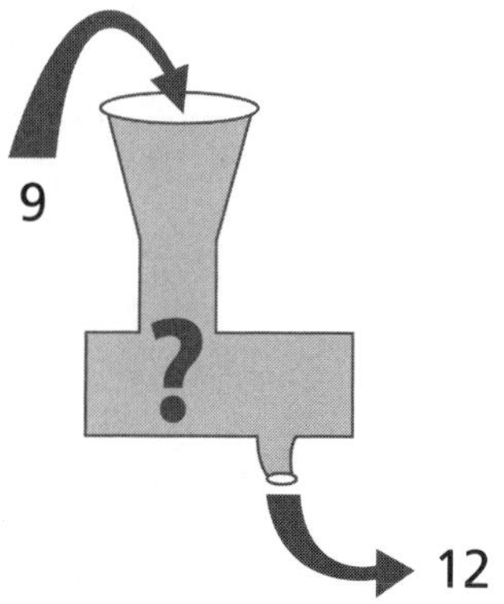

The table below shows some other input and output data for the second machine.

Input	9	11	8	☐
Output	12	14	11	?

What is the output number for 7 when it is dropped into the first machine?

(A) 10

(B) 11

(C) 12

(D) 13

HINT

Don't get confused by the two tables. Just look at the first table to answer this question.

4. If the output from the first function machine is input into the second function machine from problem 3, what is the missing output value on the table for the second machine?

(A) 9

(B) 10

(C) 14

(D) 15

HINT

The numbers in this table increase. Figure out what is added to each number in the input row to get the number in the output row.

Input/Output Tables and T-Charts

Input/output tables and **T-charts** are very similar to the function machines and the tables beneath the function machines. Look at the problem for the input/output table below:

What number is missing in the output column of the table below?

Input	Output
2	9
3	10
4	?
5	12

Ⓐ 7

Ⓑ 8

Ⓒ 10

Ⓓ 11

To answer this question, look closely at the first number in the input column and the first number in the output column. What do you have to do to the number 2 to make it 9? You add 7. Look at the second number. What do you have to do to the number 3 to make it 10? Once again, you add 7. The missing number is 7 more than 4, or 11. So answer choice D is correct.

A **T-chart** is just like an input/output table, but it is set up in a different way. Look at the T-chart below:

x	*y*
14	9
12	7
9	4
8	3

Which rule is assigned to the *x* column in order to get the number in the *y* column?

Ⓐ Add 5

Ⓑ Subtract 5

Ⓒ Multiply by 3

Ⓓ Divide by 3

To answer this question, look closely at the first number in the *x* column. It's 14. What do you have to do to 14 to get 9? You have to subtract 5. If you look at all of the numbers in the *x* column, you'll see that you have to subtract 5 to them to get the number in the *y* column. Answer choice B is correct.

Practice Questions

Practice 27: Input/Output Tables and T-Charts

DIRECTIONS:

Choose the best of the answer choices given for each of the following problems. Fill in the circle next to your choice.

1. What is the missing number in the table below?

Input	Output
6	12
8	14
10	16
12	?

Ⓐ 6

Ⓑ 8

Ⓒ 14

Ⓓ 18

HINT

Be sure to look at all of the numbers in the input/output table before making a decision about the rule.

2. **Which rule is assigned to the numbers in the *x* column to get the numbers in the *y* column?**

x	*y*
9	18
8	16
7	14
6	12

Ⓐ Add 9

Ⓑ Subtract 9

Ⓒ Multiply by 2

Ⓓ Divide by 2

Notice that the numbers in the *y* column are larger. This means using addition or multiplication.

Other Kinds of Patterns

Patterns can also relate to an activity. Look at this problem:

Pedro does a different type of exercise each day, according to this pattern:

Day 1:	Walks
Day 2:	Rides bike
Day 3:	Jogs
Day 4:	Plays basketball
Day 5:	Walks
Day 6:	Rides bike
Day 7:	Jogs
Day 8:	Plays basketball

What kind of exercise will Pedro do on Day 9?

Did you say that he will walk? That's great! Now, what kind of exercise will Pedro do on Day 22? Answering this question is harder. But you can figure it out by repeating the pattern, as shown below:

Day 1:	Walks
Day 2:	Rides bike
Day 3:	Jogs
Day 4:	Plays basketball
Day 5:	Walks
Day 6:	Rides bike
Day 7:	Jogs
Day 8:	Plays basketball
Day 9:	Walks
Day 10:	Rides bike
Day 11:	Jogs
Day 12:	Plays basketball
Day 13:	Walks
Day 14:	Rides bike
Day 15:	Jogs
Day 16:	Plays basketball
Day 17:	Walks
Day 18:	Rides bike
Day 19:	Jogs
Day 20:	Plays basketball
Day 21:	Walks
Day 22:	Rides bike

You can see from the pattern that Pedro will ride a bike on the 22nd day.

Let's try a different problem.

You are trying to save money to buy a gift for your mother's birthday. You record in the chart below the total amount of money you have at the end of each week.

Week	1	2	3	4	5
Total amount of money saved	\$2.75	\$5.50	\$8.25	\$11.00	

If you continue saving money following this pattern, how much money will you have at the end of Week 5?

Ⓐ \$8.25

Ⓑ \$11.75

Ⓒ \$13.75

Ⓓ \$14.75

To solve this problem, begin by subtracting \$2.75 from \$5.50. The answer is \$2.75. Now add \$2.75 to \$5.50. If you do this, you get the amount of money in Week 3. If you keep on going, you'll see that the pattern is to add \$2.75 each week. So you can figure out how much money you will have saved in Week 5 by adding \$2.75 to \$11.00, the amount of money you have in Week 4. The answer is \$13.75, choice C.

Practice Questions

Practice 28: Other Kinds of Patterns

DIRECTIONS:

Choose the best of the answer choices given for each of the following problems. Fill in the circle next to your choice.

1. Tammy's grandmother makes a different kind of food each day, according to this pattern:

Day 1:	Meatloaf
Day 2:	Chicken
Day 3:	Spaghetti
Day 4:	Sandwiches
Day 5:	Fish
Day 6:	Meatloaf
Day 7:	Chicken
Day 8:	Spaghetti
Day 9:	Sandwiches
Day 10:	Fish

What food will Tammy's grandmother make on Day 16?

Ⓐ Meatloaf

Ⓑ Chicken

Ⓒ Spaghetti

Ⓓ Sandwiches

HINT

Notice that there are 5 days to the pattern. Repeat the pattern to Day 16.

Directions for the Open-Ended Question

The following question is an open-ended question. Remember to:

Read the question carefully and think about the answer.

Answer all the parts of the question.

Show your work or explain your answer.

You can answer the question by using words, tables, diagrams, OR pictures. You may use your calculator, ruler, and colored shapes.

2. You are saving the money you make for babysitting your little brother. You record the total amount of money you have at the end of each week in the chart below.

Week	1	2	3	4	5
Total amount of money saved	\$5.50	\$8.75	\$12.00	\$15.25	

- **If you continue saving money following this pattern, how much money will you have at the end of Week 5? Explain the pattern you used to get your answer.**

- **A used video game you would like to buy costs \$20.00. In which single week would you first earn enough to buy the video game? Show your work or explain your answer.**

Line Graphs

A **line graph** shows the relationship between two things. If the first gets larger or smaller, it affects the second. Look at the line graph below. It shows how tall Josh has grown over the last five years.

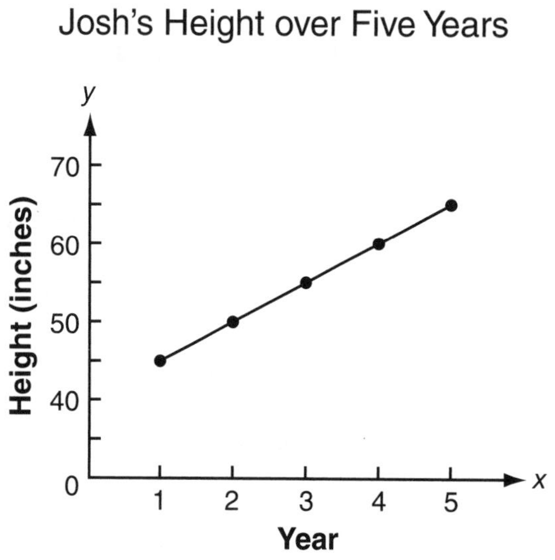

You can tell from this graph that the older Josh gets, the taller he is. This is the pattern shown by the line graph. Let's look at another.

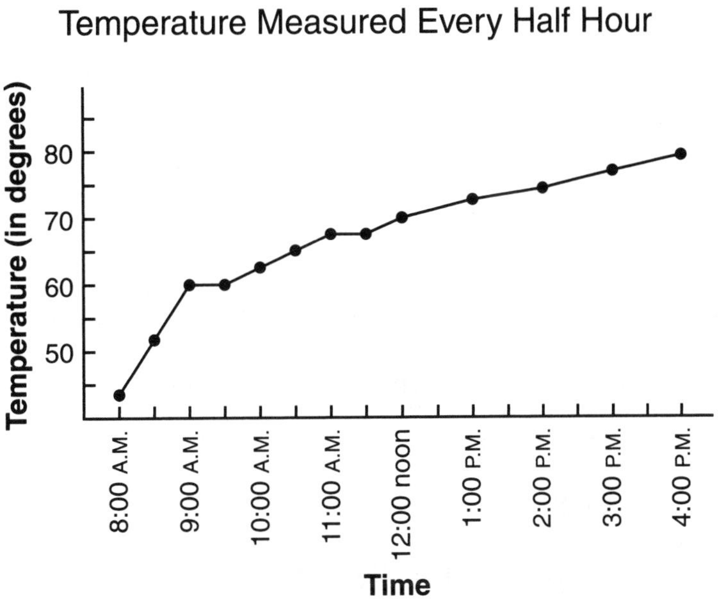

This graph shows the temperature in a town during one day. What can you tell from this graph? Write your answer on the lines below.

____

____

____

If you noticed that during the day the temperature increases, you are right.

Practice Questions

Practice 29: Line Graphs

Directions for the Open-Ended Question

The following question is an open-ended question. Remember to:

Read the question carefully and think about the answer.

Answer all the parts of the question.

Show your work or explain your answer.

You can answer the question by using words, tables, diagrams, OR pictures. You may use your calculator, ruler, and colored shapes.

1. **Look at the line graph below.**

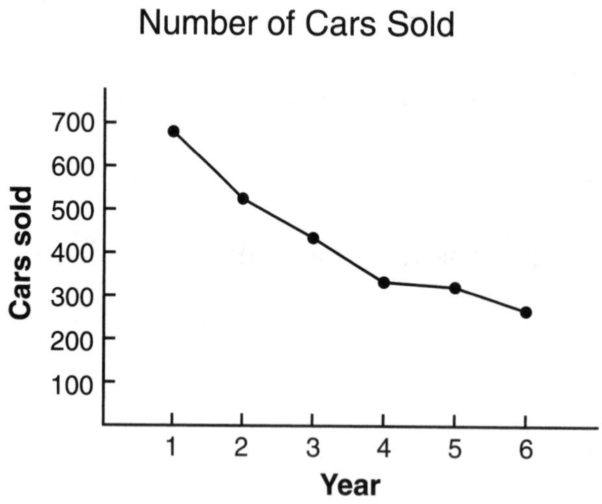

What can you conclude from the graph about the number of cars sold over the years?

____

____

____

Open Sentences

Some questions require you to fill in the blank with the correct number. These are called **open sentences**. Look at this open sentence:

$14 \div 2 = \square$

You can probably solve this problem by using mental math. You might already know that 14 divided by 2 is 7.

Let's try another.

If $24 - \square = 10$, then what is the value of $\square$?

This one is more difficult. To solve this one, you need to think, "What number subtracted from 24 gives 10?" The number is 14, because $24 - 14 = 10$.

You can also **reverse** open sentences of this type. Can you see that the missing number is the difference between 24 and 10? You can reverse subtraction and division problems, so that $24 - \square = 10$ becomes $24 - 10 = \square$.

An example using division is $12 \div \square = 6$, which reverses to $12 \div 6 = \square$. Of course, you might already have used mental math to get the correct answer, 2. Note that reversing does NOT work for addition or multiplication problems.

Sometimes a letter is used in place of the box, and you have to figure out the value of this letter. Look at this open sentence:

$n = 21 \div 3$

To solve for *n*, divide 3 into 21.

By using mental math, we see that $21 \div 3 = 7$. Therefore, $7 = 21 \div 3$, and *n* is 7.

Let's try one more:

$18 - x = 10$

By reversing the open sentence, we see that $18 - 10 = x$, so x is 8. You may have gotten this answer by mental math as well.

Now substitute 8 in the original open sentence to make sure you have the correct answer: $18 - 8 = 10$. It works!

Solve each of the following open sentences.

1. $2 \times 6 = \square$

2. $15 + \square = 32$

3. $54 - x = 24$

4. $15 + 9 = n$

5. $32 - x = 18$

You are correct if your answers are:

1. $2 \times 6 = 12$
2. $15 + 17 = 32$
3. $54 - 30 = 24$
4. $15 + 9 = 24$
5. $32 - 14 = 18$

If you missed any of these, review the section on open sentences.

Practice Questions

Practice 30: Open Sentences

DIRECTIONS:

Choose the best of the answer choices given for each of the following problems. Fill in the circle next to your choice.

1. **If 96 ÷ □ = 12, what is the value of □?**

   Ⓐ 7

   Ⓑ 8

   Ⓒ 9

   Ⓓ 11

HINT: Reverse the equation and divide 12 into 96.

2. **If 72 – □ = 38, then what is the value of □?**

   Ⓐ 28

   Ⓑ 30

   Ⓒ 32

   Ⓓ 34

HINT: Reverse the equation and subtract 38 from 72.

3. What does the *n* equal in $50 \times n = 150$?

Ⓐ 1

Ⓑ 2

Ⓒ 3

Ⓓ 4

HINT

Think: 50 times what number gives 150?

4. If $144 \div \square = 12$, then what is the value of $\square$?

Ⓐ 8

Ⓑ 10

Ⓒ 12

Ⓓ 14

HINT

Reverse the equation and divide 12 into 144.

Number Sentences

You can use open sentences to answer problems given in words, or **number sentences**.

Look at this problem:

Jennifer had 32 pencils. She gave some to her little sister, and now Jennifer has 20. Which number sentence could you use to find out how many pencils Jennifer gave her sister?

Ⓐ $20 - \square = 32$

Ⓑ $20 \times \square = 32$

Ⓒ $20 + 32 = \square$

Ⓓ $32 - 20 = \square$

For this problem, you have to find the answer choice that you could use to find out how many pencils Jennifer gave away. Answer choice A isn't correct. Subtracting a number from 20 won't tell you how many pencils she gave away. Answer choice B isn't correct either. You wouldn't multiply to find out how many pencils she gave away; you would subtract. Adding 20 and 32 (answer choice C) would give you a large number. This number wouldn't tell you how many pencils Jennifer gave away. But if you subtract 20 from 32, as in answer choice D, you would find out how many pencils she gave away. Jennifer gave away 12 pencils.

Practice Questions

Practice 31: Number Sentences

DIRECTIONS:

Choose the best of the answer choices given for each of the following problems. Fill in the circle next to your choice.

1. **Peter had 24 crayons. His mother gave him more crayons. He now has 36 crayons. Which number sentence could you use to find out how many crayons his mother gave him?**

   Ⓐ $24 + 36 = \square$

   Ⓑ $36 - 24 = \square$

   Ⓒ $24 \times \square = 36$

   Ⓓ $\square + 26 = 24$

HINT

The number of crayons Peter's mother gave him is the difference between what he has now and what he had before.

2. **Tara has 68 marbles. She gives 24 marbles to her friend. Which number sentence could you use to find out how many marbles Tara has now?**

   Ⓐ $68 + 24 = \square$

   Ⓑ $\square \times 24 = 68$

   Ⓒ $68 - 24 = \square$

   Ⓓ $24 - \square = 68$

HINT

Tara started with 68 and gave 24 away, so she has fewer now.

Multiplication Rules

The following are some rules that will help you answer questions involving multiplication.

- You can multiply numbers in any order and get the same answer. This is called the **commutative property** of multiplication.

  For example, $7 \times 3 = 21$ is the same as $3 \times 7 = 21$.

- You can also multiply numbers in any order when you are multiplying more than two numbers. The idea that you can multiply three or more numbers in any order is called the **associative property** of multiplication. Multiply the numbers in parentheses first.

  For example, $(7 \times 3) \times 2 = 42$ is the same as $7 \times (3 \times 2) = 42$.

- Any number multiplied by 1 is that number. The number 1 is called the **identity element** of multiplication.

  For example, $8 \times 1 = 8$, and $105 \times 1 = 105$.

- Any number multiplied by 0 is 0.

  For example, $9 \times 0 = 0$, and $72 \times 0 = 0$.

Practice Questions

Practice 32: Multiplication Rules

DIRECTIONS:

Choose the best of the answer choices given for each of the following problems. Fill in the circle next to your choice.

1. If 45 × ☐ = 0, what is the value of ☐?

Ⓐ 0

Ⓑ 1

Ⓒ 5

Ⓓ 45

HINT: Remember the rule about 0.

2. Which of the following is the same as 2 × (60 × 4)?

Ⓐ 2 + (60 × 4)

Ⓑ 4 ÷ (2 × 60)

Ⓒ (2 × 60) × 4

Ⓓ 2 × 2 × (60 × 4)

HINT: Go back and reread the rule about the associative property of multiplication if you don't know the answer to this question.

3. If $100 \times \square = 100$, then what is the value of $\square$?

Ⓐ 0

Ⓑ 1

Ⓒ $\frac{1}{2}$

Ⓓ 100

HINT

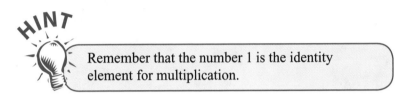

Remember that the number 1 is the identity element for multiplication.

Practice Questions

End-of-Chapter Practice Problems

DIRECTIONS:

Choose the best of the answer choices given for each of the following problems. Fill in the circle next to your choice.

1. Which rule is assigned to these numbers?

5, 14, 23, 32, 41, 50, . . .

Ⓐ Add 7

Ⓑ Add 8

Ⓒ Add 9

Ⓓ Add 11

HINT

Figure out the difference between the numbers.

2. **When 14 is dropped into this machine, it comes out as 4.**

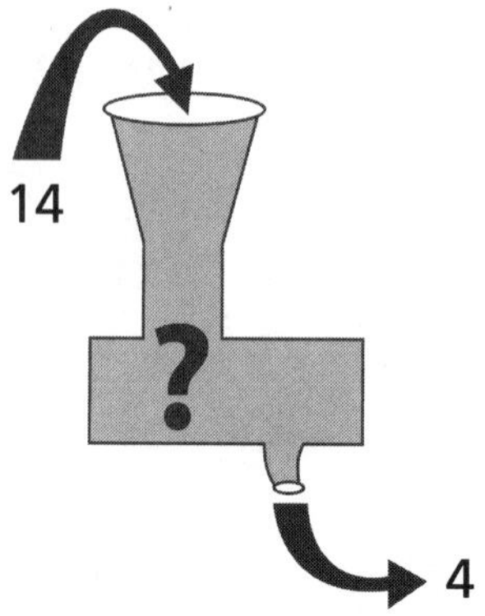

Input	14	12	38	11	28
Output	4	2	28	1	?

What is the missing number in the table?

Ⓐ 2

Ⓑ 8

Ⓒ 10

Ⓓ 18

Notice that the machine makes the numbers small, so the function involves subtraction or division.

3. Which rule is assigned to the *x* column in order to get the number in the *y* column?

x	*y*
18	12
17	11
15	9
10	4

Ⓐ Add 6

Ⓑ Subtract 6

Ⓒ Multiply by 3

Ⓓ Divide by 3

HINT

Notice that the numbers in the *y* column are smaller than the numbers in the *x* column, so the rule should involve subtraction or division.

4. If 36 ÷ □ = 3, then what is the value of □?

Ⓐ 16

Ⓑ 14

Ⓒ 12

Ⓓ 8

HINT

This is division, so you can reverse the equation.

5. What does n equal in $172 \times n = 0$?

Ⓐ 0

Ⓑ 1

Ⓒ −1

Ⓓ −172

HINT

Remember the multiplication rule about zero.

6. Brenda's class has 24 students. Brenda's teacher asks her to give each student two juice boxes. Which number sentence could be used to find out how many juice boxes Brenda needs?

Ⓐ $24 \times 2 = \square$

Ⓑ $24 \div 2 = \square$

Ⓒ $\square + 2 = 24$

Ⓓ $2 - \square = 24$

HINT

Think about what must be done to the number 24 if each of the 24 students gets two juice boxes.

Chapter 7

Data Analysis and Probability

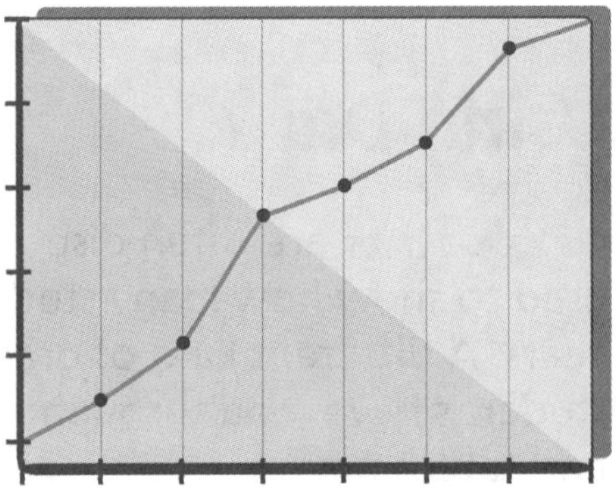

Suppose you would like to find out what kind of music most of the students in your class listen to. You grab a pencil and paper and ask each student in your class about his or her favorite music, and then you write down their answers. You use this information to reach this conclusion: Most of the students in your class like pop music!

The information you wrote down is called **data**. People use data in many different ways. The weatherperson on your television gathers data to make a prediction about the weather.

Your math teacher might give the students in your class a quiz. If the students do not do well on the quiz, your teacher might decide to spend more time teaching the lesson. The quiz your teacher gave was to gather data, or information, about whether your class understood the lesson. In this chapter, you'll learn how to reach a conclusion based on data.

Imagine that you have 10 T-shirts in your drawer. Three T-shirts are blue, two are yellow, and five are white. You reach into your drawer and pull out a T-shirt without looking. Do you think you will pull out a blue T-shirt, a yellow T-shirt, or a white T-shirt? The likelihood of pulling out one color over another color is called **probability**. In this chapter, you'll learn how to choose a fraction that represents the probability that something will happen.

Using Data

Data points are often displayed in **graphs** and **tables**. A graph might be used to show how many students played a certain sport over the past five years. A different kind of graph might be used to show how many books students have read throughout the year. Let's review some common graphs and tables now.

Bar Graphs

A **bar graph** uses bars to show data. These bars are most often **vertical** (up and down), but they can also be **horizontal** (side to side). Often the bars on a bar graph will be printed in different colors, but on the NJ ASK Mathematics test, the bars will be gray. Look at the bar graph shown below:

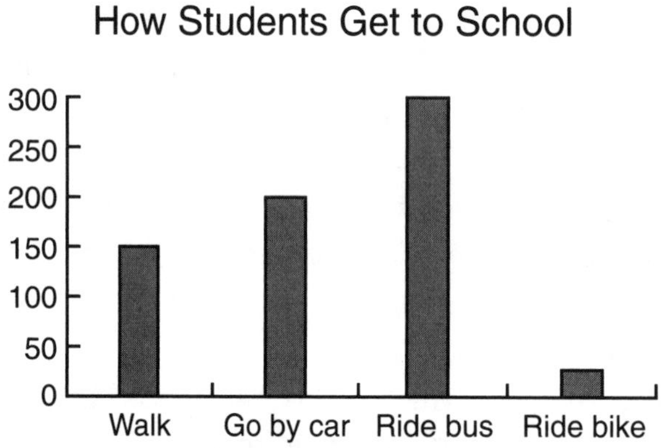

This bar graph shows how students get to school. The different ways they get to school are listed on the bottom of the graph—walk, go by car, ride the bus, and ride by bike. The numbers of students are listed on the side—0, 50, 100, and so on—and the value of each bar is determined by its height. Use this bar graph to tell how many students get to school each way. The first one is done for you.

Walk:	150 students
Car ride:	______________
Bus ride:	______________
Ride bike:	______________

How do most of the students get to school? ______________

If you wrote that 200 students get a car ride, 300 ride the bus, and 25 ride bikes, you are right. Most students get to school by bus. If any of your answers were incorrect, look more carefully at the values of the bars in the bar graph.

Pictographs

In a **pictograph,** another kind of graph, **pictures** stand for data. A picture often stands for more than one of an item. You have to look at a key to see how many things a picture stands for. Look at this pictograph. It shows how many magazines students collected for recycling during the school year:

Number of Magazines Collected for Recycling During the School Year

Caleb	[redacted]
Martin	[redacted]
Katelyn	[redacted]
Rose	[redacted]

Key [redacted] = 10 magazines

Use the pictograph and the key to tell how many magazines each friend collected. Notice that each ■ is equal to 10 magazines. So, ▌ is equal to 5 magazines. The first one is done for you.

Caleb:	100 magazines
Martin:	____________________
Katelyn:	____________________
Rose:	____________________

Who collected the most magazines? ____________________

If you wrote that Martin collected 155 magazines, Katelyn collected 125 magazines, and Rose collected 85 magazines, you are right. Martin collected the most magazines. If any of your answers were incorrect, recheck your multiplication. Remember that ▌ is equal to 5 magazines.

Line Graphs and Line Plots

You learned about line graphs in Chapter 6. A **line graph** shows the relationship between two things. If the first gets larger or smaller, it affects the second. Line graphs are used to show a **trend**. A trend is something that happens over time. Look at the line graph below. It shows the number of Eastern goldfinches, the state bird of New Jersey, Shakra counted in her yard for five months.

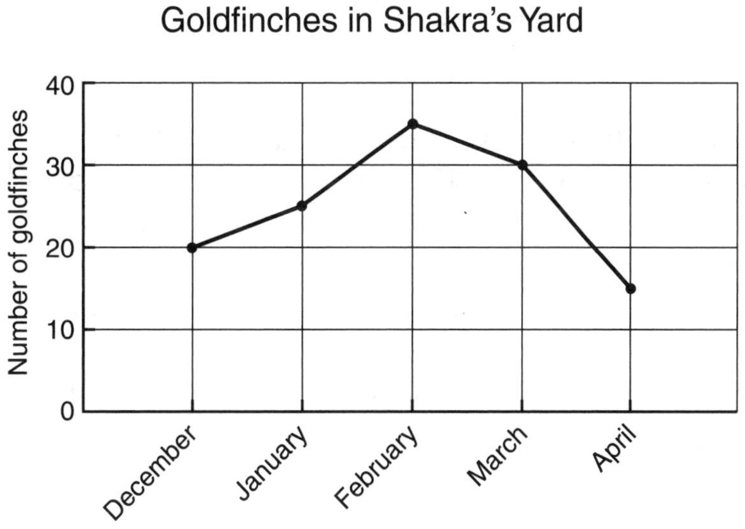

About how many goldfinches did Shakra see in her yard in December?

During which month did Shakra see the most goldfinches?

If you answered that Shakra saw 20 goldfinches in December and that she saw the most goldfinches in February, you are right. If either of your answers is incorrect, look more carefully at the graph.

A **line plot** is another type of graph. It is used to show how much of a type of data you have. Line plots are great for displaying outliers. An **outlier** is a number that is far away from the rest. Look at the line plot below.

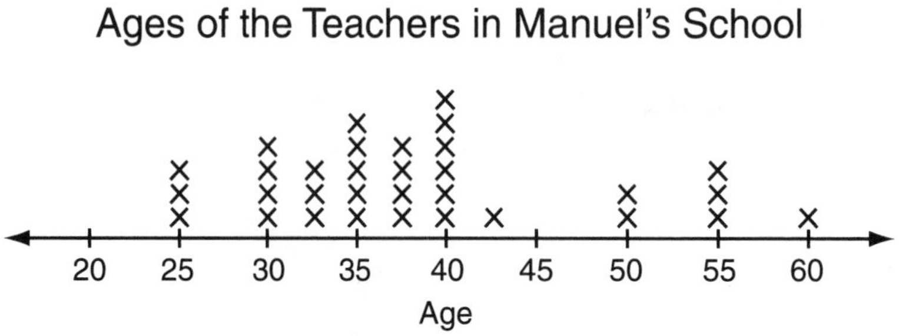

You can see from the line plot that most of the teachers in Manuel's school are between the ages of 30 and 40. What age would be considered an outlier (a data point that doesn't look like it belongs with the others)?

____

If you said 60, you are right. It lies far to the right of the group of data points.

Practice Questions

Practice 33: Using Data and Graphs

DIRECTIONS:

Choose the best of the answer choices given for each of the following problems. Fill in the circle next to your choice.

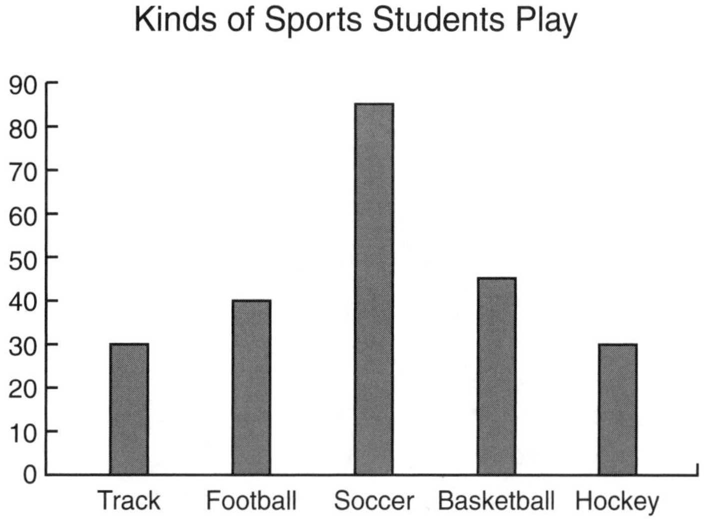

1. According to the bar graph above, how many students play football?

Ⓐ 20

Ⓑ 30

Ⓒ 40

Ⓓ 50

Look at the bar for football. What number does it go up to?

2. Which sport do most students play?

Ⓐ Track

Ⓑ Football

Ⓒ Soccer

Ⓓ Basketball

HINT

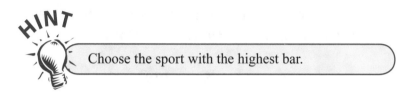

Choose the sport with the highest bar.

Probability

Probability is the chance that something will happen. Probability is often expressed as a fraction. Try this problem:

Imagine that you have a bag of 20 marbles, of which 10 are red, 5 are yellow, 3 are blue, and 2 are green. You put your hand in the bag and pull out a marble without looking. What is the chance (probability) that you will pull out a green marble?

To find out, add up all of the marbles. You have 20. This is the denominator. Then see how many marbles are green. There are 2, so the probability that you will pull out a green marble is $\frac{2}{20}$.

Let's try another.

Leslie is about to spin this spinner:

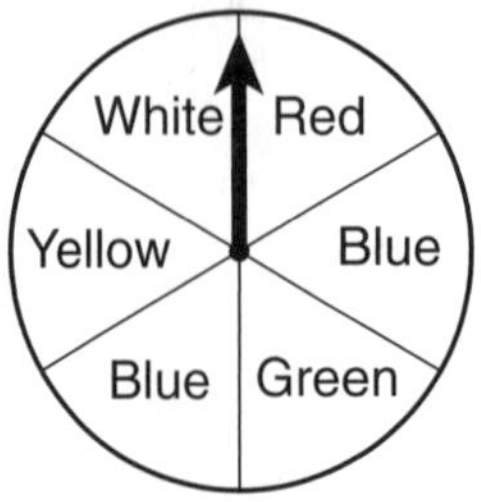

What is the probability that the spinner will land on blue?

Begin by determining how many parts are in the spinner. There are 6, so 6 is the denominator. Then see how many parts are blue. There are 2. This is the numerator. So the probability of the spinner landing on a blue part is $\frac{2}{6}$.

Practice Questions

Practice 34: Probability

DIRECTIONS:

Choose the best of the answer choices given for each of the following problems. Fill in the circle next to your choice.

1. **Rachel has a bag of 14 ribbons that contains 2 green ribbons, 3 red ribbons, 4 brown ribbons, and 5 white ribbons. If Rachel reached into the bag without looking and picked one ribbon, what is the probability that she would pick a red ribbon?**

   (A) $\frac{2}{14}$

   (B) $\frac{3}{14}$

   (C) $\frac{4}{14}$

   (D) $\frac{5}{14}$

HINT

There are 14 ribbons altogether, and 3 of these ribbons are red. Remember that probability is given as a fraction with the total number of choices on the bottom and the number of desired choices on the top.

2. **Students pick cards out of a hat to see in which group they will be. The hat contains 6 cards with Group A written on them, 4 cards with Group B, 5 cards with Group C, and 10 cards with Group D. What is the probability a student will pick a card with Group B written on it?**

(A) $\frac{4}{25}$

(B) $\frac{5}{25}$

(C) $\frac{6}{25}$

(D) $\frac{10}{25}$

HINT

Add to see the total number of cards. Four cards have Group B written on them.

Mean, Mode, and Median

The **mean, mode**, and **median** of a set of numbers are three measures of how data are spread out.

The **mean** of a set of numbers is the average. To find the mean, add up all of the numbers. Then divide by how many numbers you added. Look at this example:

Jean played piano for 2 hours one day, 3 hours the next day, 3 hours the next day, and 4 hours on the last day. What is the average number of hours Jean played the piano over the four days?

To find the mean in this problem, first add up all of the numbers:

$$\begin{array}{r} 2 \\ 3 \\ 3 \\ +\ 4 \\ \hline 12 \end{array}$$

Then divide 12 by 4, since you added four numbers.

$$12 \div 4 = 3$$

The mean number of hours Jean played the piano is 3.

Let's try one more.

On five math tests, Freddie scored 80, 80, 75, 90, and 85. What is Freddie's mean score?

$$\begin{array}{r} 80 \\ 80 \\ 75 \\ 90 \\ +\ 85 \\ \hline \end{array}$$

If you add these numbers, you get 410. Now divide this number by 5, the number of math tests. The answer is 82.

The **mode** is the number that appears the most. For example, for Freddie's test scores above, it would be 80.

Look at the data below:

7, 2, 3, 4, 4, 8, 4, 2

Which number is repeated the most? If you said 4, you are right. So the number 4 is the mode here.

Let's try one more.

Which number in this set of data appears the most?

80, 92, 45, 80, 72, 72, 80

Be careful! The number 72 is repeated, but it isn't the number that is repeated the most. The number 80 is repeated three times, so 80 is the mode.

The **median** is the number that is in the middle of a group of numbers. To find the median, you need to put numbers in order from least to greatest.

Look at this set of numbers:

6, 9, 0, 1, 4

It looks as though 0 is in the middle, but 0 isn't the median. You first have to put the numbers in order from least to greatest:

0, 1, 4, 6, 9

Now which number is in the middle? The number 4 is in the middle, so it is the median.

Let's try another one.

What is the median of this set of numbers?

32, 46, 75, 21, 88

First, put these numbers in order from least to greatest.

21, 32, 46, 75, 88

Which number is in the middle? The number 46 is the median.

Note that if there is an even amount of numbers, there are two in the middle. In that case, the median is the mean of these two middle numbers. So, for the numbers 1, 3, 4, 6, 8, 10, the median would be 5 (even though that isn't a number in the group), because 5 is the mean between the two middle numbers, 4 and 6.

Practice Questions

Practice 35: Mean, Mode, and Median

DIRECTIONS:

Choose the best of the answer choices given for each of the following problems. Fill in the circle next to your choice.

1. The table below shows the average (mean) January temperature for several years in Lindsay's hometown.

Average January Temperatures

Year	Average January Temperature
1	32
2	36
3	26
4	20
5	36

What is the average (mean) temperature for all five years?

Ⓐ 26

Ⓑ 30

Ⓒ 32

Ⓓ 36

HINT

To find the mean, add up all of the numbers. Then divide by the number of years.

2. Dale's teacher put these numbers on the chalkboard:

6, 8, 0, 2, 5 0, 2, 5, 6, 8

Which number is the middle (median)?

Ⓐ 0

Ⓑ 2

Ⓒ 5

Ⓓ 6

HINT

Remember to put the numbers in order from least to greatest.

3. Brittney scored the following points during her first seven basketball games:

2, 8, 12, 4, 4, 2, 4

Which number is the most frequent (mode)?

Ⓐ 2

Ⓑ 4

Ⓒ 8

Ⓓ 12

HINT

The mode is the number that appears the most.

Practice Questions

End-of-Chapter Practice Problems

DIRECTIONS:

Choose the best of the answer choices given for each of the following problems. Fill in the circle next to your choice.

1. The table below lists Jillian's scores on the last five social studies tests.

Jillian's Test Scores

Social Studies Test	Jillian's Score
1	85
2	90
3	92
4	78
5	90

What is her average (mean) score?

Ⓐ 85

Ⓑ 87

Ⓒ 90

Ⓓ 92

HINT

Remember to add all of the numbers. Then, in this case, you would divide by 5, the number of tests.

2. **Students pick cards out of a hat to see what kind of leaves they will collect for art class. The hat contains 8 cards with a maple leaf drawn on them, 4 cards with an oak leaf, 6 cards with a dogwood leaf, and 2 cards with an apple-tree leaf. What is the probability that a student will pick a card with an oak leaf on it?**

Ⓐ $\frac{2}{20}$

Ⓑ $\frac{4}{20}$

Ⓒ $\frac{6}{20}$

Ⓓ $\frac{8}{20}$

HINT

There are 20 cards all together. How many of these cards have an oak leaf written on them?

3. The pictograph below shows the number of laps students ran during a special event at school.

Laps Run by Students

Key: = 2 laps

How many laps did Sam run?

Ⓐ 5

Ⓑ 6

Ⓒ 12

Ⓓ 18

HINT

Determine the number of laps by using the key = 2 laps.

4. **How much did it snow in Becky's town in Year 3, according to the following bar graph?**

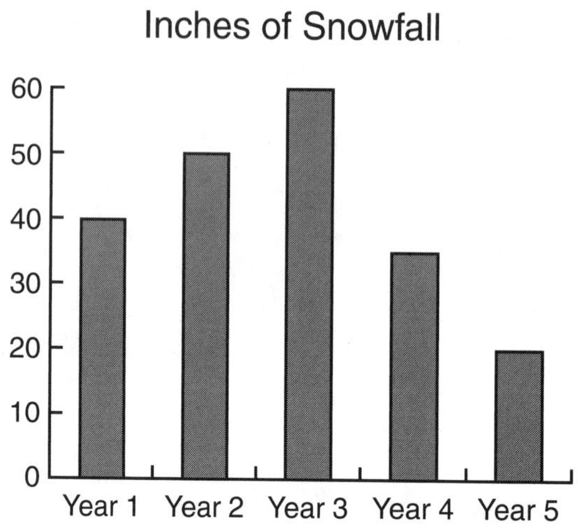

Ⓐ 40

Ⓑ 50

Ⓒ 60

Ⓓ 70

HINT

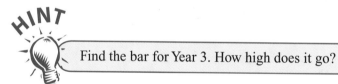

Find the bar for Year 3. How high does it go?

5. **Cecily has a bag of balloons that contains 10 red, 4 white, 5 blue, 5 green, and 6 orange balloons. If Cecily reached into the bag without looking and picked a balloon, what is the probability that she would pick an orange balloon?**

Ⓐ $\frac{4}{30}$

Ⓑ $\frac{5}{30}$

Ⓒ $\frac{6}{30}$

Ⓓ $\frac{10}{30}$

HINT

Add to find how many total balloons there are, and use the number of orange balloons to determine the probability.

6. The table below shows the number of birds at Lee's bird feeder each hour during one afternoon.

Number of Birds Each Hour

Hour	Number of Birds
1	15
2	10
3	5
4	7
5	3

What is the middle (median) number of birds for the afternoon?

Ⓐ 3

Ⓑ 5

Ⓒ 7

Ⓓ 10

HINT

Put the numbers in order from least to greatest.

Chapter 8

More About Analyzing Data

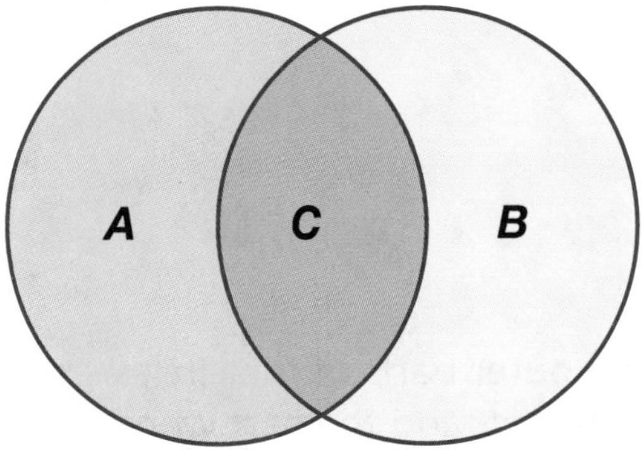

In the last chapter, Chapter 7, you learned how to analyze data in bar graphs, pictographs, line graphs, and line plots. You learned that graphs and tables show data.

Data can be shown in other ways, too. Venn and tree diagrams can be used to show data. You'll learn about these in this chapter.

You'll also learn about combinations in this chapter. Suppose you go to an ice cream stand and learn that you can have your ice cream in either a sugar cone or a waffle cone. And you can choose from chocolate, vanilla, or strawberry ice cream. How many different combinations of cones and ice cream are there? Creating a tree diagram can help you find the answer to this question.

Think about the last time you followed directions. Maybe you listened to a friend tell you how to get to her house. Or maybe you helped your grandfather cook a special dinner by following a recipe. You'll also learn about questions involving directions in this chapter.

Venn Diagrams

A **Venn diagram** is used to show how things are alike and different. It has two overlapping circles. The diagram on the next page is a Venn diagram.

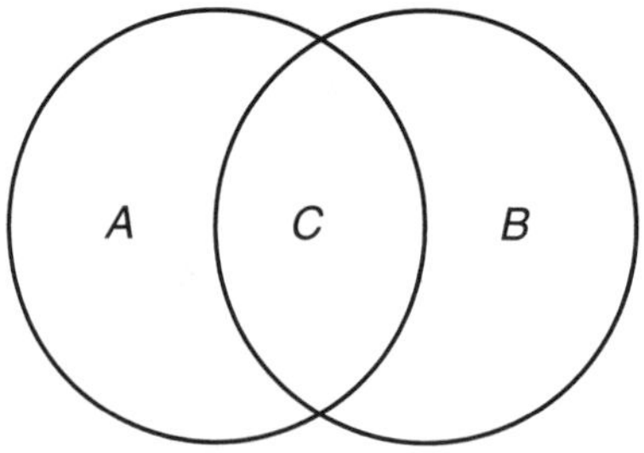

The outer parts of the circles—parts *A* and *B*—show how two things are different, and the part where the circles overlap—part *C*—shows how things are alike.

The Venn diagram below compares dogs and cats. Things about dogs are listed in circle *A* and things about cats in circle *B*. The things that dogs and cats have in common go in the part where the circles overlap.

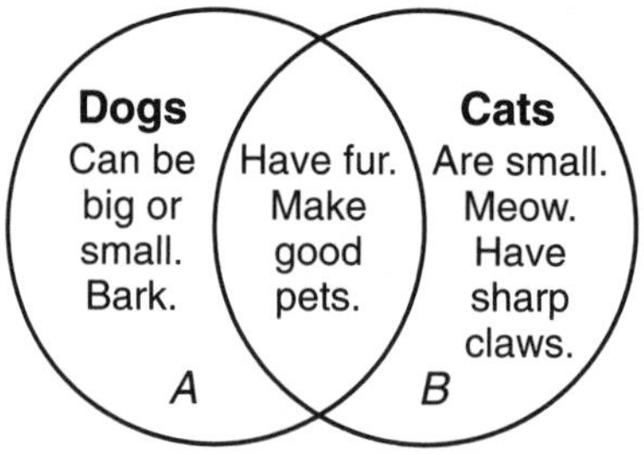

If you look at the Venn diagram, you can see that dogs and cats are alike in that they have fur and they make good pets, but dogs are different from cats in that they can be different sizes and they bark. Cats are different from dogs in that they have sharp claws, meow, and are mostly small.

Now try to make your own Venn diagram. Compare yourself and your best friend. Put things about yourself in circle *A*. Put things about your friend in circle *B*. Put some ways that you are alike in circle *C*.

Tree Diagrams

A **tree diagram** shows the **order** in which something happens. Look at the tree diagram described below.

When a boys' soccer practice is canceled, Mr. Biscotti, the coach, calls Brian and Pedro. Then Brian and Pedro each call the player listed under their name, who call the players listed under their names, and so on. This continues until every player is called.

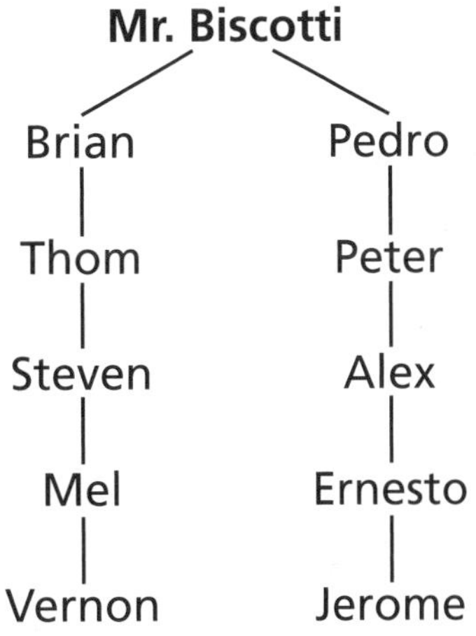

According to this telephone tree, which student will Ernesto call?

To answer this question, find Ernesto's name on the tree. Ernesto will call the person beneath his name. If you look at the tree, you can see that Ernesto will call Jerome.

Practice Questions

Practice 36: Venn Diagrams and Tree Diagrams

DIRECTIONS:

Choose the best of the answer choices given for each of the following problems. Fill in the circle next to your choice.

1. Kim used the Venn diagram below to show how her mother and grandmother are alike and different.

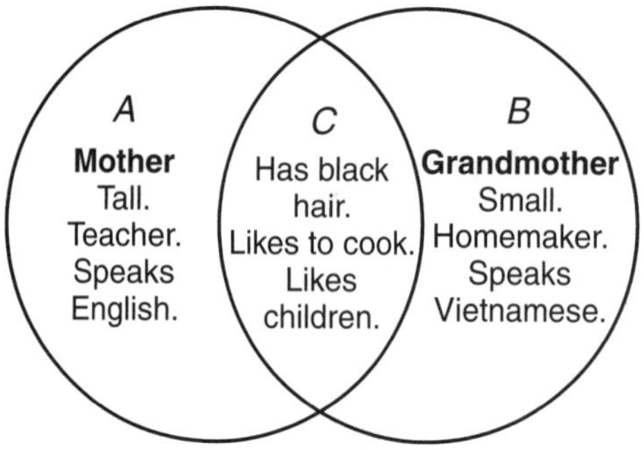

What is one way that Kim's mother and grandmother are alike?

Ⓐ Both speak English.

Ⓑ Both are homemakers.

● Both like to cook.

Ⓓ Both are small.

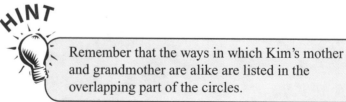

Remember that the ways in which Kim's mother and grandmother are alike are listed in the overlapping part of the circles.

2. **When the speech club is planning an activity, Rosa calls Leo and Dora. Then Leo and Dora each call the students listed directly under their names, and they follow the telephone tree shown below.**

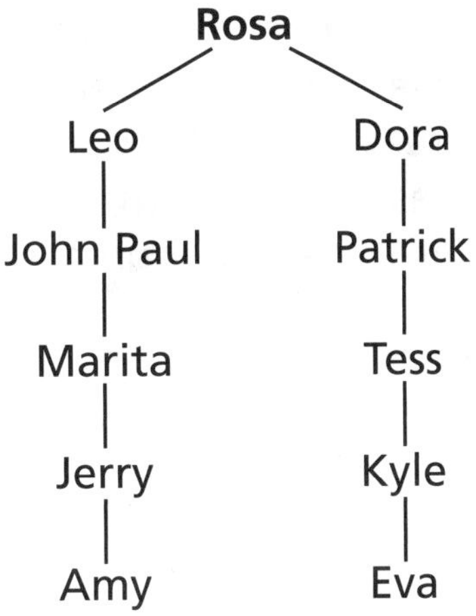

Which student does John Paul call?

(A) Patrick

(B) Marita

(C) Tess

(D) Leo

HINT: Find the name that is under John Paul.

Categories and Colors

A **category** is a group of things that are alike. Look at the diagram below:

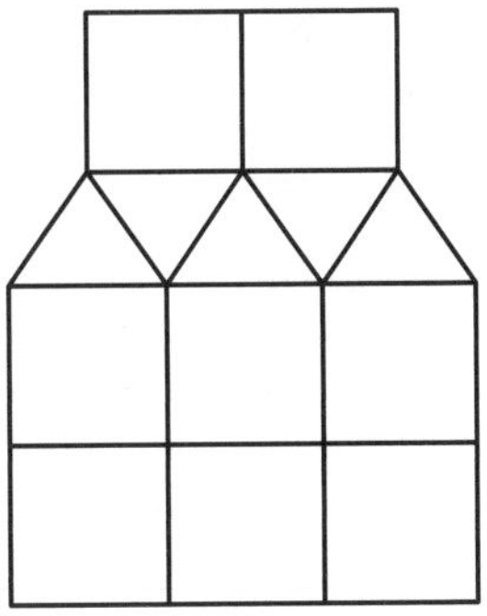

How many triangles are in this diagram? These triangles form a category. How many squares are in this diagram? These squares also form a category. If you noticed that there are five triangles and eight squares, you are right.

How many colors do you think you would need to color the diagram below, using the fewest colors possible so that no areas that touch are the same color? Note that corners of areas that touch can have the same color; only the sides of two touching areas cannot be the same color, because that would blend the two areas into one larger area.

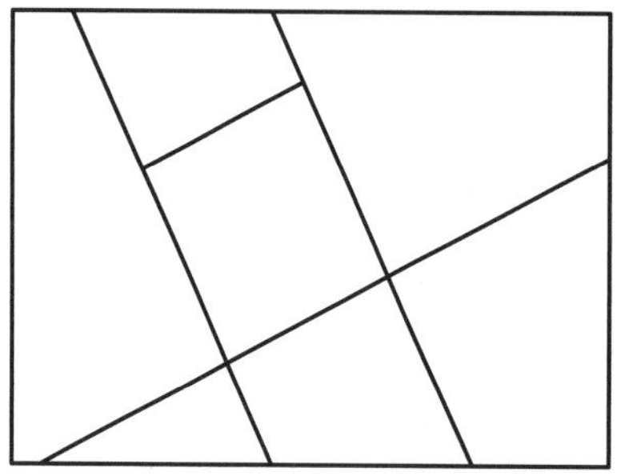

It helps if you number the areas, with each number representing a different color. Look at the numbered areas below. You can tell from the numbers that the smallest number of colors you can use is three.

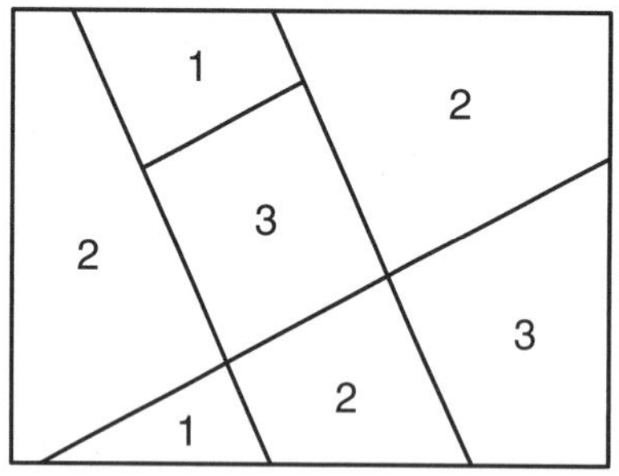

An interesting fact is that no matter how many areas are drawn, the smallest number of colors is always never more than four.

Practice Questions

Practice 37: Categories and Colors

DIRECTIONS:

Choose the best of the answer choices given for each of the following problems. Fill in the circle next to your choice.

1. A section of a quilt Jay's grandmother made is shown below. How many single-color rectangles (not counting squares) are in this section of the quilt?

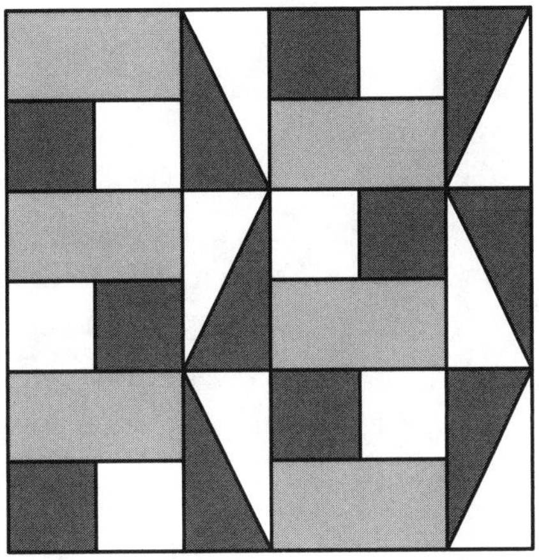

Ⓐ 5

Ⓑ 6

Ⓒ 7

Ⓓ 8

HINT

Some of the shapes in this diagram are squares. Count only the rectangles.

2. **To color the following map, you want to use as few colors as possible. What is the smallest number of colors you can use so that no areas that touch are the same color?**

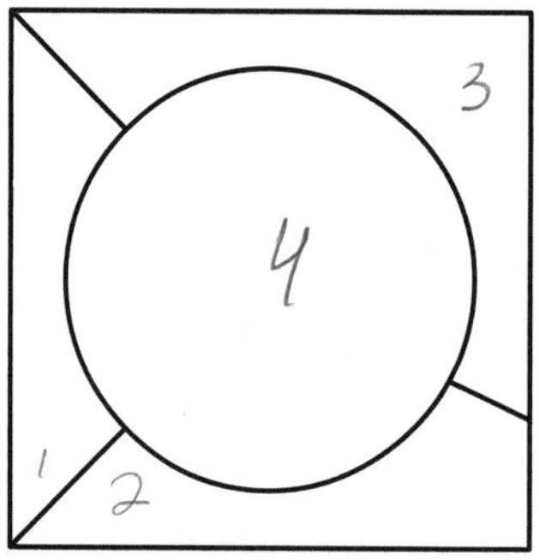

Ⓐ 2

Ⓑ 3

Ⓒ 4

Ⓓ 5

HINT

Number each color and repeat colors whenever possible.

Following Directions

Mapping questions ask you to follow or give directions by using a **grid**. Sometimes these grids will not be **coordinate grids**. This means they will not have numbers along **the *x*-axis** and ***y*-axis**. To answer these questions, you must count the number of places to the north, south, east, or west. A key showing these directions is usually provided.

Look at the map below.

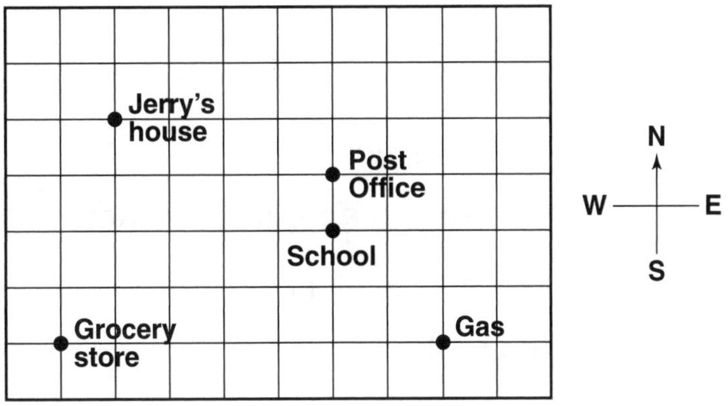

Using this map, consider the following problem:

Jerry left his house and followed this list of directions.

1. **Walk three blocks east.**
2. **Walk four blocks south.**
3. **Walk four blocks west.**

Use the map to help you list all of the places Jerry passed on his walk, including the place where he ended his walk.

To answer this problem, you need to look at the key showing the different directions: north, south, east, and west. Then you need to find Jerry's house. Follow the directions carefully. Note that each block on the grid is a block in the instructions.

First, Jerry walks three blocks east. Then he walks four blocks south. Then he walks four blocks west. This takes him to the grocery store.

Practice Questions

Practice 38: Following Directions

Directions for the Open-Ended Questions

The following questions are **open-ended** questions. Remember to:

Read each question carefully and think about the answer.

Answer all the parts of the question.

Show your work or explain your answer.

You can answer the questions by using words, tables, diagrams, OR pictures. You may use your calculator, ruler, and colored shapes.

1. Look at the map below.

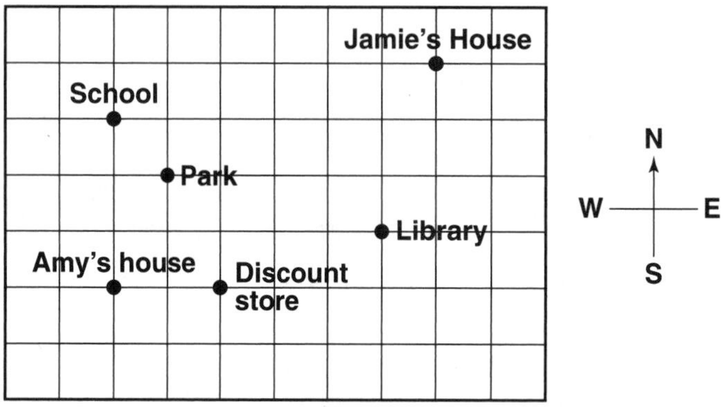

Amy left her house and followed this list of directions:

a. Walk three blocks east.

b. Walk three blocks north.

c. Walk three blocks west.

Use the map to list what Amy passed on her walk, including the place where she ended her walk.

HINT

Look at the key showing the different directions. Find Amy's house and follow the directions carefully. Note that each block on the grid is a block in the instructions.

2. **After school, Jamie is going to Amy's house to study. He wants to stop home first to get something to eat. Using the same map as for problem #1, make a list of directions that Jamie can follow to walk from school to his house and then to Amy's house.**

HINT

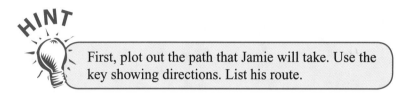

First, plot out the path that Jamie will take. Use the key showing directions. List his route.

Combinations

You can make a graph that looks like a tree diagram to help you find out how many **combinations** of something you have. Remember the combinations of ice cream cones and ice cream you read about in the beginning of this chapter? You had a choice of a sugar cone or a waffle cone. You also had a choice of chocolate, vanilla, or strawberry ice cream. To find out how many combinations of waffle and ice cream you have, you can draw a tree diagram like this:

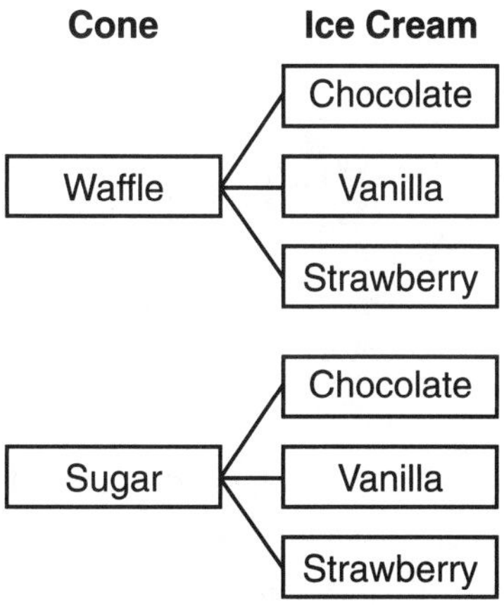

To find out how many combinations you have, count the lines. Did you count six lines? There are six different combinations of cones and ice cream.

Now try another problem that uses combinations.

Katie has 5 books in her locker: one for science, one for math, one for social studies, one for language arts, and one for art. She is going to take two books home tonight. How many different pairs of books could she take home?

Ⓐ 4

Ⓑ 6

Ⓒ 8

Ⓓ 10

Look at the diagram below. If you make a diagram like this, you can tell that Katie has 10 combinations of books.

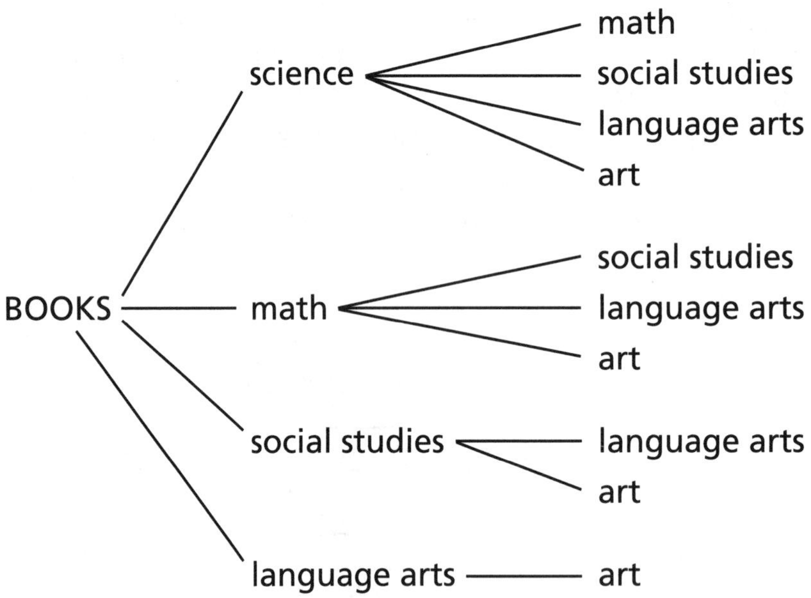

Note that only three book combinations are listed for math, because the math-science combination is already listed under science. For a similar reason, only two book combinations are listed under social studies, and only one under language arts. All of the art combinations are already listed.

Practice Questions

Practice 39: Combinations

DIRECTIONS:

Choose the best of the answer choices given for each of the following problems. Fill in the circle next to your choice.

1. Ellie wants to buy her puppy a sweater. She can choose pink, purple, green, blue, or black-and-white. She also wants to buy her puppy a collar. She can choose silver or gold. How many combinations of sweater and collar are there?

Ⓐ 4

Ⓑ 6

Ⓒ 8

● 10

HINT

Make a tree diagram. Then count the lines from each color collar to each color sweater.

2. For a brown-bag lunch, students at Veronica's school can choose from a ham sandwich, a cheese sandwich, a turkey sandwich, or a peanut-butter-and-jelly sandwich. They can also choose an apple, an orange, a banana, or a plum. How many combinations of sandwich and fruit are there?

Ⓐ 10

Ⓑ 12

● 14

Ⓓ 16

HINT

Remember to draw a diagram and count each line.

Practice Questions

End-of-Chapter Practice Problems

DIRECTIONS:

Choose the best of the answer choices given for each of the following problems. Fill in the circle next to your choice.

1. The kids in Marcy's art class use this phone tree to let students know if a class is canceled. Miss Angela calls Marcy and Kaylee, and then each student calls the person whose name is listed under his or her name. This continues until every student is called.

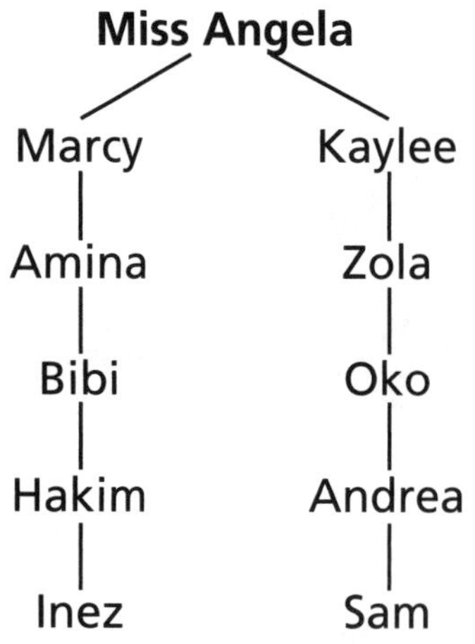

Which student will Hakim call?

Ⓐ Andrea

Ⓑ Inez

Ⓒ Sam

Ⓓ Bibi

HINT: Look for the name beneath Hakim's name.

2. **Referring to the telephone tree in #1, which student calls Zola?**

Ⓐ Oko

Ⓑ Andrea

● Kaylee

Ⓓ Amina

HINT

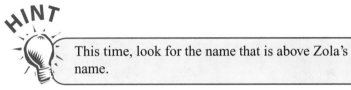

This time, look for the name that is above Zola's name.

3. **Vanessa used the Venn diagram below to show how her two favorite teachers are alike and different.**

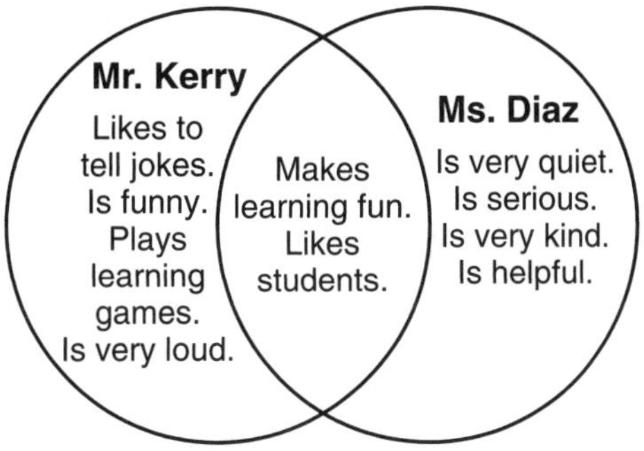
Mr. Kerry
Likes to tell jokes. Is funny. Plays learning games. Is very loud.
Makes learning fun. Likes students.
Ms. Diaz
Is very quiet. Is serious. Is very kind. Is helpful.

What is one way Mr. Kerry and Ms. Diaz are alike?

Ⓐ They are both serious.

Ⓑ They are both funny.

Ⓒ They are both helpful.

● They both make learning fun.

HINT

Look at the part where the circles overlap.

4. To color the following map, you want to use as few colors as possible. What is the smallest number of colors you can use so that no areas that touch are the same color?

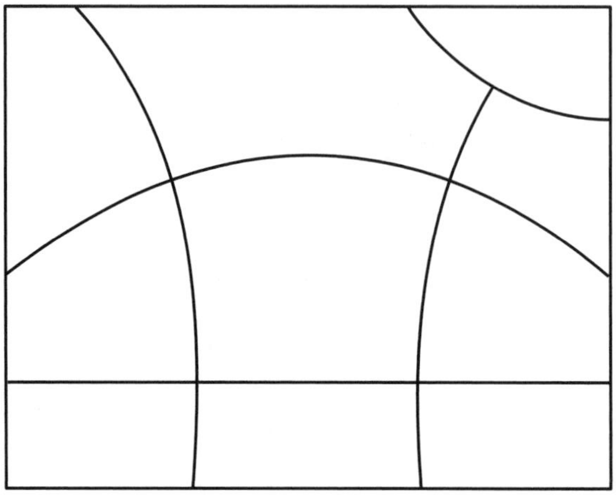

- (A) 2
- (B) 3
- (C) 4
- (D) 5

Number each section, and use as few numbers as possible.

5. Look at the map below.

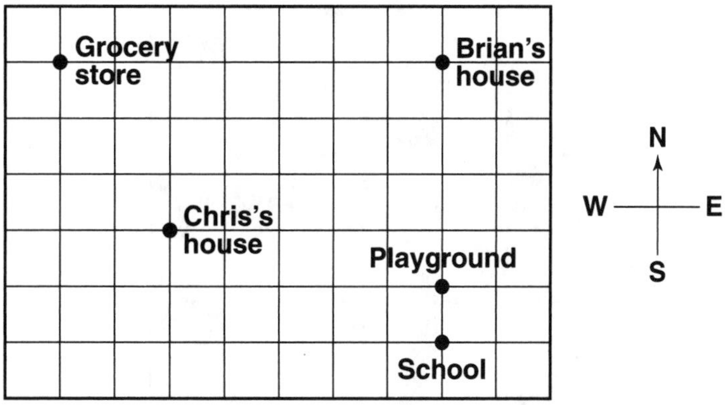

Chris left his house and followed this list of directions.

a. Walk three blocks north.

b. Walk two blocks west.

Where does Chris end up?

Ⓐ at Brian's house

● at the grocery store

Ⓒ at school

Ⓓ at the playground

HINT

Be sure to look at the direction key to make sure you are moving in the right direction.

6. **Look at the diagram below. How many single-colored squares are there?**

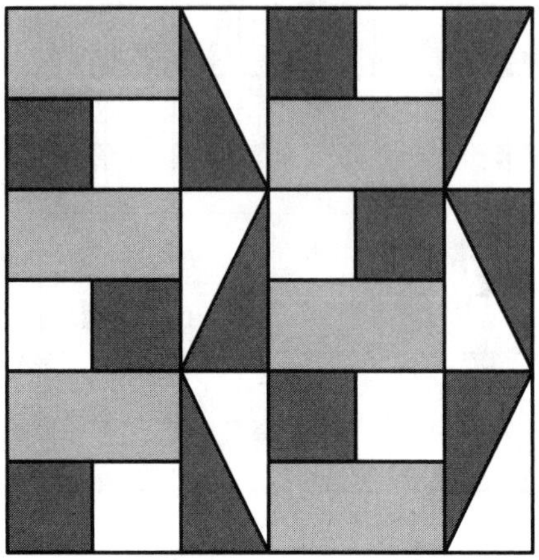

Ⓐ 10

Ⓑ 11

Ⓒ 12

Ⓓ 13

HINT

Count only the squares within the outside border, not the rectangles.

7. **For her summer job, Linda can wear a white, blue, yellow, or pink T-shirt, and tan, black, or blue shorts. How many combinations of T-shirts and shorts does she have?**

Ⓐ 7

Ⓑ 8

Ⓒ 12

Ⓓ 16

HINT

Draw a line from each color T-shirt to each color shorts, and count the lines.

New Jersey Assessment of Skills and Knowledge

MATHEMATICS Grade 4

Practice Test 1

DIRECTIONS:

When you are taking this test, remember these important things:

1. Read each question carefully and think about the answer.
2. If you do not know the answer to a question, go on to the next question. You may come back to the skipped question later if you have time.
3. When you see a STOP sign (STOP), do **not** turn the page until you are told to do so.

GO ON TO THE NEXT PAGE.

Part 1

Directions:

This part of the test contains 8 short constructed-response questions. You may NOT use a calculator for these questions. Write your answer on the line.

1. Find the exact answer: 900 − 210

Place your answer here: ____________

2. Find the exact answer: 102 ÷ 3

Place your answer here: ____________

3. Find the exact answer: 24 × 12

Place your answer here: ____________

GO ON TO THE NEXT PAGE.

4. **Find the exact answer: 702 − 105**

   Place your answer here: ____________

5. **Kendrick has a baseball card collection. He has 210 baseball cards, and his grandfather gives him 97 more. Then he gives 52 baseball cards to his brother. How many baseball cards does Kendrick have now?**

   Place your answer here: ____________

6. **Mia has a bag of beads in which 10 are blue, 8 are pink, 4 are green, and 8 are orange. If Mia reaches into the bag without looking, what is the probability that she will pull out an orange bead?**

   Place your answer here: ____________

GO ON TO THE NEXT PAGE.

7. If the following pattern continues, what is the next number?

6, 11, 16, 21, 26, 31, 36

Place your answer here: ____________

8. On five science tests, Jameel scored 90, 92, 88, 98, and 92. What is his average (mean) score?

Place your answer here: ____________

If you have time, you may review your work in this section only.

STOP

DO NOT GO ON UNTIL YOU ARE TOLD TO DO SO.

Part 2

Directions:

This part of the test contains 11 multiple-choice questions. You may NOT use a calculator for these questions. Darken the circle of the correct answer choice.

9. Estimate 824 + 397. The sum is between which numbers?

Ⓐ **50 and 400**

Ⓑ **450 and 700**

Ⓒ **750 and 1,000**

Ⓓ **1,050 and 1,300**

10. Estimate 84 × 12. The product is between which numbers?

Ⓐ **30 and 80**

Ⓑ **100 and 150**

Ⓒ **300 and 1,100**

Ⓓ **1,200 and 1,500**

11. Compare the shaded regions. Which symbol belongs in the square?

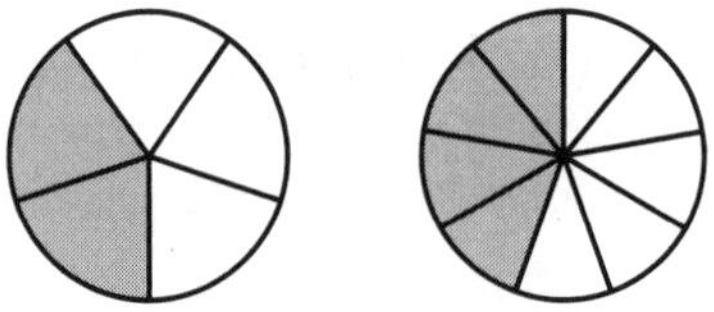

$\frac{2}{5} \square \frac{4}{9}$

Ⓐ <

Ⓑ >

Ⓒ =

Ⓓ None of the above

12. Which group of numbers is in order from least to greatest?

Ⓐ .25 1.05 1.0

Ⓑ .25 1.0 1.05

Ⓒ 1.0 1.05 .25

Ⓓ 1.05 1.0 .25

GO ON TO THE NEXT PAGE.

13. What is line segment *AB* called?

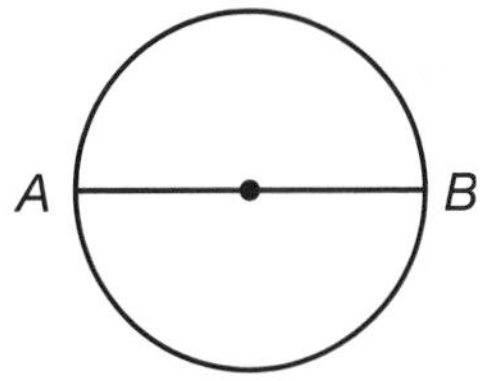

Ⓐ **a radius**

Ⓑ **a diameter**

Ⓒ **a segment**

Ⓓ **a circumference**

14. Renee wrote the following riddle to her friend:

I have 1 vertex and 1 face, and my face is a circle. What am I?

What is the answer to this riddle?

Ⓐ **cone**

Ⓑ **cylinder**

Ⓒ **sphere**

Ⓓ **pyramid**

GO ON TO THE NEXT PAGE.

15. Which of these shows parallel lines?

Ⓐ 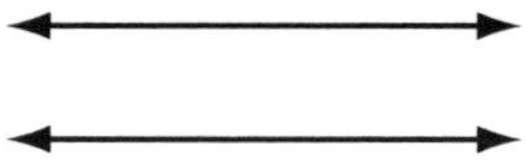

Ⓑ 

Ⓒ 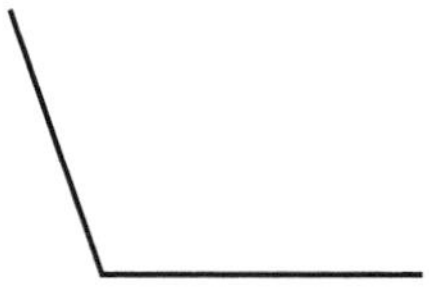

Ⓓ 

GO ON TO THE NEXT PAGE.

16. Which angle below is a right angle?

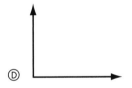

Ⓐ 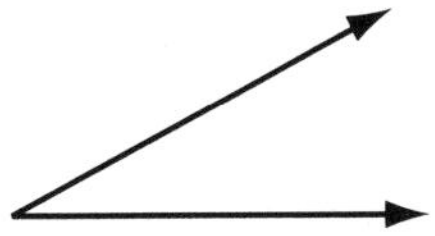

Ⓑ 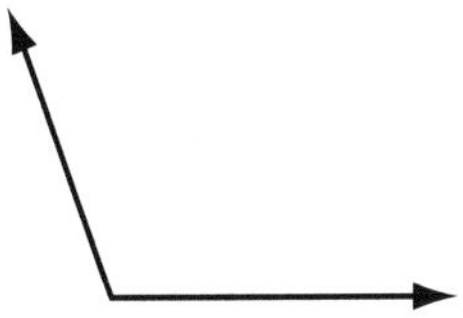

Ⓒ 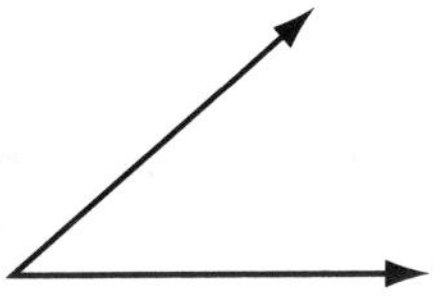

Ⓓ 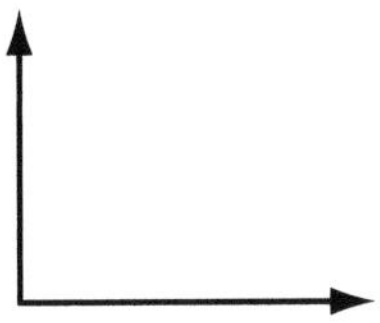

GO ON TO THE NEXT PAGE.

17. What is the most reasonable estimate of the amount of water in a pond?

Ⓐ 100,000 cups

Ⓑ 100,000 pints

Ⓒ 100,000 quarts

Ⓓ 100,000 gallons

18. The population of Trenton, New Jersey, at the 2000 census was 85,403. What is the value of 4 in the number 85,403?

Ⓐ 4 thousands

Ⓑ 4 hundreds

Ⓒ 4 tens

Ⓓ 4 ones

GO ON TO THE NEXT PAGE.

19. **To color the following flag, you want to use as few colors as possible. What is the smallest number of colors you can use so that no areas that touch are the same color?**

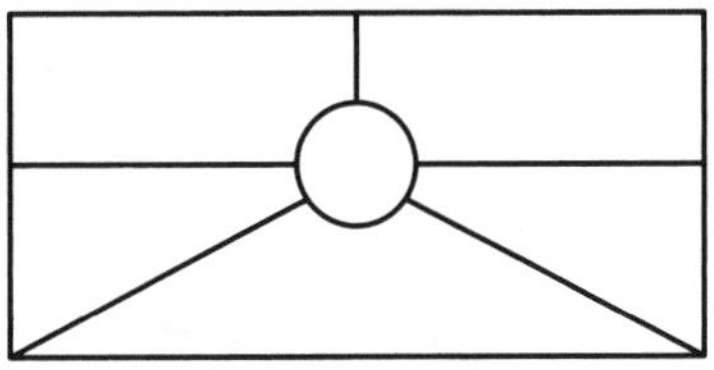

Ⓐ **2**

Ⓑ **3**

Ⓒ **4**

Ⓓ **5**

If you have time, you may review your work in this section only.

STOP

DO NOT GO ON UNTIL YOU ARE TOLD TO DO SO.

Part 3

Directions:

This part of the test contains 8 multiple-choice questions and one extended constructed-response question. You may NOT use a calculator for this part of the test. Darken the circle of the correct answer choice. Follow the directions for the ECR.

20. Enrico had 52 stickers. He gave his sister some of the stickers. He now has 35 stickers. Which number sentence could you use to find out how many stickers he gave to his sister?

Ⓐ $52 - \square = 35$

Ⓑ $\square - 52 = 35$

Ⓒ $52 + 35 = \square$

Ⓓ $52 \div \square = 35$

21. What does n equal in $124 \times n = 372$?

Ⓐ 2

Ⓑ 3

Ⓒ 4

Ⓓ 5

GO ON TO THE NEXT PAGE.

22. There are 10 houses on Angel's street. Mary lives 3 houses to the right of Angel. Carmen lives 4 houses to the right of Mary.

How many houses to the left of Carmen does Angel live?

Ⓐ **1**

Ⓑ **4**

Ⓒ **5**

Ⓓ **7**

23. Which of these figures has more than one line of symmetry?

Ⓐ 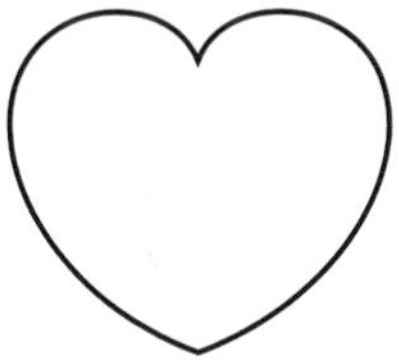

Ⓑ 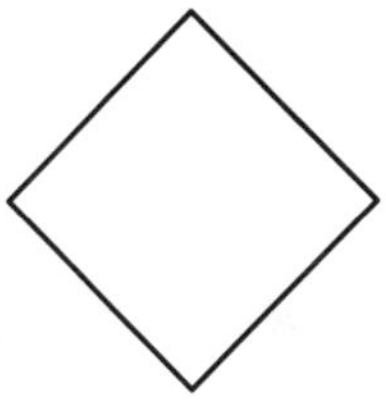

Ⓒ 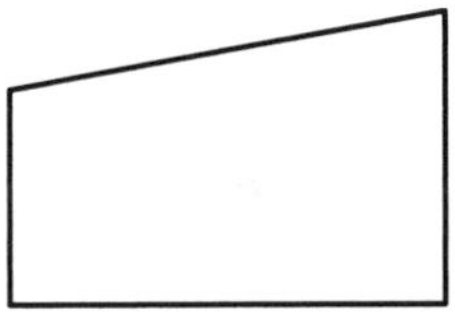

Ⓓ 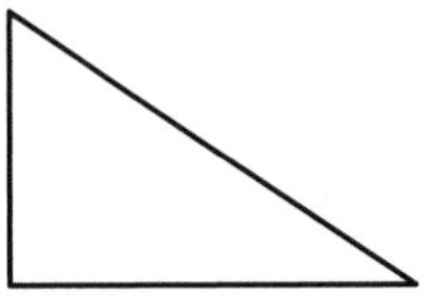

24. The temperature at 7:00 A.M. one winter morning was 24°F. If the temperature went up three degrees every hour, what was the temperature at 2:00 P.M.?

Ⓐ **21°F**

Ⓑ **36°F**

Ⓒ **42°F**

Ⓓ **45°F**

25. What is the missing number in the output column of the table below?

Input	7	9	11	13
Output	13	15		19

Ⓐ **6**

Ⓑ **14**

Ⓒ **17**

Ⓓ **19**

GO ON TO THE NEXT PAGE.

26. If 87 – ☐ = 38, then what is the value of ☐?

Ⓐ **46**

Ⓑ **48**

Ⓒ **49**

Ⓓ **125**

GO ON TO THE NEXT PAGE.

27. When 4 is dropped into the function machine, it comes out as 12.

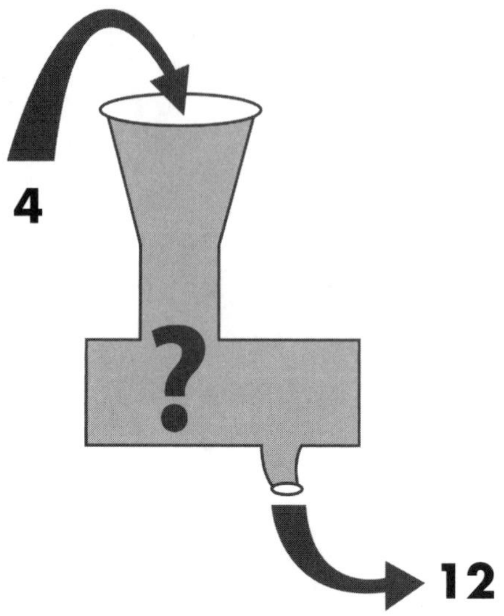

Input	4	3	12	8	7
Output	12	9	36	24	

What is the missing number in the table?

Ⓐ **14**

Ⓑ **15**

Ⓒ **21**

Ⓓ **28**

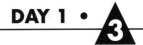

Directions for the Extended Constructed-Response Question

The following question is an extended constructed-response question. Remember to:

- Read the question carefully and think about the answer.
- Answer all parts of the question.
- Show your work or explain your answer.

You may write and/or draw your answer.

GO ON TO THE NEXT PAGE.

28. A machine charges 45¢ to play a game and accepts only nickels, dimes, and quarters. The machine requires exact change.

What combination of coins could you put into the machine to play a game?

Show your work or explain your answer.

If you have time, you may review your work in this section only.

STOP

DO NOT GO ON UNTIL YOU ARE TOLD TO DO SO.

Part 4

Directions:

This part of the test contains 8 multiple-choice questions and one extended constructed-response question. You MAY use a calculator for this part of the test. Darken the circle of the correct answer choice. Follow the directions for the ECR.

29. In Miss Clark's class of 36 students, $\frac{2}{3}$ of the students have blue eyes. If the class consists of 9 boys who have blue eyes, how many girls have blue eyes?

Ⓐ **6**

Ⓑ **12**

Ⓒ **15**

Ⓓ **18**

30. How many numbers between 80 and 100 can be divided by 3, with no remainder?

Ⓐ **8**

Ⓑ **7**

Ⓒ **6**

Ⓓ **5**

GO ON TO THE NEXT PAGE.

31. Katherine bought hamburgers and hot dogs for a total of $20.75. Each hamburger costs $2.25 and each hot dog costs $3.50. Which of the following shows the number of hamburgers and hot dogs that she bought?

Ⓐ 5 hamburgers and 3 hot dogs

Ⓑ 3 hamburgers and 5 hot dogs

Ⓒ 4 hamburgers and 3 hot dogs

Ⓓ 3 hamburgers and 4 hot dogs

32. Building A has 40 floors. Each floor has 16 offices. Building B has 55 floors. Each of its floors has 19 offices. How many more offices are in building B than in building A?

Ⓐ 425

Ⓑ 405

Ⓒ 130

Ⓓ 120

33. Paul took ten quizzes in his math class. He had a grade of 75 on three quizzes, a grade of 85 on two quizzes, and a grade of 100 on all the rest. What is his average (mean) grade for all the quizzes?

Ⓐ **89.5**

Ⓑ **88**

Ⓒ **86.5**

Ⓓ **85**

34. In a company of 88 people, 24 of them are absent today. Of the people who are present, $\frac{3}{4}$ of them are working overtime. How many people in the company are working overtime?

Ⓐ **66**

Ⓑ **60**

Ⓒ **54**

Ⓓ **48**

GO ON TO THE NEXT PAGE.

35. During a four-hour period, Maria spent 40 minutes doing her math homework, 30 minutes doing her English homework, and one-half of the remaining time watching television. How many minutes did Maria spend watching television?

Ⓐ 170

Ⓑ 120

Ⓒ 85

Ⓓ 35

36. Miss Roberts bought 25 large boxes of crayons for her classes. Each box contains 150 crayons. She gave each student 30 crayons. If she has a total of 122 students, how many crayons were left over?

Ⓐ 92

Ⓑ 90

Ⓒ 88

Ⓓ 86

GO ON TO THE NEXT PAGE.

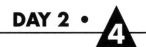

Directions for the Extended Constructed-Response Question

The following question is an extended constructed-response question. Remember to:

- Read the question carefully and think about the answer.
- Answer all parts of the question.
- Show your work or explain your answer.

You may write and/or draw your answer.

GO ON TO THE NEXT PAGE.

37. Mrs. Miller is planning to put up a wallpaper border in the community room of her apartment building. She plans to use 72 feet of wallpaper border, and the room is 16 feet wide.

How long is the community room? Show how you got your answer.

If Mrs. Miller adds a star on the border every three feet, how many stars will she need? Show all of your work to explain your answer.

If you have time, you may review your work in this section only.

STOP

DO NOT GO ON UNTIL YOU ARE TOLD TO DO SO.

Part 5

Directions:

This part of the test contains 8 multiple-choice questions and one extended constructed-response question. You may NOT use a calculator for this part of the test. Darken the circle of the correct answer choice. Follow the directions for the ECR.

38. Debbie has four notebooks: one for social studies, one for language arts, one for math, and one for reading. She is going to take two notebooks home tonight.

How many different pairs of notebooks can she take home?

Ⓐ **4**

Ⓑ **5**

Ⓒ **6**

Ⓓ **10**

39. You and your brothers and sister pick cards out of a hat to see what chore you will do on Saturday. The hat contains 4 cards with "clean garage" written on them, 2 with "mow lawn" on them, and 3 with "clean attic" on them. What is the probability that you will pick a card with "mow lawn" on it?

Ⓐ $\frac{1}{9}$

Ⓑ $\frac{2}{9}$

Ⓒ $\frac{3}{9}$

Ⓓ $\frac{4}{9}$

GO ON TO THE NEXT PAGE.

40. The table below shows the highest temperature for 5 days in Jeremy's hometown.

Day	Temperature
1	90°F
2	90°F
3	95°F
4	98°F
5	93°F

What is the median temperature?

Ⓐ **90°F**

Ⓑ **93°F**

Ⓒ **95°F**

Ⓓ **98°F**

GO ON TO THE NEXT PAGE.

41. This graph shows the number of each kind of school supply Ben purchased last week.

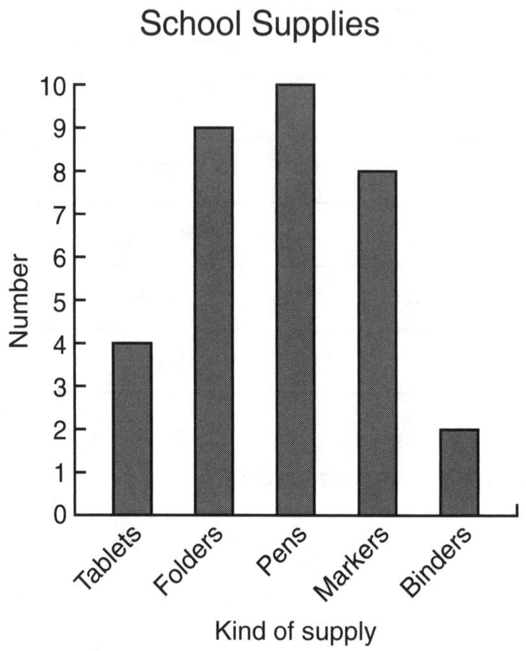

How many pens and markers did Ben purchase?

Ⓐ **8**

Ⓑ **10**

Ⓒ **18**

Ⓓ **20**

42. Jay kept track of how many students in his school had birthdays in September, October, November, and December.

Student Birthdays

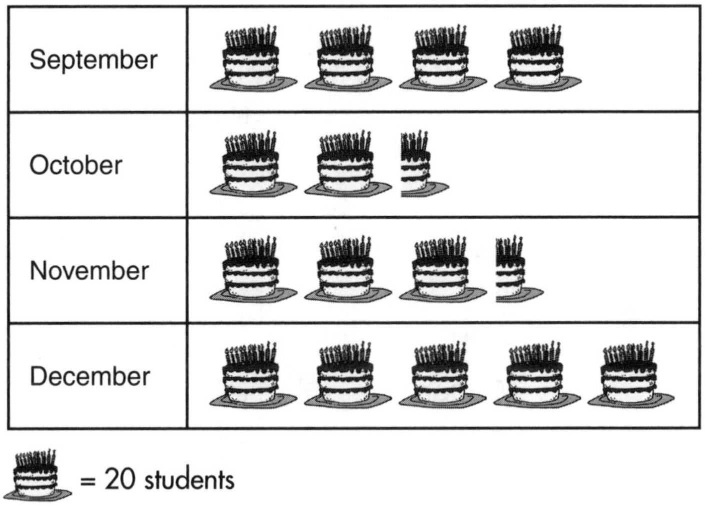

How many students have a birthday in November?

Ⓐ $3\frac{1}{2}$

Ⓑ **60**

Ⓒ **70**

Ⓓ **80**

43. When a girls' field hockey practice is canceled, Ms. Vitale, the coach, calls Missy and Kate. Then Missy and Kate call the players listed under their names. This continues until every player is called.

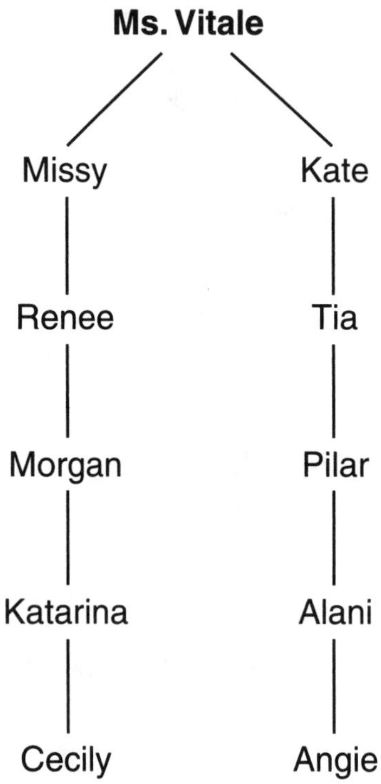

Which player will Katarina call?

Ⓐ **Morgan**

Ⓑ **Alani**

Ⓒ **Cecily**

Ⓓ **Angie**

44. During the year, two thousand one hundred thirty-two books were checked out of the school library. What is another way to write this number?

Ⓐ **232**

Ⓑ **2,123**

Ⓒ **2,132**

Ⓓ **2,232**

45. Use your ruler to help you solve this problem.

The drawing below shows the bookmark Charlene bought.

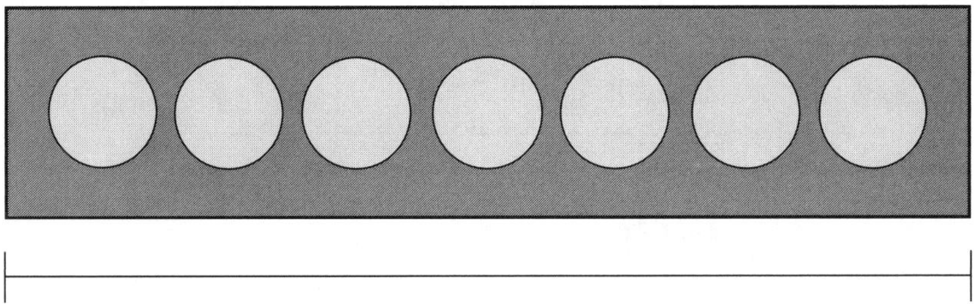

How many centimeters long is Charlene's bookmark?

Ⓐ **10**

Ⓑ **11**

Ⓒ **12**

Ⓓ **13**

Directions for the Extended Constructed-Response Question

The following question is an extended constructed-response question. Remember to:

- Read the question carefully and think about the answer.
- Answer all parts of the question.
- Show your work or explain your answer.

You may write and/or draw your answer.

46. Look at the three input-output tables below.

Table A

Input	6	8	11	15
Output	18	20	23	☐

Table B

Input	6	8	11	15
Output	18	24	33	☐

Table C

Input	6	8	11	15
Output	24	32	44	☐

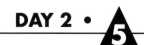

Each table has a different rule to change the input numbers to get the output numbers.

- **What is the rule for Table A?**
- **What is the rule for Table B?**
- **What is the rule for Table C?**
- **What are the output values for the number 15 in each table? Which table gives the greatest output? Explain your answers.**

If you have time, you may review your work in this section only.

STOP

DO NOT GO ON UNTIL YOU ARE TOLD TO DO SO.

Part 6

Directions:

This part of the test contains 8 multiple-choice questions and one extended constructed-response question. You may NOT use a calculator for this part of the test. Darken the circle of the correct answer choice. Follow the directions for the ECR.

47. Hakeem read a 120-page book in 10 days. He read the same number of pages each day. How many pages did Hakeem read each day?

Ⓐ **12**

Ⓑ **10**

Ⓒ **9**

Ⓓ **8**

48. Lucy covered a poster board with square stickers, as shown below.

POSTER BOARD

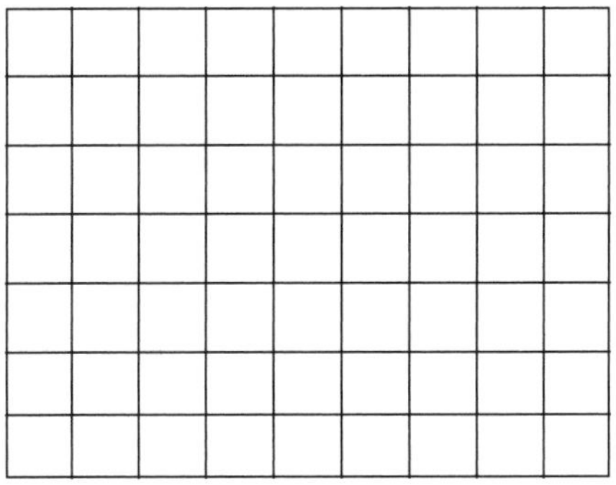

KEY

□ = **1 square unit**

What is the area, in square units, of the poster board?

Ⓐ **60**

Ⓑ **63**

Ⓒ **70**

Ⓓ **72**

49. The Bedford Bugle newspaper has 9,017 readers. What is another way to write this number?

Ⓐ **nine hundred seventeen**

Ⓑ **nine thousand seven**

Ⓒ **nine thousand seventeen**

Ⓓ **nine thousand seventy-one**

50. Which number when multiplied by any odd number *always* results in an even number?

Ⓐ **1**

Ⓑ **5**

Ⓒ **7**

Ⓓ **8**

51. Tanya bought 7 packages of candles for her aunt's birthday cake. Each package contained 8 candles. How many candles did Tanya buy in all?

Ⓐ **49**

Ⓑ **54**

Ⓒ **56**

Ⓓ **63**

52. Patrick drew a quadrilateral on the blackboard. The figure had the same number of sides and angles. What is that number?

Ⓐ **3**

Ⓑ **4**

Ⓒ **5**

Ⓓ **6**

GO ON TO THE NEXT PAGE.

53. Lucy wants to check that she correctly solved the number sentence below.

$$15 \times 3 = 45$$

What number sentence should Lucy use to see if her answer is correct?

Ⓐ $45 \times 15 = \square$

Ⓑ $15 \div 3 = \square$

Ⓒ $45 \times 3 = \square$

Ⓓ $45 \div 3 = \square$

GO ON TO THE NEXT PAGE.

54. Which input-output table follows the rule below?

Input ÷ 3 = Output

Ⓐ

Input	Output
16	8
14	7
12	6
10	5

Ⓑ

Input	Output
9	3
10	4
11	5
12	6

Ⓒ

Input	Output
18	6
21	7
24	8
27	9

Ⓓ

Input	Output
6	18
7	21
8	24
9	27

Directions for the Extended Constructed-Response Question

The following question is an extended constructed-response question. Remember to:

- Read the question carefully and think about the answer.
- Answer all parts of the question.
- Show your work or explain your answer.

You may write and/or draw your answer.

GO ON TO THE NEXT PAGE.

55. **J.D. has $5.00 to spend on food at the carnival. Prices for items at the carnival are shown below.**

Carnival Snack Bar	
Hot Dog	$2.25
Peanuts	$1.45
Pizza Slice	$3.50
Fudge Bar	$0.90
Shake	$3.00

Write three different items that J.D. can buy that total less than $5.00.

_______________ _______________ _______________

If J.D. buys the items, how much money will he have left over?

Show your work.

Answer $ _______________

STOP

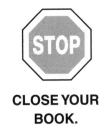

CLOSE YOUR BOOK.

New Jersey Assessment of Skills and Knowledge

MATHEMATICS

Grade 4

Practice Test 2

DIRECTIONS:

When you are taking this test, remember these important things:

1. Read each question carefully and think about the answer.
2. If you do not know the answer to a question, go on to the next question. You may come back to the skipped question later if you have time.
3. When you see a STOP sign (STOP), do not turn the page until you are told to do so.

GO ON TO THE NEXT PAGE.

Part 1

Directions:

This part of the test contains 8 short constructed-response questions. You may NOT use a calculator for these questions. Write your answer on the line.

1. Find the exact answer: 956 − 311

Place your answer here: ____________

2. Find the exact answer: 610 ÷ 5

Place your answer here: ____________

3. Find the exact answer: 48 × 14

Place your answer here: ____________

GO ON TO THE NEXT PAGE.

4. **Find the exact answer: 395 + 724**

Place your answer here: ______________

5. **Patrick has a book collection. He has 290 books, and his friend gives him 24 more. Then Patrick gives 125 books to a local library. How many books does Patrick have now?**

Place your answer here: ______________

6. **Latisha's teacher put these numbers on the chalkboard:**

0, 3, 8, 10, 2, 5, 7, 3, 12

What is the mode of these numbers?

Place your answer here: ______________

GO ON TO THE NEXT PAGE.

7. Simone wrote the following riddle to her friend:

   I have 6 faces, 8 vertices, and I look like a block. What am I?

   What is the answer to this riddle?

   Place your answer here: ____________

8. A newspaper sold 2,083,660 copies during one year. What is the value of 8 in the number 2,083,660?

   Place your answer here: ____________

If you have time, you may review your work in this section only.

STOP

DO NOT GO ON UNTIL YOU ARE TOLD TO DO SO.

Part 2

Directions:

This part of the test contains 11 multiple-choice questions. You may NOT use a calculator for these questions. Darken the circle of the correct answer choice.

9. Estimate 289 ÷ 3. The quotient is between which numbers?

Ⓐ **30 and 100**

Ⓑ **150 and 300**

Ⓒ **400 and 800**

Ⓓ **1,000 and 1,500**

10. Estimate 310 − 178. The difference is between which numbers?

Ⓐ **100 and 300**

Ⓑ **400 and 600**

Ⓒ **700 and 900**

Ⓓ **1,000 and 1,200**

GO ON TO THE NEXT PAGE.

11. A toll machine charges 80¢ to drive on a road and accepts only nickels, dimes, and quarters. The toll machine requires exact change.

What combination of coins could you put in the toll machine to drive on the road?

Ⓐ 

Ⓑ 

Ⓒ 

Ⓓ 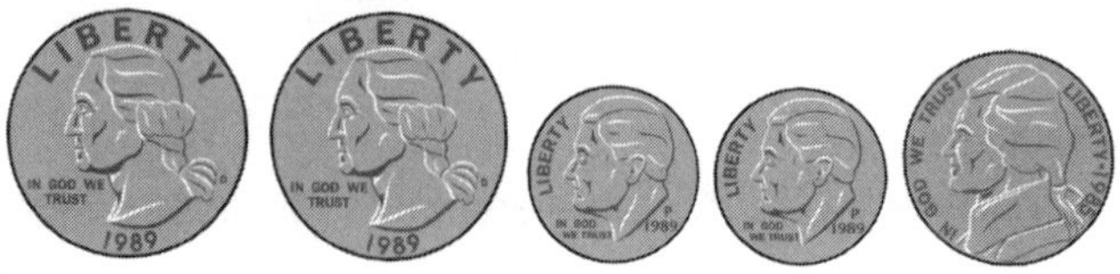

12. What is the most reasonable estimate of the length of your arm?

Ⓐ **5 centimeters**

Ⓑ **1 centimeter**

Ⓒ **1 meter**

Ⓓ **1 kilometer**

13. Which of these shapes is a pentagon?

Ⓐ 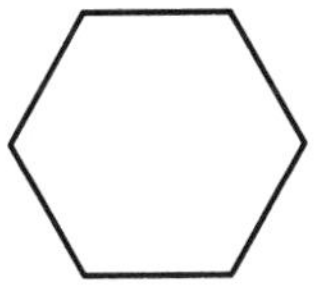

Ⓑ 

Ⓒ 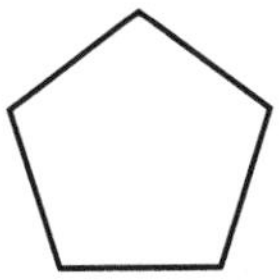

Ⓓ 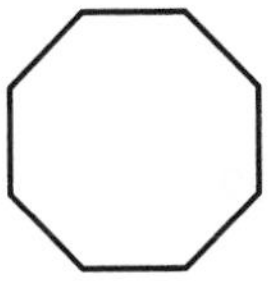

GO ON TO THE NEXT PAGE.

14. Look at the figure below.

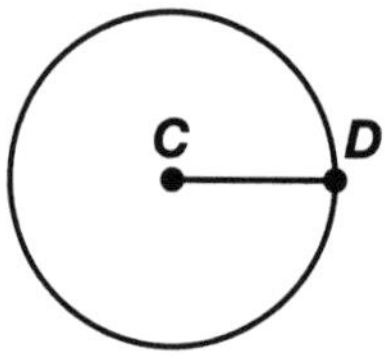

What is the line segment *CD* called?

Ⓐ **a radius**

Ⓑ **a diameter**

Ⓒ **a circumference**

Ⓓ **a line**

15. Which group of numbers is in order from least to greatest?

Ⓐ .90 9.0 9.10

Ⓑ 9.0 .90 9.10

Ⓒ 9.10 9.0 .90

Ⓓ 9.0 9.10 .90

16. If the pattern below continues, what is the next number?

4, 9, 14, 19, 24, 29, 34

Ⓐ 36

Ⓑ 37

Ⓒ 38

Ⓓ 39

GO ON TO THE NEXT PAGE.

17. Which of the following is a tessellation?

Ⓐ 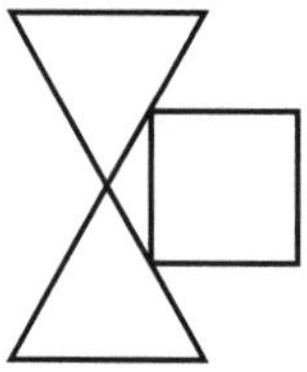

Ⓑ 

Ⓒ 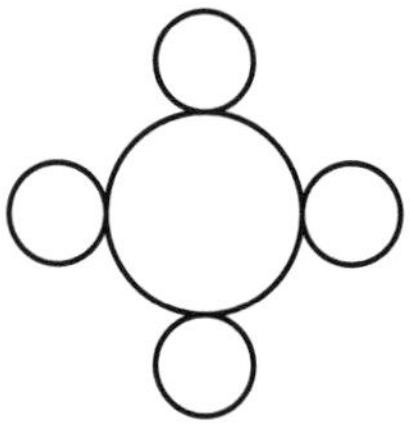

Ⓓ 

GO ON TO THE NEXT PAGE.

18. On the following grid, which ordered pair shows the location of the pond?

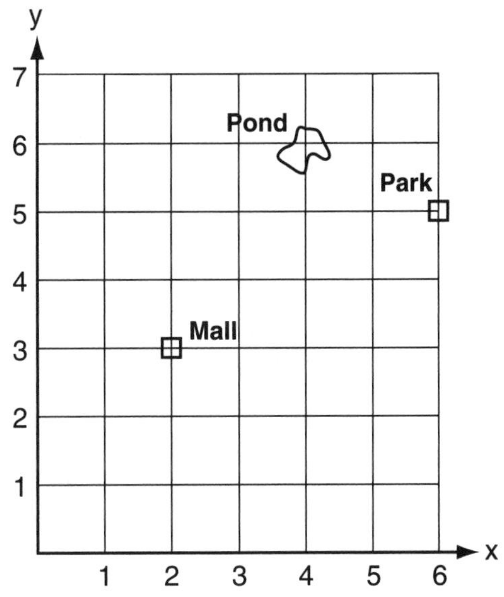

Ⓐ **(4, 6)**

Ⓑ **(6, 4)**

Ⓒ **(5, 4)**

Ⓓ **(4, 5)**

19. Dawn had 78 marbles. Her mother gave her some more marbles. She now has 96 marbles. Which number sentence could you use to find how many marbles her mother gave her?

Ⓐ $\square - 78 = 96$

Ⓑ $78 + \square = 96$

Ⓒ $\square \times 78 = 96$

Ⓓ $78 + 96 = \square$

If you have time, you may review your work in this section only.

STOP

DO NOT GO ON UNTIL YOU ARE TOLD TO DO SO.

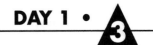

Part 3

Directions:

This part of the test contains 8 multiple-choice questions and one extended constructed-response question. You may NOT use a calculator for this part of the test. Darken the circle of the correct answer choice. Follow the directions for the ECR.

20. Which of the following angles is an obtuse angle?

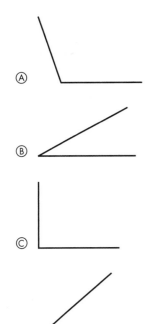

Ⓐ 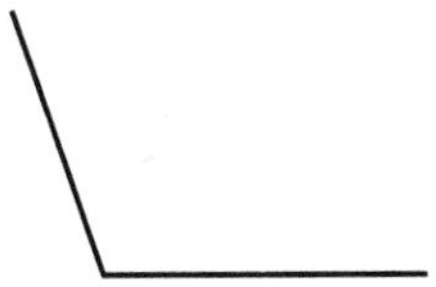

Ⓑ 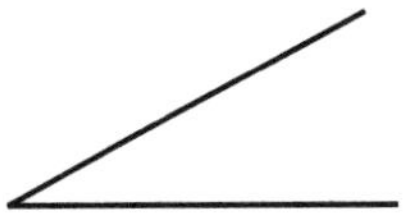

Ⓒ 

Ⓓ 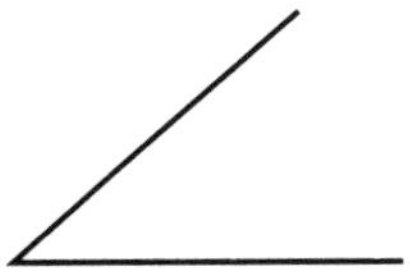

21. Ms. Owens's class kept track of how many tin cans they collected for recycling.

Cans Collected

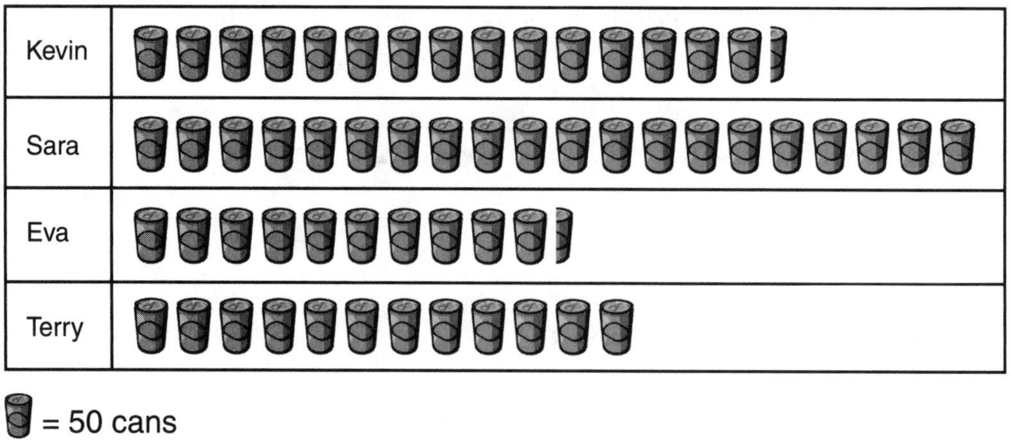

How many cans did Kevin collect?

Ⓐ **150**

Ⓑ **175**

Ⓒ **750**

Ⓓ **775**

22. Erin made these cutouts for a school project. Which cutout has more than one line of symmetry?

Ⓐ 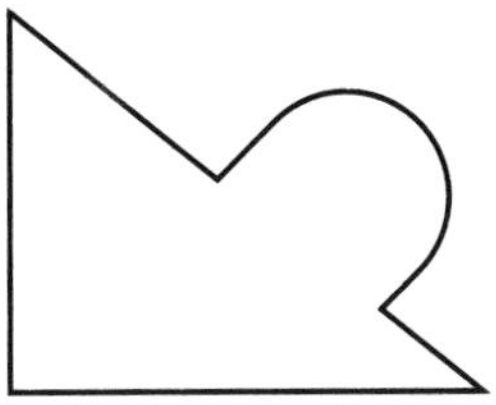

Ⓑ 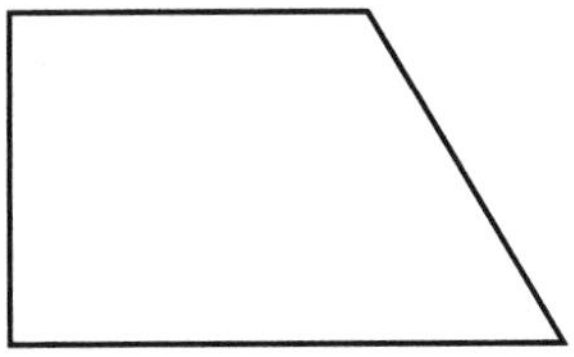

Ⓒ 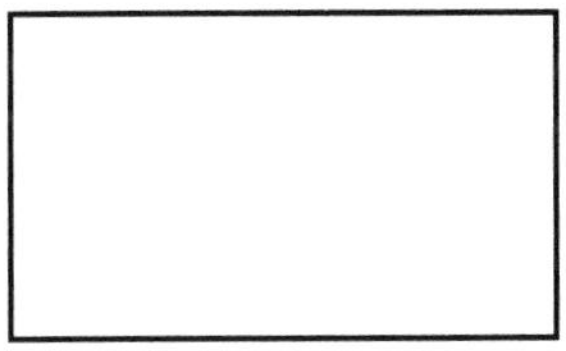

Ⓓ 

GO ON TO THE NEXT PAGE.

23. If $96 \div \square = 12$, then what is the value of $\square$?

Ⓐ **6**

Ⓑ **8**

Ⓒ **12**

Ⓓ **84**

24. Which of these shows perpendicular lines?

Ⓐ 

Ⓑ 

Ⓒ 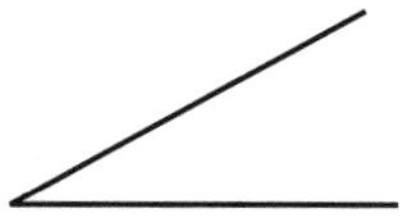

Ⓓ 

25. What does n equal in $147 \times n = 294$?

Ⓐ **1**

Ⓑ **2**

Ⓒ **3**

Ⓓ **4**

26. A section of Kerry's wallpaper border is shown here.

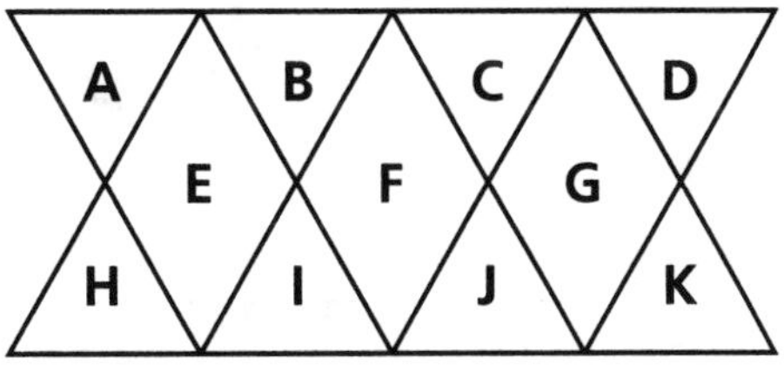

How many lettered sections are triangles?

Ⓐ **4**

Ⓑ **5**

Ⓒ **8**

Ⓓ **9**

GO ON TO THE NEXT PAGE.

27. When 24 is dropped into this machine, it comes out as 12.

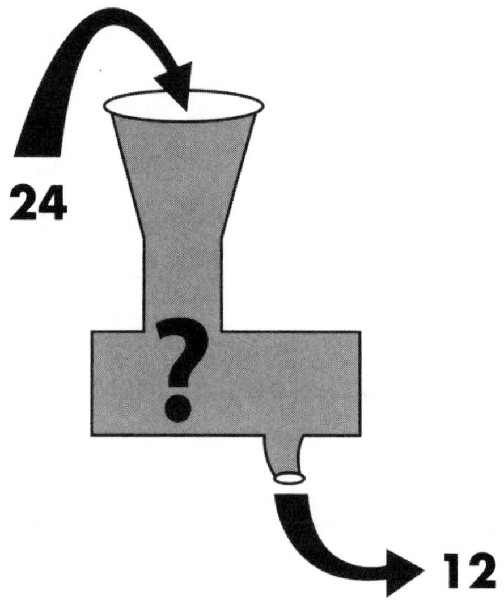

Input	24	12	48	56
Output	12	6	24	

What is the missing number in this table?

Ⓐ **2**

Ⓑ **13**

Ⓒ **28**

Ⓓ **32**

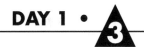

Directions for the Extended Constructed-Response Question

The following question is an extended constructed-response question. Remember to:

- Read the question carefully and think about the answer.
- Answer all parts of the question.
- Show your work or explain your answer.

You may write and/or draw your answer.

 GO ON TO THE NEXT PAGE.

28. Danielle went to her friend's house at 2:30 P.M. Her mother told her to be home in 2 hours and 30 minutes.

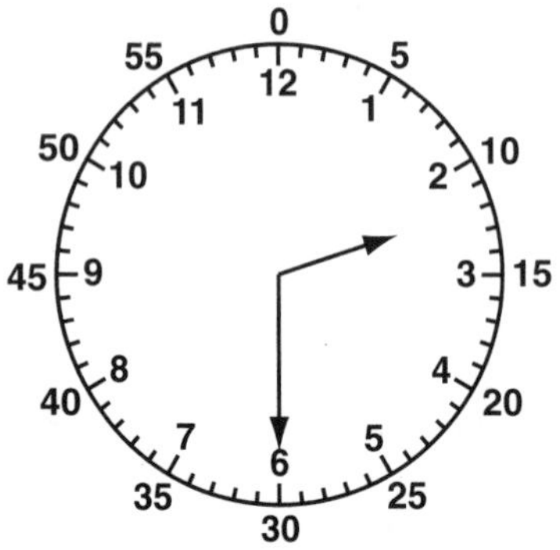

What time did Danielle need to come home?

As soon as Danielle gets home, she has a piano lesson that lasts 45 minutes. What time will her piano lesson end?

Show all your work or explain your answers.

If you have time, you may review your work in this section only.

STOP

DO NOT GO ON UNTIL YOU ARE TOLD TO DO SO.

Part 4

Directions:

This part of the test contains 8 multiple-choice questions and one extended constructed-response question. You MAY use a calculator for this part of the test. Darken the circle of the correct answer choice. Follow the directions for the ECR.

29. Megan practices a different mathematics skill each day, according to this pattern:

Day 1:	Adding numbers
Day 2:	Subtracting numbers
Day 3:	Multiplying numbers
Day 4:	Dividing numbers
Day 5:	Adding numbers
Day 6:	Subtracting numbers
Day 7:	Multiplying numbers
Day 8:	Dividing numbers

What skill will she practice on Day 23?

Ⓐ **Multiplying numbers**

Ⓑ **Dividing numbers**

Ⓒ **Adding numbers**

Ⓓ **Subtracting numbers**

GO ON TO THE NEXT PAGE.

30. The temperature on a summer day was 90°F at noon. If the temperature dropped 4°F every hour, what was the temperature at 6:00 P.M.?

Ⓐ **60°F**

Ⓑ **64°F**

Ⓒ **66°F**

Ⓓ **70°F**

31. The table below shows Ashley's first five test scores in social studies class.

Ashley's Social Studies Test Scores

Test	Score
1	82
2	80
3	85
4	88
5	90

What is Ashley's average (mean) test grade?

Ⓐ **80**

Ⓑ **83**

Ⓒ **85**

Ⓓ **90**

32. Lisa can build 20 toy boats in one hour and Billy can build 18 toy boats in one hour. If Lisa works 8.4 hours and Billy works 10.5 hours, what is the total number of boats they can build?

Ⓐ **361**

Ⓑ **357**

Ⓒ **353**

Ⓓ **349**

33. Oreo needs a collar and a name tag. Cara is looking at collars in pink, peach, white, and black, and name tags in red or yellow.

Cara also wants a matching leash for Oreo. The leash can be short, medium, or long.

How many total combinations of collars, name tags, and leashes are possible?

Ⓐ **9**

Ⓑ **12**

Ⓒ **18**

Ⓓ **24**

 GO ON TO THE NEXT PAGE.

34. Mr. London buys a board at the lumber yard. The board is 5 yards 8 inches long. How long, in inches, is the board?

Ⓐ 68

Ⓑ 108

Ⓒ 148

Ⓓ 188

35. Andrew writes a total of 44 names on 7 blank cards. On each of the first 6 cards he writes 7 names. How many names does Andrew write on the last card?

Ⓐ 4

Ⓑ 3

Ⓒ 2

Ⓓ 1

36. Tamara is making 15 bracelets with beads. She puts 6 blue beads on each bracelet. What is the total number of blue beads that Tamara uses for her bracelets?

Ⓐ **70**

Ⓑ **85**

Ⓒ **90**

Ⓓ **95**

GO ON TO THE NEXT PAGE.

Directions for the Extended Constructed-Response Question

The following question is an extended constructed-response question. Remember to:

- Read the question carefully and think about the answer.
- Answer all parts of the question.
- Show your work or explain your answer.

You may write and/or draw your answer.

GO ON TO THE NEXT PAGE.

37. Jolene has $10.00 to spend on food at the football game. Prices for food items at the stadium snack bar are shown below.

Stadium Snack Bar

Pizza Slice	$4.75
Hot Dog	$3.25
Cheese Nachos	$3.50
Chicken Sandwich	$6.25
Lemonade	$2.50

Write three different items that Jolene can buy that total less than $10.00.

________________ ________________ ________________

If Jolene buys the three items, what amount of money will she have left over?

Show your work.

Answer $____________

If you have time, you may review your work in this section only.

DO NOT GO ON UNTIL YOU ARE TOLD TO DO SO.

Part 5

Directions:

This part of the test contains 8 multiple-choice questions and one extended constructed-response question. You may NOT use a calculator for this part of the test. Darken the circle of the correct answer choice. Follow the directions for the ECR.

38. According to the bar graph below, how many more people lived on Yi Min's block in Year 5 than in Year 4?

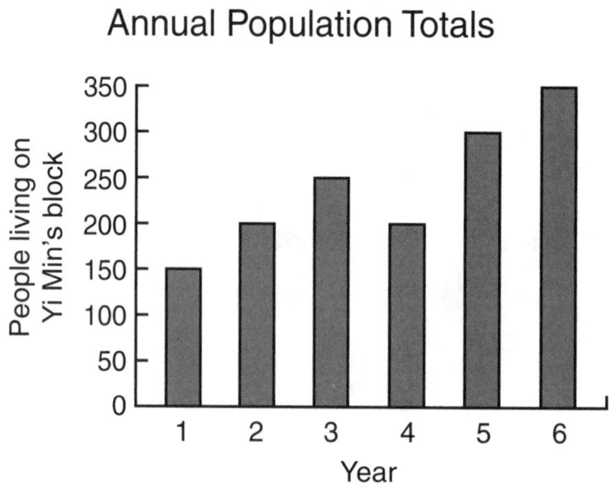

Ⓐ **50**

Ⓑ **100**

Ⓒ **150**

Ⓓ **200**

39. A diagram of a park is shown below. Part of the park is covered with grass, and part of the park is covered with sand.

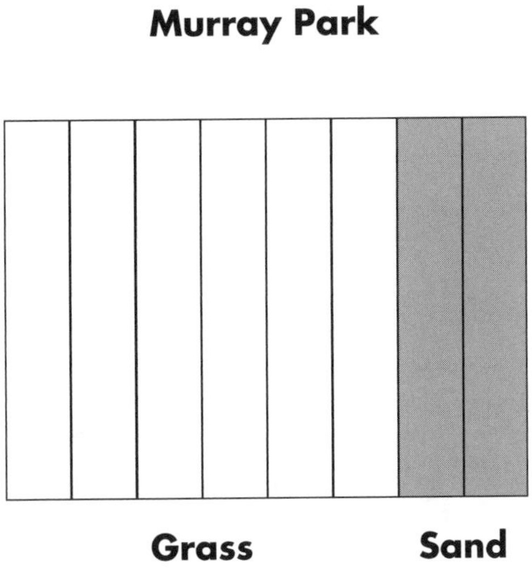

What fraction of the park is covered with sand?

Ⓐ $\frac{1}{8}$

Ⓑ $\frac{1}{3}$

Ⓒ $\frac{1}{2}$

Ⓓ $\frac{1}{4}$

GO ON TO THE NEXT PAGE.

40. At Gabby's gymnastics school, there are 30 more girls than boys. If there are 120 girls, how can you find the number of boys?

Ⓐ add 30 to 120

Ⓑ subtract 30 from 120

Ⓒ multiply 120 by 30

Ⓓ divide 120 by 30

41. At the U.S. Open tennis tournament, nine thousand seven hundred thirty-eight people bought tickets for one session. What is another way to write this number?

Ⓐ 9,738

Ⓑ 9,378

Ⓒ 9,038

Ⓓ 938

42. Use your ruler to help you solve this problem.

How many centimeters long is the pencil shown below?

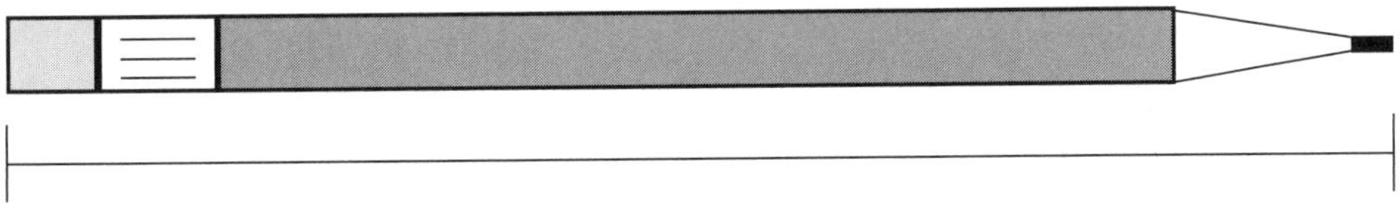

Ⓐ **11**

Ⓑ **12**

Ⓒ **13**

Ⓓ **14**

43. Douglass Elementary has 932 books in its library. What is 932 rounded to the nearest hundred?

Ⓐ **800**

Ⓑ **900**

Ⓒ **930**

Ⓓ **1,000**

44. Lena shoots 100 free throws every day for practice. How many days does it take Lena to shoot 800 free throws?

Ⓐ **7**

Ⓑ **8**

Ⓒ **10**

Ⓓ **12**

45. Daniel used a ruler to draw a pattern of squares on a sheet of paper. The squares cover the sheet completely.

SHEET OF PAPER

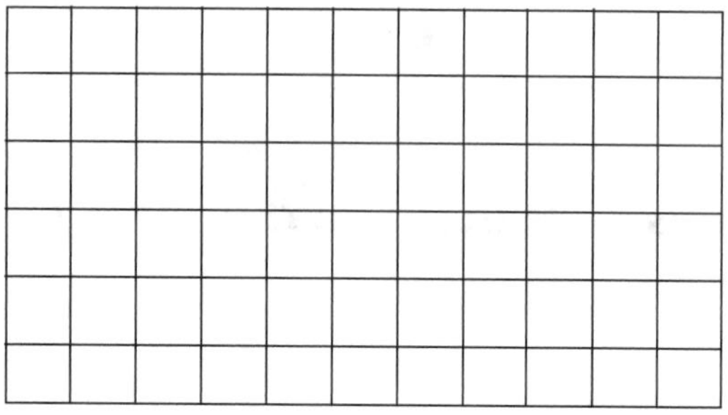

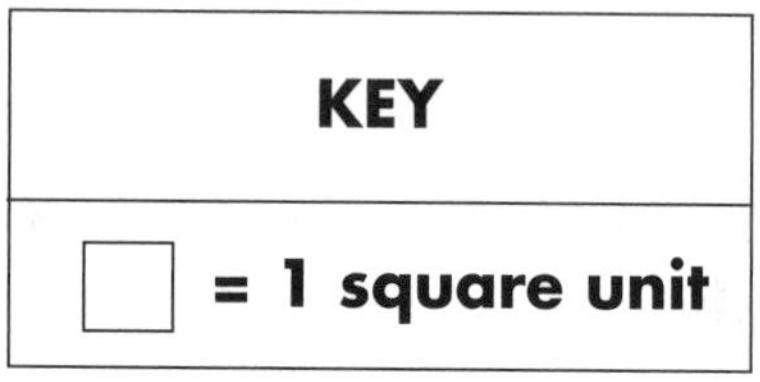

What is the area, in square units, of the sheet of paper?

Ⓐ **56**

Ⓑ **60**

Ⓒ **63**

Ⓓ **66**

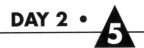

Directions for the Extended Constructed-Response Question

The following question is an extended constructed-response question. Remember to:

- Read the question carefully and think about the answer.
- Answer all parts of the question.
- Show your work or explain your answer.

You may write and/or draw your answer.

46. Lucinda, Alex, and Marta held a contest to read the most books in the summer. The table below shows the number of books each student read over 3 months.

BOOKS READ IN THE CONTEST

Student	Number of Books		
	June	July	August
Lucinda	5	3	6
Alex	4	5	7
Marta	7	4	8

Part A

On the lines below, write the total number of books each student read over the three months.

Lucinda _______ books

Alex _______ books

Marta _______ books

Part B

On the grid below, make a bar graph to show the total number of books each student read.

Be sure to:

- **title the graph**
- **label both axes**
- **provide a scale for the graph**
- **graph all the data**

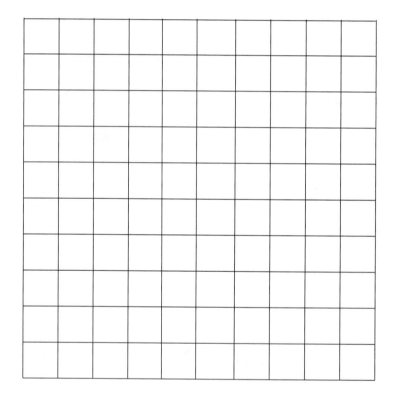

If you have time, you may review your work in this section only.

STOP

DO NOT GO ON UNTIL YOU ARE TOLD TO DO SO.

Part 6

Directions:

This part of the test contains 8 multiple-choice questions and one extended constructed-response question. You may NOT use a calculator for this part of the test. Darken the circle of the correct answer choice. Follow the directions for the ECR.

47. The number of vehicles in a parking lot are shown below.

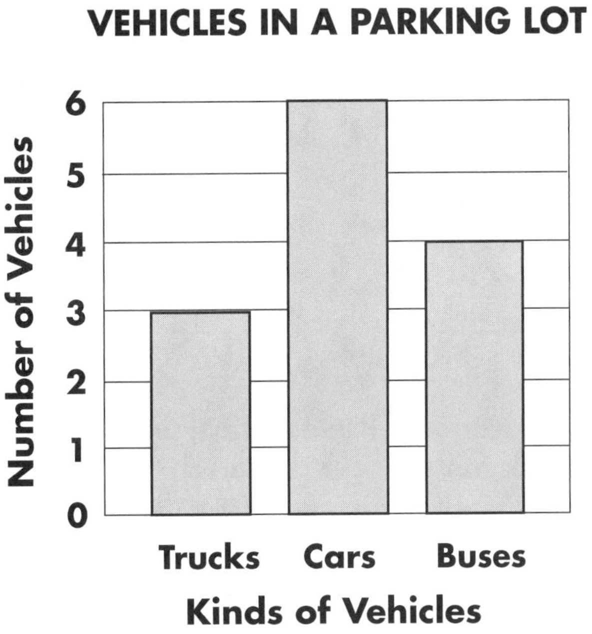

Based on the information in the bar graph, which statement is true?

Ⓐ **More than half of all the vehicles are cars.**

Ⓑ **The number of cars is two times the number of trucks.**

Ⓒ **The number of cars is two times the number of buses.**

Ⓓ **Exactly half of all the vehicles are cars.**

48. Which input-output table follows the rule below?

Input × 2 = Output

Ⓐ

Input	Output
20	10
16	8
14	7
12	6

Ⓒ

Input	Output
23	25
26	28
29	31
31	33

Ⓑ

Input	Output
4	12
6	18
8	24
10	30

Ⓓ

Input	Output
1	2
3	6
5	10
7	14

49. Each school bus at Roosevelt Elementary can carry 42 students. There are 392 students going on the school field trip. Miguel estimates that 10 buses are needed for the trip. Which expression can be used to check whether Miguel's estimation is reasonable?

Ⓐ **400 ÷ 30**

Ⓑ **400 ÷ 40**

Ⓒ **300 ÷ 30**

Ⓓ **300 ÷ 40**

50. The two statements below describe the number of dogs, cats, and hamsters living in Jason's house.

the number of hamsters > the number of dogs

the number of cats < the number of dogs

Which could be the number of dogs, cats, and hamsters living in Jason's house?

Ⓐ **5 dogs, 3 cats, 4 hamsters**

Ⓑ **4 dogs, 3 cats, 5 hamsters**

Ⓒ **3 dogs, 4 cats, 5 hamsters**

Ⓓ **4 dogs, 5 cats, 3 hamsters**

GO ON TO THE NEXT PAGE.

51. Which pair of figures are similar?

Ⓐ 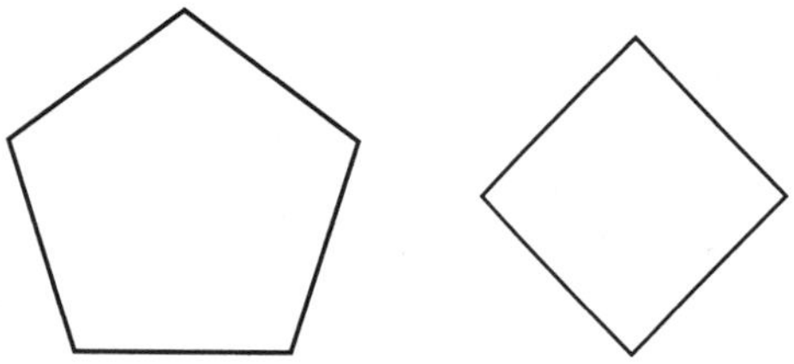

Ⓑ 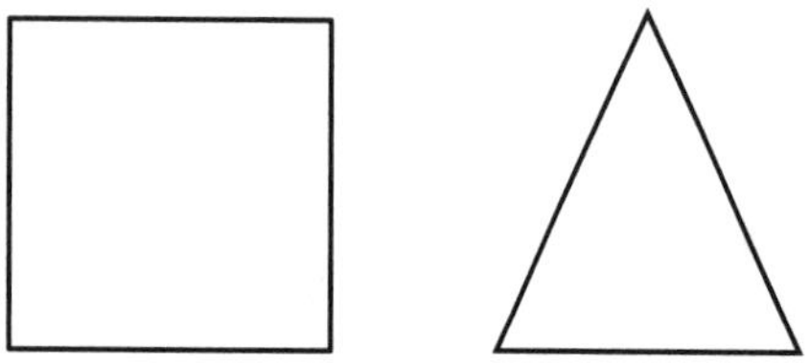

Ⓒ 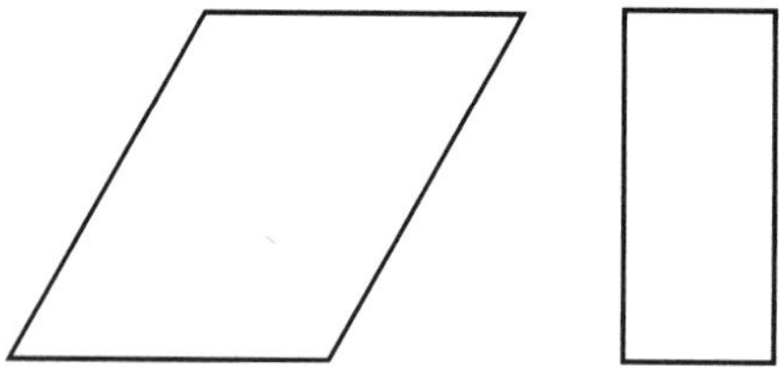

Ⓓ 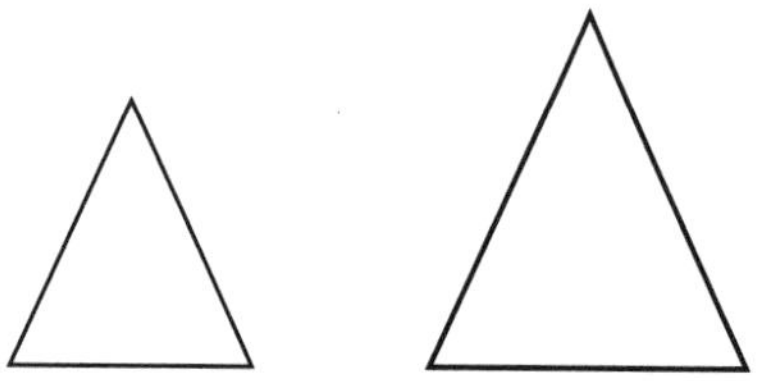

 GO ON TO THE NEXT PAGE.

52. Dustin drew the circles below. Two of the 6 circles are black.

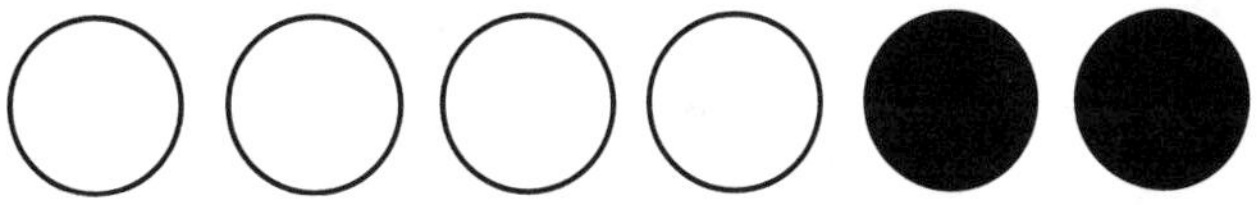

Which fraction is equivalent to $\frac{2}{6}$?

Ⓐ $\frac{1}{3}$

Ⓑ $\frac{1}{4}$

Ⓒ $\frac{1}{2}$

Ⓓ $\frac{2}{3}$

53. Paula opens a 22-ounce jar of salsa. She pours 3 ounces of salsa on each of 5 enchiladas. How many ounces of salsa are left in the jar?

Ⓐ **5**

Ⓑ **7**

Ⓒ **8**

Ⓓ **10**

54. Claire can do 3 times as many sit-ups as Tim. Tim can do 5 more sit-ups than Whitney. Whitney can do 15 sit-ups. How many sit-ups can Claire do?

Ⓐ **60**

Ⓑ **62**

Ⓒ **65**

Ⓓ **70**

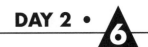

Directions for the Extended Constructed-Response Question

The following question is an extended constructed-response question. Remember to:

- Read the question carefully and think about the answer.
- Answer all parts of the question.
- Show your work or explain your answer.

You may write and/or draw your answer.

GO ON TO THE NEXT PAGE.

55. Mr. Sanchez is making 75 fancy belt buckles. The table below shows the total number of buckles he has made by the end of weeks 3 through 6.

MR. SANCHEZ'S BELT BUCKLES

Week	Total Number of Belt Buckles
3	21
4	28
5	35
6	42

Part A

If the pattern in the table continues, how many belt buckles will Mr. Sanchez have made by the end of Week 8?

Answer ______________ **buckles**

On the lines below, explain how you found your answer.

____

____

____

____

____

GO ON TO THE NEXT PAGE.

Part B

If the pattern in the table continues, by the end of which week will Mr. Sanchez have made the 75th belt buckle?

Answer **Week** _______________

CLOSE YOUR BOOK.

Answer Key
Chapter 1 Answer Explanations

Practice 1: Whole Numbers and Place Value

1. C

This number is two hundred and fifty thousand. The 5 is in the ten thousands place.

2. D

The 8 in the number 8,717,925 stands for 8 millions.

Practice 2: Fractions

1. B

By carefully looking at the shaded areas, you can see that $\frac{5}{12}$ is larger than $\frac{3}{16}$.

2. A

If you look carefully at the shaded areas, you can see that $\frac{4}{11}$ is smaller than $\frac{3}{7}$.

Practice 3: Decimals

1. B

A decimal is always smaller than a mixed decimal (which has a decimal and a whole number). So, .34 is definitely the smallest number and should come first. The next two numbers in answer choice B are 1.0 and 1.24. Zero is smaller than 24, so 1.0 is smaller than 1.24.

2. D

The decimal should come first, then the mixed number 1.23, and then 1.50. For the mixed decimals in these answer choices, the whole number parts are equal, so compare the decimal parts.

Practice 4: Negative Numbers

1. D

In this group of numbers, -10 is the smallest, because it is negative. The remaining two numbers, 9 and 10, are whole numbers, and you know that 9 is smaller than 10.

2. A

To answer this question correctly, you need to remember that -5 is smaller than -3 and that 0 is greater than both of these numbers.

End-of-Chapter Problems

1. B

Remember that the decimal is the smallest. Since both mixed numbers include the whole number 2, choose the one with the smaller decimal after it for the next number.

2. B

If you look closely at the shaded areas, you'll see that $\frac{5}{9}$ is greater than $\frac{3}{8}$.

3. C

The 1 in the number 9,125,000 has a place value of one hundred thousand.

4. A

The decimal is smallest, and then for the mixed decimals, compare the whole number parts.

5. **B**

   The 4 in the number 6,234,000 has a place value of 4 thousands.

6. **A**

   If you look closely at the shaded areas, you'll see that $\frac{2}{7}$ is less than $\frac{5}{9}$.

7. **B**

   Remember that with negative numbers, the highest digit is the smallest negative number (look at the number line).

Chapter 2 Answer Explanations

Practice 5: Adding and Subtracting Numbers

1. **D**

   When you correctly add up the numbers, you get 872. Remember to carry the 1 in your addition.

2. **C**

   When you subtract 310 from 809, you get 499. Remember to borrow in your subtraction.

3. **D**

   When you add 210 and 679, you get 889.

4. **D**

   To solve this problem correctly, add 125 and 98. The correct answer choice is D, 223.

5. Open-ended question

$210 + 30 = 240$

$240 - 53 = 187$

To solve this problem, you need to first add 210 and 30, and then subtract 53 from this number.

Practice 6: Multiplying and Dividing Numbers

1. C

When you divide 2 into 360, the answer is 180.

2. D

When you set up the problem correctly and multiply 38×24, you get 912.

3. Open-ended question

$$\begin{array}{r} 21 \\ 8\overline{)168} \\ -16 \\ \hline 8 \end{array} = 21 \text{ stickers}$$

Practice 7: Counting Money

1. D

For this question, you need to add up the coins in each answer choice and choose the combination that equals 95¢. The coins in answer choice A add up to 55¢, so this is not the correct answer. The coins in answer choice B add up to 65¢, so this isn't the correct answer. The coins in answer choice C add up to 90¢, so this isn't the right answer. The coins in answer choice D add up to 95¢. This is the correct answer choice.

2. Open-ended question

Sample answer: "I would put two quarters and two dimes into the machine." Other answers include two quarters, one dime, and two nickels, or even seven dimes.

3. **B**

   When you add \$2.75 and \$0.50, you get \$3.25. When you subtract \$3.25 from \$5.00, you get \$1.75.

End-of-Chapter Practice Problems

1. **B**

   If you add 251 and 300, you get 551.

2. **C**

   The only given number that 12 divides into evenly is 36.

3. **B**

   The number 2 divides evenly into each digit in 242, giving you 121.

4. **D**

   Answer choice A is 60¢, B is 55¢, C is 45¢, and D is 65¢.

5. **B**

   Set the problem up with 592 on top, 356 on the bottom, and the numbers aligned on the right, and subtract. Note that you have to use borrowing with these numbers.

6. Open-ended question

   If Miguel gives away 86 of his 124 coins, he will have the difference, 38, left.

7. **C**

   Remember to carry the 6. Your result should be 1,273.

8. **B**

   Four apples at \$0.35 each equals \$1.40. The change from \$2.00 is \$0.60.

Chapter 3 Answer Explanations

Practice 8: Estimating Addition

1. C

The number 720 rounded to the nearest hundred is 700. The number 292 rounded to the nearest hundred is 300. If you add 700 + 300, you get 1,000. This number is between the 1,000 and 1,200 range in answer choice C.

2. B

The number 109 rounded to the nearest hundred is 100. The number 258 rounded to the nearest hundred is 300. If you add 100 + 300, you get 400. This number is between 300 and 600, the range in answer choice B.

Practice 9: Estimating Subtraction

1. C

When you round 780 to the nearest hundred, you get 800. When you round 349 to the nearest hundred, you get 300. When you subtract these numbers, the answer is 500. Answer choice C is correct.

2. D

When you round 836 to the nearest hundred, you get 800. When you round 432 to the nearest hundred, you get 400. If you subtract 400 from 800, you get 400. That is between 200 and 500.

Practice 10: Estimating Multiplication

1. C

If you round 43 to 40 and 18 to 20 and multiply, you get 800, so the range 300 to 800 is the correct answer choice, C.

2. C

If you round 29 to 30 and 11 to 10 and multiply, you get 300. Answer choice C is correct.

Practice 11: Estimating Division

1. **C**

   If you round 148 to 100 and divide by 4, you get 25. Answer choice C is correct.

2. **A**

   If you round 246 to 200 and divide by 6, you get a number close to 33. Another way to do this problem is to round 6 to 5. The number 200 divided by 5 is 40. If you recognize by mental math that 6 divides evenly into 246, giving an actual quotient of 41, you also get answer choice A.

End-of-Chapter Practice Problems

1. **C**

   If you round 795 to 800 and 116 to 100 and add 800 and 100, you get 900.

2. **D**

   If you round 85 to 90 and 12 to 10, you get 900. You could also round 85 to 100 and multiply by 12 to get 1,200. Both answers are in the range in answer choice D.

3. **B**

   If you round 252 to 300 and divide by 2, you get 150.

4. **C**

   If you round 925 to 900 and 347 to 300 and subtract 300 from 900, you get 600.

5. **B**

   If you round 372 to 400 and 108 to 100 and add them, you get 500.

6. **D**

   If you round 87 to 90 and 12 to 10 and multiply them, you get 900.

7. **B**

   If you round 114 to 100 and 6 to 10 and divide them, you get 10. (You can divide 100 by 6 by mental math to get the range. You don't need an exact answer.)

Chapter 4 Answer Explanations

Practice 12: Lines

1. **C**

   A ray has one endpoint and one arrow.

2. **C**

   The points at the end of a line segment are called endpoints.

3. **B**

   Two lines going in exactly the same direction are called parallel lines.

Practice 13: Angles

1. **B**

   An acute angle is smaller than a right angle. It is less than 90°.

2. **A**

   The other answer choices are either larger or smaller than a right angle.

Practice 14: Two-Dimensional Shapes

1. **B**

   An octagon is any eight-sided figure. The sides don't have to be equal.

2. C

This riddle defines a circle.

3. D

The only figure in the answer choices that has four sides is a rectangle.

Practice 15: Three-Dimensional Shapes

1. B

A sphere looks like a ball. It does not have faces or vertices.

2. C

A triangular pyramid meets this description.

Practice 16: Lines of Symmetry:

1. B

Because this diamond has four equal sides, it has horizontal, vertical, and diagonal symmetry.

2. A

Of the letters E, F, G, and J, only E (answer choice A) can be divided into two equal halves (horizontally).

Practice 17: Congruent Shapes

1. A

The rectangles in answer choice A are exactly the same size and shape, so they are congruent.

2. C

These rectangles are different sizes and shapes, so they are not congruent.

Practice 18: Moving Shapes

1. **D**

   Answer choice D is the only answer choice that isn't turned or flipped.

2. **A**

   Answer choice A looks like a reflection of the first figure.

3. **B**

   Answer choice B shows a turn.

4. **B**

   The shape in answer choice B fits into the tessellation without a gap.

Practice 19: Coordinate Grids

1. **B**

   The coordinates for the playground are (4, 6).

2. **A**

   Andy's house is located at (3, 1).

3. **B**

   The school is located at (8, 3).

End-of-Chapter Practice Problems

1. **A**

   The figure shown here has a horizontal, a vertical and a diagonal line of symmetry.

2. **D**

   Answer choice D has an obtuse angle, which is greater than 90°.

3. B

The triangles in answer choice B are flipped a different way, but they are the same size and shape and are therefore congruent.

4. C

A rectangular prism has 6 faces and 8 vertices and looks like a box.

5. D

Answer choice D shows an angle greater than 90°.

6. C

Because the line segment extends from one end of the circle to the other through the center of the circle, it is the diameter.

7. A

Lines that go in the same direction and don't intersect are called parallel lines.

8. B

The point where two rays meet is called the vertex.

9. C

A hexagon is a two-dimensional figure with six sides.

10. Open-ended question

Sample answer: The figure on the left is a cone, and the figure on the right is a cylinder.

A cone has one face, and a cylinder has two.

They are the same in that the faces are circles. They are different in that a cone has a vertex and a cylinder doesn't.

11. A

Point A is located at (2, 4).

12. C

Remember that a flip is like a reflection. Answer choice C shows a flip.

Chapter 5 Answer Explanations

Practice 20: Length

1. B

It might seem like a pretty long way from your bedroom floor to the ceiling, but try to remember the size of each unit of measurement. Inches are too small to use. Miles are used for long distances. Yards would make your bedroom ceiling about three stories high! The best answer choice would be in feet.

2. A

Think of how small a penny is. It's pretty small. Right away you should be able to see that meters, decimeters, and kilometers are far too big to measure such a small object. The correct choice is in centimeters.

Practice 21: Weight

1. A

A car is very heavy, so answer choice A, in tons, is the best answer.

2. B

One gram is a very light weight, and a piece of lettuce is very light.

Practice 22: Capacity

1. A

Two cups of liquid is equal to one pint.

2. D

A swimming pool holds a lot of water. If you measured the amount of water in a pool in cups, it would be a very high number. Pints and quarts are also a little too small to use. The best answer is gallons.

Practice 23: Perimeter and Area

1. C

When you add up all of the unit edges on the sides of the rectangle, you get $7 + 7 + 4 + 4 = 22$.

2. D

There are 28 blocks inside the rectangle.

3. D

If you add $10 + 10$, you get 20 for the two lengths. When you subtract 20 from 36, the total length of fencing, you get 16. Sixteen divided by 2 is 8, the width of the deck.

Practice 24: Measuring Time

1. D

If you add 1 hour and 15 minutes to 2:30, you get 3:45.

2. C

If you add 30 minutes to 9:10, you get 9:40.

End-of-Chapter Practice Problems

1. D

The most reasonable estimate for the weight of a truck would be in tons. Ounces and pounds are too small.

2. B

There are two lengths and two widths, so multiply 10 by 2 and 4 by 2 and add these numbers.

3. D

If you subtract 20, which is twice the width of the room, from 64, you get 44. When you divide this number by 2, you get 22.

4. C

A sidewalk would be measured in meters.

5. C

If you add 1 hour and 30 minutes to 9:30, you get 11:00.

Chapter 6 Answer Explanations

Practice 25: Patterns

1. C

The rule assigned to these numbers is to add 8. For example, $6 + 8 = 14$, and $14 + 8 = 22$.

2. B

Each number decreases by 3. For example, $52 - 3 = 49$.

Practice 26: Function Machines

1. B

Each number is increased by 9. If you add 9 to 12, the answer is 21.

2. B

Each number is decreased by 3. If you subtract 3 from 9, the answer is 6.

3. C

In the first table, each number is increased by 5. The number 7 in the input row becomes 12 in the output row.

4. D

In the second table, each number is increased by 3. The output from the first machine becomes the input for the second machine. If you add 3 to 12, you get 15.

Practice 27: Input/Output Tables and T-Charts

1. D

Each number is increased by 6. If you add 6 to 12, you get 18.

2. C

The numbers in the x column are multiplied by 2 to get the numbers in the y column. When the numbers increase but not by the same amount, as here, you should think of multiplication.

Practice 28: Other Kinds of Patterns

1. A

If you repeat the pattern three times, on Day 15 Tammy's grandmother would make fish. On Day 16, the pattern would begin again, and she would make meatloaf.

2. Open-ended

Sample answer: The pattern is that you add \$3.25 each week. If you add \$3.25 to \$15.25, you get \$18.50. In week 6 you would earn enough money in that week to buy the used video game. In Week 6, you would make \$21.75.

Practice 29: Line Graphs

1. Open-ended

Sample answer: The number of cars sold decreased over the years.

Practice 30: Open Sentences

1. B

By reversing the open sentence, you get $96 \div 12 = \square$, and you can determine that the missing number is 8.

2. D

By reversing the open sentence, you get $72 - 38 = \square$, and you can determine that the missing number is 34.

3. C

This is a multiplication problem, so you cannot use reversal. Think—what number times 50 gives 150? You should be able to answer this by using mental math.

4. C

This is the same as $144 \div 12 = \square$, so the missing number is 12.

Practice 31: Number Sentences

1. B

If you know that Peter had 24 crayons and now has 36, you can subtract the two numbers to find out how many crayons his mother gave him.

2. C

This problem also requires subtraction. You need to subtract 24 from 68.

Practice 32: Multiplication Rules

1. A

Any number multiplied by 0 is 0.

2. C

This question asks about the associative property. If you multiply three numbers, you can move the parentheses and still get the same answer.

3. B

Any number multiplied by 1 is that number.

End-of-Chapter Practice Problems

1. C

The numbers are increased by 9. For example, $5 + 9 = 14$.

2. D

The numbers are decreased by 10. If you subtract 10 from 28, the answer is 18.

3. B

The numbers are decreased by 6. For example, $18 - 12 = 6$.

4. C

Reverse to get $36 \div 3 = \square$, and you can see that the missing number is 12.

5. A

Any number multiplied by 0 is 0.

6. A

The first number sentence is the correct answer. You need to multiply the number of students, 24, by 2, the number of juice boxes each student will receive.

Chapter 7 Answer Explanations

Practice 33: Using Data and Graphs

1. C

Look for football on the bottom of the bar graph. The bar above football goes up to 40.

2. C

The highest bar is soccer. More than 80 students play soccer.

Practice 34: Probability

1. B

There are 14 ribbons altogether, and 3 of these ribbons are red. So the probability that Rachel will pick a red ribbon is $\frac{3}{14}$.

2. A

There are 25 cards in the hat, and 4 of the cards have "Group B" written on them, so the probability that a student will pick a card with "Group B" on it is $\frac{4}{25}$.

Practice 35: Mean, Mode, and Median

1. B

If you add up all of the numbers in the table, you get 150. If you divide this number by 5, the answer is 30. Answer choice B is correct.

2. C

If you put the numbers in order from least to greatest, they look like this: 0, 2, 5, 6, 8. The median is the number in the middle. Number 5 is in the middle.

3. B

The number 4 is listed three times. It is the mode.

End-of-Chapter Practice Problems

1. B

If you add up Jillian's scores on the last five social studies tests, you get 435. When you divide 435 by 5 (the number of tests), the answer is 87.

2. B

There are 20 cards altogether, so 20 is the denominator. The question asks you to find the probability that a student will pick a card with an oak leaf on it. There are 4 cards with an oak leaf on them, so 4 is the numerator.

3. C

To solve this problem, you need to look at how many runners are after Sam's name. There are 6. Then you have to multiply this number by 2, which gives you 12.

4. C

The bar for Year 3 goes up to the number 60.

5. C

There are 30 balloons altogether and 6 of the balloons are orange, so the answer is $\frac{6}{30}$.

6. C

The median number is the middle number. If you put the numbers in order from least to greatest, you'll see that the number 7 is in the middle.

Chapter 8 Answer Explanations

Practice 36: Venn Diagrams and Tree Diagrams

1. C

In the part where the circles overlap, it says that both women like to cook.

2. B

John Paul calls Marita.

Practice 37: Categories and Colors

1. B

There are 6 rectangles in this section of the quilt.

2. C

Four colors are needed so that no areas that touch each other have the same color.

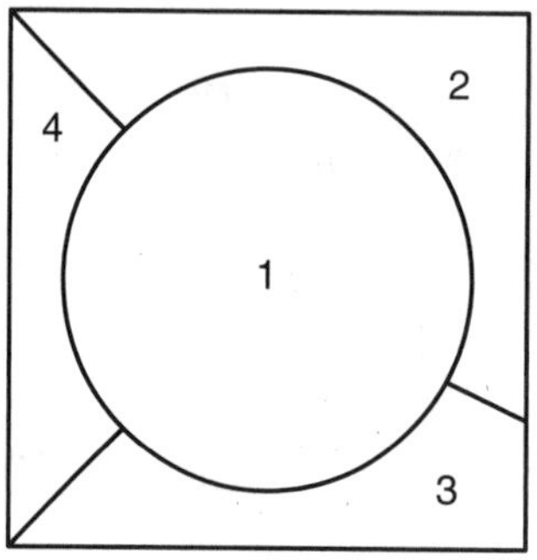

Practice 38: Following Directions

1. Open-ended

Sample response: Amy will pass the discount store on her walk. Her walk ends when she reaches the school.

2. Open-ended

Sample response: Directions for Jamie to get from the school to his house:

1. Walk six blocks east.

2. Walk one back north.

Directions for Jamie to get from his house to Amy's house:

1. Walk four blocks south.

2. Walk six blocks west.

Practice 39: Combinations

1. D

If you draw lines for each combination, you can see that there are 10 combinations of sweater and collar.

2. D

There are 16 combinations of sandwich and fruit. Count the lines after you list them (as with the example in the chapter that uses books).

End-of-Chapter Practice Problems

1. B

Hakim will call Inez, because her name is under his name.

2. C

Kaylee calls Zola, because Zola's name is under her name.

3. D

In the area where the circles overlap, it says that both Mr. Kerry and Ms. Diaz make learning fun.

4. B

If you number the sections, you'll see that you need only three colors.

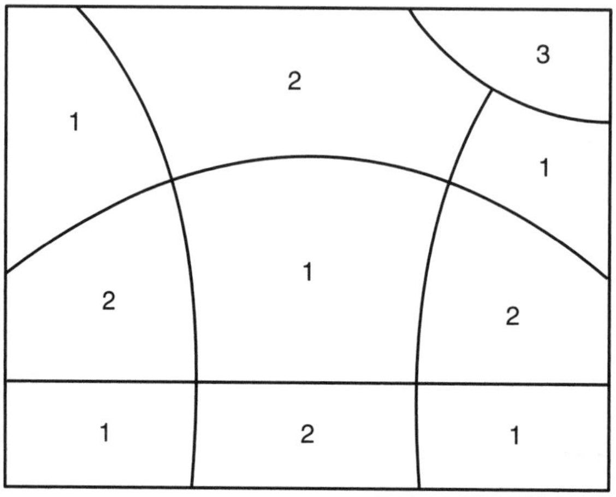

5. B

Chris is at the grocery store. If you didn't answer this question correctly, check the key next to the map to make sure that you've moved in the correct directions.

6. C

There are 12 single-colored squares.

7. C

If you draw lines from each T-shirt to each color of shorts, you'll see that there are 12 combinations.

Practice Test 1 Answer Explanations

1. (Standard Assessed: Numerical Operations)

If you set up this problem so that 900 is above 210, and subtract carefully, you'll see that the correct answer is 690.

2. (Standard Assessed: Numerical Operations)

When you divide 3 into 102, you find that the correct answer is 34.

3. (Standard Assessed: Numerical Operations)

To multiply these numbers correctly, put the 12 under the 24 and multiply. The correct answer is 288.

4. (Standard Assessed: Numerical Operations)

If you put the number 702 on top and the number 105 on the bottom and carefully subtract, you should get the correct answer: 597. This subtraction involves borrowing.

5. (Standard Assessed: Numerical Operations)

To solve this problem, you have to add 210 and 97. Then subtract 52 from this sum to get the answer, 255.

6. (Standard Assessed: Probability)

Mia has 30 beads in the bag, so this number is the denominator. Eight of the beads are orange, so this is the numerator. The answer is $\frac{8}{30}$.

7. (Standard Assessed: Patterns)

The pattern for these numbers is to add 5. If you add 5 to 36, you get 41, which is the next number in the pattern.

8. Open-ended (Standard Assessed: Data Analysis)

If you add Jameel's five test scores and divide by 5, you get 92. This is his mean score.

9. **D** (Standard Assessed: Estimation)

To answer this question correctly, you need to round 824 to 800 and round 397 to 400, and then add 800 and 400, to find the range that contains the sum, 1,200.

10. C (Standard Assessed: Estimation)

To answer this question correctly, you need to round 84 to 80 and round 12 to 10. Then multiply and find the range that contains 800.

11. A (Standard Assessed: Number Sense)

If you look carefully at the shaded areas, you can see that $\frac{2}{5}$ is not as large as $\frac{4}{9}$. Therefore, you need to choose the less-than sign.

12. B (Standard Assessed: Number Sense)

The decimal .25 is smaller than the mixed numbers, which have a number to the left of the decimal point. The number 1.0 is smaller than 1.05. Therefore, answer choice B is the best answer.

13. B (Standard Assessed: Geometric Properties)

A line segment extending across a circle through its center is its diameter.

14. A (Standard Assessed: Geometric Properties)

The correct answer is a cone. A cylinder has two faces, a sphere has none, and a pyramid has five.

15. A (Standard Assessed: Geometric Properties)

Parallel lines go in the same direction and don't intersect.

16. D (Standard Assessed: Geometric Properties)

A right angle measures 90°. Answer choice D shows a right angle.

17. D (Standard Assessed: Units of Measure)

A pond would contain a lot of water. It would be measured in gallons.

18. B (Standard Assessed: Number Sense)

In the number 85,403, the 8 is in the ten thousands place, the 5 is in the thousands place, the 4 (which this question asks about) is in the hundreds place, the 0 is in the tens place, and the 3 is in the ones place.

19. C (Standard Assessed: Discrete Mathematics)

The smallest number of colors you can use is four, as shown in the diagram, where each number represents a different color.

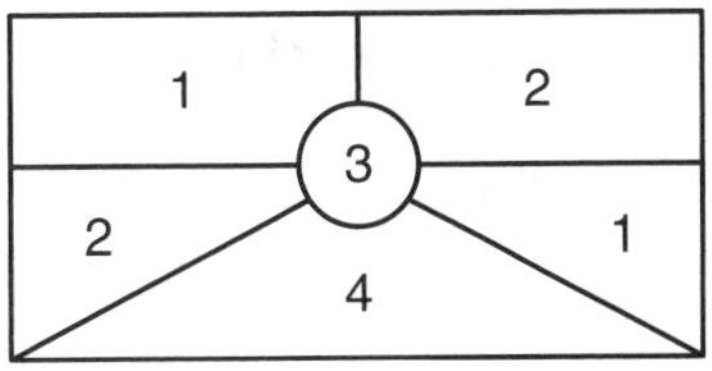

20. A (Standard Assessed: Modeling)

You know that Enrico had 52 stickers, gave some away, and now has 35, so this is a subtraction problem. The unknown number, the number of stickers Enrico gave away, should be in the box.

21. B (Standard Assessed: Modeling)

If you multiply 3 by 124, you get 372. So the correct answer is 3.

22. D (Standard Assessed: Units of Measurement)

If you make 10 *x*'s and each *x* stands for one house on Angel's street, you'll see that Angel lives 7 houses to the left of Carmen.

23. B (Standard Assessed: Geometric Properties)

Remember that a line of symmetry divides an object into two halves that are reflections of each other. In order for an object to have two lines of symmetry, it needs to be able to be divided into exact halves in two different ways.

24. D (Standard Assessed: Patterns)

There are seven hours between 7:00 A.M. and 2:00 P.M. If you multiply 7 hours by 3, the number of degrees the temperature rises every hour, you get 21. Add 21 to 24°F , the temperature at 7:00 A.M. The temperature at 2:00 P.M. is 45°F.

25. C (Standard Assessed: Functions and Relationships)

Six is added to each number in the input table. If you add 6 to the number 11, you get 17.

26. C (Standard Assessed: Modeling)

You can reverse the numbers to solve this problem. Subtract 38 from 87 to get 49.

27. C (Standard Assessed: Functions and Relationships)

Each number dropped into the function machine is multiplied by 3. If you multiply 7 by 3, you get 21. Answer choice C is correct.

28. Open-ended (Standard Assessed: Numerical Operations)

Sample answer: I would use 1 quarter and 2 dimes to play the game.

Other answers include 1 quarter, 1 dime, and 2 nickels, or 4 dimes and 1 nickel, among many other combinations.

29. C

The number of students who have blue eyes is $\left(\frac{2}{3}\right)(36) = 24$. Since 9 boys have blue eyes, there must be $24 - 9 = 15$ girls who have blue eyes.

30. B

The lowest number in this group that can be divided by 3 is 81. The other numbers are 84, 87, 90, 93, 96, and 99. Thus, there are seven numbers.

31. D

The cost of three hamburgers and four hot dogs is (3)($2.25) + (4)(($3.50) = $6.75 + $14 = $20.75. The total for answer choice (A) is $21.75, the total for (B) is $24.25, and the total for (C) is $19.50.

32. B

The number of offices in building A is (40)(16) = 640 and the number of offices in building B is (55)(19) = 1045. Building B has 1045 – 640 = 405 more offices than building A.

33. A

Paul scored 100 on the remaining five quizzes. To find his total points on all quizzes we need to multiply and then add:

(3)(75) + (2)(85) + (5)(100) = 225 + 170 + 500 = 895.

His average for the ten quizzes is $\frac{895}{10} = 89.5$.

34. D

There are 88 – 24 = 64 people in the company who are present today. Thus, the number of people working overtime is $\left(\frac{3}{4}\right)(64) = 48$.

35. C

Four hours is equal to (4)(60) = 240 minutes. Since 240 – 40 – 30 = 170. Then Maria's free time after she completes her homework is 170 minutes. So, the time spent watching television is $\left(\frac{1}{2}\right)(170) = 85$ minutes.

36. B

The number of crayons that Miss Roberts bought is (25)(150) = 3750. Since each student received 30 crayons, she handed out (30)(122) = 3660 crayons. This means she had 3750 – 3660 = 90 crayons left over.

37. Open-ended (Standard Assessed: Measuring Geometric Objects)

The perimeter of the room is 72 feet. If the width is 16 feet, it takes up 32 feet of the perimeter. If you subtract 32 from 72, you get 40. If you divide 40 by 2—because there are two lengths to the perimeter of the room—you get 20 feet. The community room is 20 feet long. To find out how many stars Mrs. Miller needs, you have to divide 3 into 72. She needs 24 stars.

38. C (Standard Assessed: Discrete Mathematics)

If you draw a tree diagram, you'll see that there are six combinations of notebooks.

39. B (Standard Assessed: Probability)

There are 9 cards in the hat, and 2 of them have "mow lawn" written on them. The probability that you will pick a card that says "mow lawn" is $\frac{2}{9}$, or 2 out of 9.

40. B (Standard Assessed: Data Analysis)

The median temperature is in the middle. If you put the temperatures in order from least to greatest, you can see that 93 is the median: 90, 90, 93, 95, 98.

41. C (Standard Assessed: Data Analysis)

To answer this question, you have to add the number of pens and markers Ben purchased. He purchased 10 pens and 8 markers, so the correct answer is 18.

42. C (Standard Assessed: Data Analysis)

Each cake picture stands for 20 students, so you need to multiply $3\frac{1}{2}$ cakes by 20. So $3 \times 20 = 60$ students. Then add the $\frac{1}{2}$ cake, equal to 10 students. Therefore, 70 students have a birthday in November.

43. C (Standard Assessed: Discrete Mathematics)

Katarina will call the player whose name is listed under hers. She will call Cecily.

44. C (Standard Assessed: Number Sense and Operations)

"Two thousand one hundred thirty-two" is the same as the number 2,132. Answer choice C is correct.

Answer choice A is incorrect because it is "two hundred thirty-two." Answer choice B is incorrect because it is "two thousand one hundred twenty-three." Answer choice D is incorrect because it is "two thousand two hundred thirty-two."

45. B (Standard Assessed: Measurement)

If you use the centimeters part of your ruler, you'll see that the bookmark is 11 centimeters long.

Answer choices A, C, and D are incorrect because they are the wrong measurements for the bookmark.

46. Open-ended (Standard Assessed: Functions and Relationships)

Sample answer: The rule for Table A is to add 12. The rule for Table B is to multiply by 3. The rule for Table C is to multiply by 4. The values for 15 in each table are shown below:

Table A 27

Table B 45

Table C 60

Table C gives the greatest value.

47. A (Standard Assessed: Number Sense and Operations)

120 is a multiple of 10. 120 divided by 10 = 12. Answer choice A is correct.

Answer choices B, C, and D are all incorrect due to faulty division.

48. B (Standard Assessed: Geometry)

The poster board is divided into 7 rows, with 9 squares in each row. To get the area, multiply 7 x 9, which is 63. Answer choice B is correct.

Answer choices A, C, and D are incorrect because of miscounting the squares or faulty multiplication.

49. C (Standard Assessed: Number Sense and Operations)

The correct words for the number 9,017 are "nine thousand seventeen." Answer choice C is correct.

Answer choice A is the same as 917. Answer choice B is the same as 9,007. Answer choice D is the same as 9,071.

50. D (Standard Assessed: Number Sense and Operations)

An even number multiplied by an odd number always results in an even number. The only even number among the answers is 8. Thus, answer choice D is correct.

Answer choices A, B, and C are all incorrect because they are odd numbers.

51. C (Standard Assessed: Number Sense and Operations)

Seven packages of 8 candles is 7 x 8, or 56. Answer choice C is correct.

Answer choices A, B, and D are incorrect products of 7 and 8.

52. B (Standard Assessed: Geometry)

A quadrilateral is a polygon with 4 sides and 4 angles. The word part *quad-* means "four." Answer choice B is correct.

Answer choice A is incorrect because it is the number for a triangle. Answer choice C is incorrect because it is the number for a pentagon. Answer choice D is incorrect because it is the number for a hexagon.

53. D (Standard Assessed: Number Sense and Operations)

Use the inverse operation to check if an answer is correct. The inverse operation of multiplication is division. One way to check if this number sentence is correct is to divide 45 by 3. Answer choice D is correct.

Answer choices A and C are incorrect because they do not use the inverse operation and use the wrong numbers. Answer choice B is incorrect because it divides the wrong numbers to check the correct answer.

54. C (Standard Assessed: Functions and Relationships)

$18 \div 3 = 6$
$21 \div 3 = 7$
$24 \div 3 = 8$
$27 \div 3 = 9$

55. Hot Dog, Peanuts, and Fudge Bar (Standard Assessed: Measurement)

Add the cost of the three items together:

Hot Dog ($2.25) + Peanuts ($1.45) + Fudge Bar ($0.90) = $4.60.

Then subtract the total from $5.00:

$5.00 – $4.60 = $0.40.

J.D. would have $0.40 left over.

Practice Test 2 Answer Explanations

1. 645 (Standard Assessed: Numerical Operations)

If you subtract 311 from 956, you should get 645.

2. 122 (Standard Assessed: Numerical Operations)

If you carefully divide 5 into 610, you should get 122.

3. 672 (Standard Assessed: Numerical Operations)

If you set up this problem so that 48 is on the top and 14 is on the bottom and then you multiply, you should get the correct answer: 672.

4. 1,119 (Standard Assessed: Numerical Operations)

If you set up this problem so that 724 is on the top and 395 is on the bottom and then you carefully add, you should get the correct answer: 1,119. Note that this addition involves carrying.

5. 189 (Standard Assessed: Numerical Operations)

$290 + 24 = 314$

$314 - 125 = 189$

To solve this problem, you need to first add 290 and 24. Then subtract 125 from this number.

6. 3 (Standard Assessed: Data Analysis)

The mode is the number that occurs most frequently. The number 3 is the only number that appears twice, so it is the mode.

7. Cube (Standard Assessed: Geometric Properties)

The correct answer is a cube. It has six faces and looks like a block.

8. Ten thousands (Standard Assessed: Number Sense)

In the number 2,083,660, the number 2 is in the millions place, the first 0 is in the hundred thousands place, the 8 (which is what the question asks about) is in the ten thousands place, the 3 is in the thousands place, the first 6 is in the hundreds place, the second 6 is in the tens place, and the last 0 is in the ones place.

9. **A** (Standard Assessed: Estimation)

To answer this problem correctly, round 289 to 300. Then you need to divide 3 into 300 and choose the range that includes this number.

10. **A** (Standard Assessed: Estimation)

To answer this problem correctly, you need to round 310 to 300 and 178 to 200. Then find the difference between 300 and 200 and choose the range that includes this number.

11. **A** (Standard Assessed: Numerical Operations)

Answer choice A is correct. These coins add up to 80¢. The coins in answer choice B add up to 70¢, the coins in answer choice C add up to 85¢, and the coins in answer choice D add up to 75¢.

12. **C** (Standard Assessed: Units of Measurement)

Of these answer choices, a meter is the best unit of measurement to measure your arm.

13. **C** (Standard Assessed: Geometric Properties)

A pentagon has five sides. Answer choice A is a hexagon, answer choice B is a square, and answer choice D is an octagon.

14. A (Standard Assessed: Geometric Properties)

A radius extends from the center of a circle to a point on the circle.

15. A (Standard Assessed: Number Sense)

You have to look closely at the numbers to correctly answer this question. The decimal .90 is the smallest, so this number should go first. The number 9.0 is smaller than 9.10, so answer choice A is correct.

16. D (Standard Assessed: Patterns)

The pattern is to add 5 to each number. If you add 5 to 34, you get 39.

17. B (Standard Assessed: Transforming Shapes)

In a tessellation, shapes fit together without any spaces between them. Answer choice B is a tessellation.

18. A (Standard Assessed: Coordinate Geometry)

If you move along the *x*-axis until you get to the pond, you'll stop at number 4. Then if you go up, you'll stop at number 6. Remember that the *x* value goes first, so (4, 6) is the correct answer.

19. B (Standard Assessed: Modeling)

You know that Dawn had 78 marbles, and, after her mother gave her some, she has 96 marbles. What you don't know is how many marbles Dawn's mother gave her. This number should be the □. Answer choice B is the correct answer.

20. A (Standard Assessed: Geometric Properties)

An obtuse angle is greater in degrees than a right angle. Answer choice A is an obtuse angle.

21. D (Standard Assessed: Data Analysis)

To find out how many cans Kevin collected, multiply each  by 50, since each  stands for 50; thus, a  stands for 25. There are $15\frac{1}{2}$ cans after Kevin's name. $15 \times 50 = 750$, and $750 + 25 = 775$.

22. C (Standard Assessed: Geometric Properties)

Remember that a line of symmetry divides an object into two halves that look like reflections. In order for an object to have two lines of symmetry, it needs to be able to be divided into exact halves in two different ways.

23. B (Standard Assessed: Modeling)

To find the answer to this question, you can reverse the problem to $96 \div 12 = \square$. Divide 12 into 96 to get the answer, 8.

24. D (Standard Assessed: Geometric Properties)

Remember that perpendicular lines are two lines that intersect at right angles.

25. B (Standard Assessed: Modeling)

Substitute the answer choices to find the correct one. $147 \times 2 = 294$, so answer B, 2, is correct.

26. C (Standard Assessed: Discrete Mathematics)

Only the triangles—and not the diamonds—should be counted here. The answer is eight; there are eight triangles. Four of these triangles are on the top, and four are on the bottom.

27. C (Standard Assessed: Functions and Relationships)

The pattern is to divide by 2. If you divide 56 by 2, you get 28.

28. Open-Ended (Standard Assessed: Units of Measurement)

Sample answer: If you add 2 hours and 30 minutes to 2:30 P.M., you get 5:00 P.M. Danielle needs to come home at 5:00. If Danielle's piano lesson is 45 minutes long, it ends at 5:45 P.M.

29. A (Standard Assessed: Patterns)

Every four days, Megan repeats a pattern. So on days 4, 8, 12, 16, and 20, Megan will practice dividing numbers. On Day 23, therefore, she will practice multiplying numbers.

30. C (Standard Assessed: Units of Measurement)

There are 6 hours between noon and 6:00 P.M., and the temperature drops 4 degrees an hour, so it will drop 24 degrees by 6:00 P.M. Subtract 24 from 90°F. The answer is 66°F.

31. C (Standard Assessed: Data Analysis)

If you add the scores on Ashley's first five tests, you get 425. If you divide 425 by 5, the number of tests Ashley has taken, you get 85, her mean test score.

32. B

In 8.4 hours, Lisa can build (8.4)(20) = 168 toy boats. In 10.5 hours, Billy can build (10.5)(18) = 189 toy boats. Their total is 168 + 189 = 357 toy boats.

33. D (Standard Assessed: Discrete Mathematics)

If you make a tree diagram, you can see that there are 24 lines, or possible combinations of collar, name tag, and leash.

34. D (Standard Assessed: Measurement)

Five yards is equal to (36)(5) = 180 inches. The length of the board is 180 + 8 = 188 inches.

35. C (Standard Assessed: Number Sense and Operations)

$6 \times 7 = 42$

$44 - 42 = 2$

36. C (Standard Assessed: Number Sense and Operations)

$15 \times 6 = 90$

37. Hot Dog, Cheese Nachos, and Lemonade (Standard Assessed: Measurement)

Add the cost of the three items together:

Hot Dog ($3.25) + Cheese Nachos ($3.50) + Lemonade ($2.50) = $9.25.

Then subtract the total from $10.00:

$10.00 − $9.25 = $0.75.

Jolene would have $0.75 left.

38. B (Standard Assessed: Data Analysis)

To answer this question, you have to find out how many people lived on Yi Min's block in Year 5 and Year 4 and subtract these numbers. There were 300 people in Year 5 and 200 in Year 4, so the answer is 100.

39. D (Standard Assessed: Number Sense and Operations

The diagram of the park is divided into 8 parts. 2 of the parts are shaded to represent sand. The fraction $\frac{2}{8} = \frac{1}{4}$. Answer choice D is correct.

Answer choices A, B, and C are incorrect fractions to show the relationship of the shaded area to the whole park.

40. B (Standard Assessed: Modeling)

If there are 30 more girls than boys and 120 girls, you need to subtract 30 from 120 to find the number of boys.

41. A (Standard Assessed: Number Sense and Operations)

"Nine thousand seven hundred thirty-eight" is the same as the number 9,738. Answer choice A is correct.

Answer choice B is incorrect because it is "nine thousand three hundred seventy-eight." Answer choice C is incorrect because it is "nine thousand thirty-eight." Answer choice D is incorrect because it is "nine hundred thirty-eight."

42. C (Standard Assessed: Measurement)

Measure the pencil with the centimeters part of your ruler. The pencil is exactly 13 centimeters long.

Answer choices A, B, and D are incorrect because they are the wrong measurements for the pencil.

43. B (Standard Assessed: Number Sense and Operations)

To round 932 to the nearest hundred, look at the digit in the tens place. This digit is 3, which is less than 5. Round down to the nearest hundred. The correct answer is 900.

Answer choice A is incorrect because it was rounded down to 800, not 900. Answer choice C is incorrect because it was rounded to the nearest ten. Answer choice D is incorrect because it was rounded up to 1,000 instead of down to 900.

44. B (Standard Assessed: Number Sense and Operations)

800 is a multiple of 100. 800 divided by 100 = 8. It takes 8 days for Lena to shoot 800 free throws. Answer choice B is correct.

Answer choices A, C, and D are all incorrect due to faulty division.

45. D (Standard Assessed: Geometry)

The sheet of paper is divided into 6 rows, with 11 squares in each row. To get the area, multiply 6 x 11, which is 66. Answer choice D is correct.

Answer choices A, B, and C are incorrect because of miscounting the squares or faulty multiplication.

46. Part A: (Standard Assessed: Statistics and Probability)

Lucinda: 14

Alex: 16

Marta: 19

Part B:

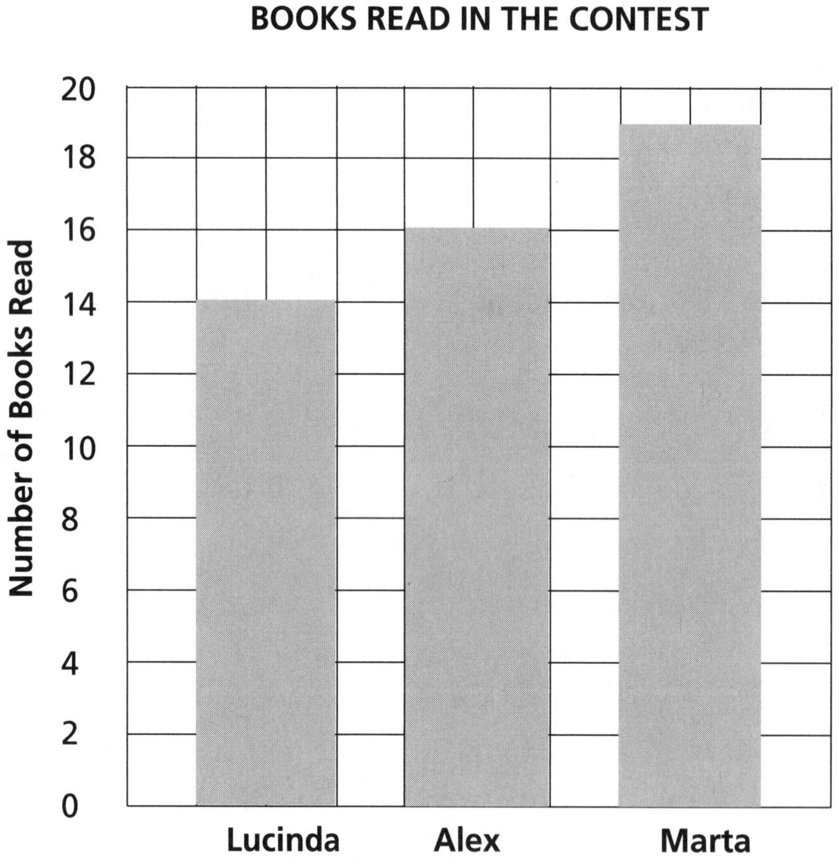

47. B (Standard Assessed: Data Analysis and Probability)

Check each statement by reading the numbers in the graph. There are 6 cars in the parking lot, and 3 trucks. Six is exactly two times 3. Answer choice B is correct.

Answer choice A is incorrect because there are 13 total vehicles and 6 is not one-half of 13. Answer choice C is incorrect because there are 4 buses and 2 x 4 is not 6. Answer choice D is incorrect because there are 6 cars and 6 is not one-half of 13.

48. D (Standard Assessed: Algebra)

Answer choice D is correct.

$1 \times 2 = 2$
$3 \times 2 = 6$
$5 \times 2 = 10$
$7 \times 2 = 14$

Answer choice A is incorrect because the rule for it is input $\div$ 2 = output.
Answer choice B is incorrect because the rule for it is input $\times$ 3 = output.
Answer choice C is incorrect because the rule for it is input + 2 = output.

49. B (Standard Assessed: Number Sense and Operations)

To estimate, round 42 down to 40 and round 392 up to 400. 400 divided by 40 = 10. Answer choice B is correct.

Answer choice A is incorrect because it rounds 42 down to 30. Answer choice C is incorrect because it rounds 42 down to 30 and 392 down to 300. Answer choice D is incorrect because it rounds 392 down to 300.

50. B (Standard Assessed: Algebra)

Answer choice B is correct because:

the number of hamsters (5) > the number of dogs (4)

the number of cats (3) < the number of dogs (4)

Answer choice A is incorrect because:

the number of hamsters (4) is not greater than the number of dogs (5)

Answer choice C is incorrect because:

the number of cats (4) is not less than the number of dogs (3)

Answer choice D is incorrect because:

the number of hamsters (3) is not greater than the number of dogs (4)

51. D (Standard Assessed: Geometry)

Figures that are similar are the same shape but not necessarily the same size. The triangles in answer choice D are similar figures.

The other answer choices are incorrect because the figures in each pair are not the same shape.

52. A (Standard Assessed: Number Sense and Operations)

For the fraction $\frac{2}{6}$, both the numerator and denominator can be divided by 2. This gives you the fraction $\frac{1}{3}$. Answer choice A is correct.

Answer choices B, C, and D are not equivalent fractions to $\frac{2}{6}$.

53. B (Standard Assessed: Number Sense and Operations)

The number sentence for this situation is:

$22 - (5 \times 3)$
$= 22 - 15$
$= 7$

Answer choices A, C, and D are incorrect remainders for this problem.

54. A (Standard Assessed: Number Sense and Operations)

Claire can do 3 times as many sit-ups as Tim, and Tim can do 5 more than 15. The number sentence for this problem is:

$3 \times (5 + 15)$
$= 3 \times 20$
$= 60$

Answer choice A is correct.

Answer choices B, C, and D are incorrect due to faulty calculations.

55. Part A: (Standard Assessed: Algebra)

56 belt buckles

Each week Mr. Sanchez adds 7 more belt buckles to the total number. On Week 6, he had made 42. So on Week 8 he would have 42 + 7 + 7 or 56 belt buckles.

Part B: Week 11

By week 9, he would have 56 + 7 = 63 belt buckles.
By week 10, he would have 63 + 7 = 70 belt buckles.
By week 11, he would have 70 + 7 = 77 belt buckles.